Prayers of the Eucharist: Early and Reformed

R.C.D. Jasper and G.J. Cuming

Prayers of the Eucharist: Early and reformed

Texts translated and edited with commentary

Third edition, revised and enlarged

Pueblo Publishing Company

New York

Design: Frank Kacmarcik

Material from *Formula Missae* 1523 and *Deutsche Messe* 1526 are from LUTHER'S WORKS, volume 53. Copyright © 1965 by Fortress Press. Used by permission of the publisher.

First edition published in Great Britain in 1975 by Collins Publishers, Liturgical Publications.

Second edition published in the United States in 1980 by Oxford University Press, New York, New York.

ISBN: 0-916134-85-7

Printed in the United States of America

Contents

PREFACE

The object of this collection of eucharistic prayers is to introduce readers with little or no knowledge of Greek or Latin or modern languages other than English into the treasure house of the Church's worship. The first edition (1975) contained thirty-six prayers; the second (1980) had forty. This third edition, besides some small additions in Part I (chs. 1, 2, and 13), has been carried down to the end of the eighteenth century, a point which marks a pause in liturgical revision which, as far as the eucharistic prayer is concerned, extended until the 1920s.

The new prayers are from the Neuchâtel liturgy (1713), the Nonjurors' rite (1718), the first American Lutheran liturgy (1748), the Scottish Communion Office (1764), and the first American Book of Common Prayer (1789). These additions register the development of the 1549–1637 strain in Anglican worship, and document the entry of America into the liturgical scene.

In addition, the introductions to the various prayers have been considerably enlarged so as to deal with the content of the prayers as well as their provenance. The Bibliographies have been brought up to date; as before, they are intended for English-speaking students beginning the serious study of liturgy, rather than for experienced scholars. They indicate where the original text may be found, and list books and articles that are in English and relatively easily accessible. Failing these, we have included a few titles in French.

We have tried to indicate how each rite handles the four main actions of the eucharist: taking, giving thanks, breaking, and giving. The remainder of each rite has been set out in skeleton form.

All translations are our own, except where otherwise specified. We have used "you" rather than "thou," except in texts actually written in a "thou" form in English: in these the spelling, punctuation, and capitalization have been modernized. The translations aim at literal exactitude rather than elegance. Every effort has been made to utilize the oldest and most reliable sources, including some which have come to light only during the last thirty years.

Some of the technical terms used in the introductions below may need explanation. The communion service is also known as "the eucharist" (which means thanksgiving), and its central prayer as "the eucharistic prayer." These names are used in most modern services. In the East the service is called "the liturgy" and the prayer "the anaphora" (which means "offering"); in the West the corresponding terms were "the Mass" and "the Canon"; in the Book of Common Prayer of 1662, "the Holy Communion" and "the Prayer of Consecration".

The liturgical account of the Last Supper is called "the Institution Narrative," and is followed in most liturgies by "the anamnesis" (which means remembrance), a section in which Christ's death and resurrection are "remembered."

Invocation of the Holy Spirit on the elements or on the worshippers or both is called "the epiclesis." The first section of the prayer is called "the preface," which here means "proclamation," not "introduction"; and the prayer ends with "the doxology," giving glory to God.

An "embolism" is a short insertion into a longer prayer.

A "Church Order" was a document containing doctrinal statements, disciplinary rules, and forms of worship. The oldest known example is the *Didache*; the *Apostolic Tradition* and the *Apostolic Constitutions* are included in a Church Order known as the *Octateuch*. After the fourth century the genre fell into disuse, but was revived by the Reformers, especially in Germany, where over 100 *Kirchenordnungen* appeared during the sixteenth century.

In the Bibliographies, references are given wherever possible to the following collections of texts:

F. E. Brightman, *Liturgies Eastern and Western* (1896, reprinted 1965)—quoted as *LEW*.
A. Hänggi and I. Pahl, *Prex Eucharistica* (1968)—quoted as *Prex Eucharistica*.
I. Pahl, *Coena Domini I* (1983)—quoted as *Coena Domini*.

Bard Thompson, *Liturgies of the Western Church* (1961)—quoted as Bard Thompson.

Other frequently-cited works are:

G. Dix, *The Shape of the Liturgy* (1945)—quoted as Dix, *The Shape*.
L. Bouyer, *Eucharist* (1970)—quoted as Bouyer.

R. C. D. JASPER
G. J. CUMING

Translator's note

Anamnesis has been translated "remembrance," and *memnēmenoi* "remembering"; but the Greek has overtones of "proclamation" which the English does not suggest.

Logikos has been translated "reasonable," as in the King James Bible, in order to preserve the flavor of scriptural quotation, but "spiritual" is probably nearer to the sense of the word in its liturgical use.

PART I

Early Prayers of the Eucharist

INTRODUCTION: THE STUDY OF EARLY LITURGY

Why are the early liturgies worth studying? Two good reasons spring to mind at once. First, the early liturgies, whether in the form of texts for use or as described by the Fathers, give us a picture of Christian worship in its simplest and purest form ("the springtime of liturgy," as it has been called), before complication and distortion distract attention from the essentials. This reason would be sufficient in itself, but it has recently been reinforced by the fact that virtually all revisions of the last thirty years have been strongly influenced by the early liturgies, and a knowledge of the latter enriches our appreciation of contemporary services.

But first, it is important to understand the complex factors that must be taken into account in the presentation of a text to the modern reader. Strictly speaking, there is no such thing as a specific early liturgy. Definitive texts only came into existence with the invention of printing, and by then many early liturgies had gone out of use. Until then, one can speak of any particular liturgy only in terms of the surviving manuscripts of that liturgy: for example, Vatican MS gr. 2281 of the *Liturgy of St. Mark*, which is by no means identical with Vatican MS gr. 1970 of the same liturgy. There are only three complete manuscripts of *St. Mark*, but there are twenty or thirty of *St. James*, and about 1800 of *St. John Chrysostom*, of which 249 are of interest to specialists. Even manuscripts of approximately the same date may differ widely in content, though the later manuscripts became increasingly stereotyped. Liturgical manuscripts were normally written for use in services which may reflect the local usage of a church or monastery. Some of the most important manuscripts were written in southern Italy, whither numbers of monks had fled before the advance of the Arabs; their content is very different from those which preserve the use of Constantinople.

Very few manuscripts bear the date of writing; Vatican 2281 (mentioned above) is an exception, being dated A.D. 1209. The handwriting can usually be dated within a hundred years either way; and sometimes an indication is given by the mention of a patriarch in the intercessions. The great majority of manuscripts date from a period after A.D. 800, unlike those of the New Testament, some of which go back to *c.* 400. Thus there may be a gap of centuries between composition and copying. A very important exception is the ever-increasing corpus of liturgical papyri preserved in the sands of Egypt, some of which were probably written as early as the fourth century. There are also one or two Latin sacramentaries which were written in the sixth or seventh centuries.

It is important to distinguish between the date of writing of a manuscript and the date of its contents. For instance, *The Prayers of Sarapion* survive only in one manuscript written in the eleventh century; yet they were composed probably in the fourth century, certainly not later than the fifth. It is unlikely that these prayers have been altered in the meantime, but in some cases it is possible to trace a steady development over seven or eight hundred years.

Besides Greek and Latin, liturgies are extant in Syriac, Arabic, Coptic, Ethiopic, Armenian, Georgian, and Old Slavonic. Especial value attaches to those which were translated from the Greek, since the translations were mostly made some centuries before the oldest surviving Greek manuscript. They thus bear witness to an early state of the text, and have usually undergone less alteration and expansion than the Greek.

There is one other important source of information about the liturgies, namely *catecheses*. These were addresses given by a bishop to a group of baptismal candidates. Those of Cyril of Jerusalem, Ambrose, and Theodore of Mopsuestia all give us facts about the celebration of the eucharist, and often quotations from the text. This is true also of the sermons of John Chrysostom (not to be confused with the liturgy named after him) and Augustine. These Fathers often refer explicitly to what their hearers have just seen or heard. All these sources belong to the second half of the fourth century and the early fifth, so that we have a fairly complete picture of the order of service in such places as Jerusalem, Antioch, Milan, and Carthage at a date much earlier than that of most liturgical manuscripts. Unfortunately, none of these Fathers deals in

Introduction: The study of early liturgy

full detail with the text of the eucharistic prayer, which was probably regarded as a subject to be treated with some reserve.

The attribution of a liturgy to one or all of the apostles is unlikely to be acceptable nowadays, though it was an understood convention in the early centuries. However, the liturgy in Book VIII of the *Apostolic Constitutions*, sometimes called the "Clementine Liturgy," was highly regarded in the seventeenth and eighteenth centuries because of the attribution, and despite growing doubts of its authenticity. Argument continues about the authorship of the liturgies of *St. Basil* and *St. John Chrysostom*. These attributions need to be treated with caution, though it is by no means impossible in either case that the saint concerned may have contributed a part of the liturgy which bears his name. In the earliest days it is clear that the bishop was free to compose the eucharistic prayer for himself. Origen mentions certain "conventions" which had to be observed, though he does not say what they were. Hippolytus provides a specimen prayer, but adds that a bishop need not use it, provided that his own prayer is orthodox. By the end of the fourth century, unorthodox prayers were becoming a problem in North Africa, leading to the imposition of controls; and finally in 535 the emperor Justinian insists that no one should be consecrated bishop until he can repeat the prayer by heart, which implies the existence of an accepted text for him to learn.

Until fairly recently, scholars attempted to trace all extant eucharistic prayers back to one original, but for the last fifty years the evidence has been read as showing that an original variety was gradually reduced to uniformity. Early eucharistic prayers are always closely associated with places: Rome, Jerusalem, Alexandria, Antioch, Constantinople, with corresponding variations in structure. But there was considerable interchange of content and, in the rest of the liturgy, borrowing of complete prayers.

Scholars have laid down "laws" of liturgical development, of which the two most important are, first, that a shorter version of a text is likely to be earlier than a longer version (almost always true, but not quite invariably); and secondly, that accurate quotations from the Bible are likely to be later than inexact quotations (compare New Testament quotations from the Old Testament). Certainly, the normal development of a liturgy is by a process of expansion, even if only in such small details as the widespread change of "holy" to "all-holy."

By the end of the fourth century the pattern of the anaphora had been standardized as follows:

1. Sursum corda
2. Preface
3. Pre-Sanctus
4. Sanctus
5. Post-Sanctus
6. Institution Narrative
7. Anamnesis
8. Offering
9. Epiclesis
10. Intercessions
11. Doxology

This pattern is now usually called "West Syrian," though sometimes "Antiochene" or "Syro-Antiochene." It is found in *St. John Chrysostom*, *St. Basil*, *St. James*, and the *Apostolic Constitutions*.

The two main variations from this pattern are the "East Syrian" or "Chaldaean," which places the epiclesis *after* the intercessions; and the "Egyptian," which places the intercessions after the preface. In each case the primitive link between the intercessions and the offering is preserved (the Egyptian preface includes an offering).

Introduction: The study of early liturgy

1 Jewish Prayers

Jesus and his disciples, as devout Jews, would be familiar with the statutory Jewish prayers. But, as with Christian liturgy, most of the manuscripts are late and undated, so that it is uncertain whether the prayers were extant in their present form in the first century. Indeed, it is unlikely that they had a fixed form at that date. So it is not surprising that verbal quotation from Jewish sources is hard to find in Christian liturgy. To some extent also, Christians would feel the need to distance their worship from actual Jewish prayers; but the structure and the style would not so easily be discarded, and are clear to see.

Jewish liturgy included the sacrifices in the temple, the services of the synagogue, and prayer in the home. Although the Christian Church soon began to use sacrificial language in the eucharistic prayer, this was not derived from the Old Testament: Leviticus gives copious instructions about the performance of the various types of sacrifice, but says nothing about what was said. The synagogue service almost certainly contributed the Sanctus, together with its introduction. But the most influential source seems to have been the domestic blessing (*berakah*), and especially the common grace (*birkath ha-mazon*, blessing over food), a thanksgiving after a meal. This may well have been the ultimate origin of the Christian anaphora.

It consists of three short paragraphs, beginning respectively "Blessed are you, Lord our God," "We will give thanks to you," and "Have mercy on us." Each ends with a short blessing summarizing the paragraph. This is known as the *chatimah*, and its purpose is to retain the framework of blessing, even though the intervening paragraph is concerned with thanksgiving or intercession. Joseph Heinemann rather unfortunately refers to it as "the eulogy." Scholars have been divided on the question whether blessing and thanksgiving (*berakah* and *tōdah*) are significantly different. At present, the general trend seems to emphasize their difference, and to associate thanksgiving with a form of prayer in which thanksgiving is followed by intercession, producing a structure of two "panels," as against the three panels of the *berakah*.

Heinemann distinguishes three main topics in Jewish prayer: creation, revelation (the giving of the Law), and redemption. These are associated with the beginning, the critical turning-point, and the end of history respectively, redemption being viewed as still to come. Prayer is based on thanking God for these things, or blessing him for them. This can be clearly seen in the Psalms, where the chief emphasis is on creation and redemption, though the two themes are usually kept apart. To declare the mighty works of God, the Psalmist uses such verbs as "remember" and "proclaim." In the *Birkath ha-mazon* God is blessed in the first paragraph for creating the world; in the second for giving his people food; and in the third, prayer is made for the restoration of Jerusalem. These themes all appear in the earliest Christian prayers, though there the food has become the spiritual food of the eucharist, and Jerusalem has become the Christian Church.

As one would expect, it is above all at the Passover that "pre-echoes" of the eucharist are to be found. The ritual as recorded *c.* A.D. 200 may be summarized thus:

Blessing over the first cup
Hors d'oeuvres (herbs and sauce)
Explanation (*haggadah*) by the head of the house
First part of the *hallel* (Psalm 113 or Psalms 113–114)
The second cup
Blessing over the (unleavened) bread
The Passover lamb
Blessing (*Birkath ha-mazon*) over the third cup ("the cup of blessing")
Second part of the *hallel* (Psalms 114–118 or 115–118)
Praise over the fourth cup.

The New Testament narratives fit easily into this framework. All the three themes mentioned by Heinemann occur in the words of the rite, which includes one or two phrases which have survived in the Christian anaphora. At the Passover a paragraph is added to the *Birkath ha-mazon* in which God is asked to remember the Messiah and all the house of Israel, and this may have prompted

Jewish prayers

Jesus' "Do this for my remembrance." The word "remembrance" denotes no mere calling to mind. In the Passover, past, present, and future are simultaneously involved. The past, by being "re-membered," becomes a present reality, while the future coming of God's judgement is symbolized by the four cups. The *haggadah* begins with a series of verbs of "acknowledgement" in a way that was picked up in some of the earliest liturgies, and became a constant style for beginning the anaphora (see *b*. below).

As time went on, the Sanctus began to appear in the Christian anaphora. It is always introduced by a passage describing the worship of the angels in heaven, and this must have arisen from the similar introduction to the Sanctus in the synagogue service (see *c*. below), though the time and manner of its transfer to the eucharist remain unknown.

The rite for the Day of Atonement included a prayer *Attah konanta* (see *d*. below), which begins with Creation and goes on to the Fall; this again becomes a prominent feature in the Eastern anaphoras.

Some scholars have pointed to the *kiddush*-cup (the blessing of a cup before a meal) as a possible source of the anaphora; and some have argued that Jesus and the Twelve formed a *chaburah* (a group of like-minded men who met to take meals together); but there is no evidence that these existed as early as Jesus' time.

However much or little importance is attached to individual details, there seems to be a growing consensus among scholars that Jewish prayers provided the soil from which Christian liturgy grew.

a. The text translated below is that of the *Siddur Rav Saadya Gaon* (tenth-century manuscript).
b. Mishnah, *Pesahim*, 10.5.
c. *Prex Eucharistica*, below.
d. As *a*.

BIBLIOGRAPHY
Prex Eucharistica, pp. 9–12, 24, 36–7, 56.
J. Heinemann, *Prayer in the Talmud* (1977).

L. Ligier, (1) "From the Last Supper to the Eucharist," in L.C. Sheppard (ed.), *The New Liturgy* (1970), pp. 113–50. (2) "The Origins of the Eucharistic Prayer," in *Studia Liturgica,* 9(1973), pp. 161–85.

R. T. Beckwith, "The Daily and Weekly Worship of the Primitive Church in relation to its Jewish Antecedents," in *The Evangelical Quarterly,* 56(1984), pp. 64–80, 138–58. *Daily and Weekly Worship—from Jewish to Christian* (1987).

T. J. Talley, "The Literary Structure of the Eucharistic Prayer," in *Worship,* 58(1984), pp. 404–20.

B. D. Spinks, "The Jewish Sources for the Sanctus," in *The Heythrop Journal,* 21(1980), pp. 168–79.

Dix, *The Shape,* pp. 50–6, 214–25.

Bouyer, pp. 50–90.

a. Blessing for food

Blessing of him who nourishes
Blessed are you, Lord our God, King of the universe, for you nourish us and the whole world with goodness, grace, kindness, and mercy.

Blessed are you, Lord, for you nourish the universe.

Blessing for the land
We will give thanks to you, Lord our God, because you have given us for our inheritance a desirable land, good and wide, the covenant and the law, life and food.

(*On the feasts of* Hanukkah *and* Purim, *here follows an embolism.*)

And for all these things we give you thanks and bless your name for ever and beyond.

Blessed are you, Lord, for the land and for food.

Blessing for Jerusalem
Have mercy, Lord our God, on us your people Israel, and your city Jerusalem, on your sanctuary and your dwelling place, on Zion, the habitation of your glory, and the great and holy house over which your name is invoked. Restore the kingdom of the house of David to its place in our days, and speedily build Jerusalem.

(*On the feast of* Passover, *here follows this embolism:*

Our God and God of our fathers, may there arise in your sight, and come, and be present, and be regarded, and be pleasing, and be heard, and be visited, and be remembered, our remembrance and our visitation, and the remembrance of our fathers, and the remembrance of the Messiah, the son of your servant David, and the remembrance of Jerusalem, the city of your holiness, and the remembrance of all your people, the house of Israel: for escape, for prosperity, for grace, and for loving-kindness and mercy, for life and for peace, on this day of the Feast of Unleavened Bread. Remember us on this day, Lord our God, for prosperity, and visit us on it for blessing, and save us on it for life. And by the word of salvation and mercy spare us, and grant us grace, and have mercy on us, and save us: for our eyes look to you, for you, O God, are a gracious and merciful king.)

Blessed are you, Lord, for you build Jerusalem. Amen.

[*Blessing of the good and beneficent*

Blessed are you, Lord our God, King of the universe, God, our father, our king, our creator, our redeemer, good and beneficent king, who day by day is concerned to benefit us in many ways, and himself will increase us for ever in grace and kindness and spirit and mercy and every good thing.]

b. The Passover Haggadah
   At the elevation of the cup:

Wherefore we ought to celebrate, praise, glorify, magnify, exalt, honor, bless, extol, and proclaim him victor, who did all these signs among our fathers and among us: he brought us out of slavery into freedom, from sorrow to joy, from mourning to a feast-day, from darkness into a great light, from purchase to ransom. Let us therefore say before him, "Hallelujah."

c. The Yōtser

. . . May you be blessed, our rock, our king, our redeemer, who creates the saints. May your name be glorified for ever, our king,

who makes the angels. Your angels stand over the world and proclaim aloud, in fear, with one voice the great words of the living
God and king of the universe. All beloved, all the chosen, all powers, and all (men) do the will of their creator in fear and trembling; and all open their mouths in holiness and purity, singing
melodiously, and bless and glorify and magnify and adore the
holy king, the name of God, mighty king, great and terrible: holy
is he. And all, one from another, take upon them the yoke of the
heavenly kingdom and give each other in turn to proclaim the
holy creator with a quiet mind, a bright tongue, and a holy gentleness, all with one mind answering and saying in fear:

Holy, holy, holy (is the) Lord of hosts; the whole earth is full of
his glory.

And the wheels and the holy living creatures raise themselves
with great thunder, give glory from the other side and say:

Blessed be the glory of the Lord from his place . . .

d. Attah konanta

You founded the world in the beginning; you established the
globe, and made the universe, and molded the creatures.

When you saw the empty void, the darkness, and the spirit on
the face of the deep, you scattered the blackness and aroused the
light . . .

He fell away from your word and was expelled from Eden; and
you did not destroy him, because he was the workmanship of
your hands . . .

2 The New Testament

There is a close connection between the four accounts of the Last Supper (Matthew, Mark, Luke, 1 Corinthians) and the structure and language of the early liturgies. Joachim Jeremias, indeed, held that the accounts embodied already existing liturgical units, while Heinz Schürmann concluded that the accounts were written for liturgical use. Most probably the gospels influenced the liturgical forms and *vice versa*. It should not be forgotten that almost the entire New Testament originated in readings at the liturgical assembly.

A sequence of four actions over the bread (taking, blessing, breaking, and distributing) is deeply embedded in the tradition, appearing also in the feedings of the four thousand and the five thousand, and in the meal at Emmaus. Three of the actions are repeated over the cup at the Last Supper, making seven actions in all, which form the framework upon which all the early liturgies are built. It is the great merit of Dom Gregory Dix to have emphasized this fact so strongly that almost all modern liturgies have adopted this framework, and have taken pains to make it clear to the worshipper. All the early liturgies telescope the seven actions into four, taking and giving thanks over the bread and the cup simultaneously, and delaying the breaking and distribution of the bread until the cup also has been blessed.

The Christian Church clearly saw itself as bound to obey the command "Do this for my remembrance," even though it is absent from Mark and Matthew. The first name given to the resultant service was "the breaking of the bread," as in the quotations from Acts below, and this action has always remained part of the service; but by the second century the name had been superseded by "eucharist" (thanksgiving). The first action, "taking," was identified by Dix with the later offertory, but this identification has been generally rejected. As Jeremias has shown, the use of the word "take" is a stylistic mannerism without theological significance. It refers to the action of the paterfamilias at the Passover, who raises the bread a handsbreadth from the table, not to anyone bringing it there, still less offering it.

The four accounts fall into two pairs: Mark and Matthew, Paul and Luke. It is not possible to decide which is the earlier tradition, since each contains a primitive feature which the other has discarded (see below). Already in the New Testament there is evidence of parallelism, i.e. shaping the form of words so that what is said of the bread is also said of the cup, and *vice versa*. In later centuries the accounts are harmonized and expanded to considerable length by the addition of such phrases as "looking up to heaven" (Mark 6:41), "in his holy and venerable hands," and "to his holy and blessed disciples and apostles."

The Fourth Gospel holds that the Last Supper took place the night before the Passover, and presents Jesus as the Passover lamb, crucified while the lambs were being slaughtered. The others all clearly regard the Supper as having been the Passover meal: such features as Luke's first cup and Matthew's "hymn" belong to the Passover ritual. The liturgies follow suit, indicating this by such phrases as "the night before he suffered." No attempt to reconcile the Johannine dating with the Synoptic has been generally accepted.

One textual problem must be mentioned: all MSS of Luke include a cup before the bread, and some omit the cup after the bread, producing the order cup—bread. Scholars are divided as to which reading should be preferred. The cup before the bread appears also in the *Didache* (see below, p. 20), and in 1 Corinthians 10:16 ("The cup of blessing . . ."), and it is possible that it may represent a very early usage which soon disappeared.

The precise meaning of "remembrance" (*anamnesis*) is also a matter of debate. Jeremias urged that the phrase meant "Do this to put God in remembrance of me," and is able to quote such passages as Isaiah 62:6–7 in his support: "You who put the Lord in remembrance, take no rest . . ." Dix, on the other hand, proposed that it means a "re-calling" or "re-presenting" before God, but in all three examples that he quotes from the Old Testament, what is recalled is the *sin* of the person concerned, so their relevance may be questioned. In Jewish usage the word includes proclamation, and Paul emphasizes this in 1 Corinthians: "You proclaim the Lord's death till he comes." The injunction is carried out in the liturgies in the special section of the eucharistic prayer known as the "anamnesis," which follows immediately after the Institution Narrative, and proclaims the Passion, Resurrection, and Ascension of Jesus Christ.

It is possible to trace within the New Testament the process by which the words over the bread at the beginning of the Supper and those over the cup "after supper" (still clearly distinguished in Paul and Luke) were combined in a single thanksgiving. Mark and Matthew already have the cup following the bread without anything intervening, so that it was only a short step to combining the two graces into a single prayer. Since the grace over bread was shorter and less impressive than that over the cup, it was easily absorbed into the latter. At the same time the seven actions would be reduced to four, with thanks being given over the cup before the bread was broken and distributed.

Another debated question is whether the words "bless" and "give thanks over" have significantly different meanings. Mark and Matthew preserve the distinction between blessing the bread and giving thanks over the cup, which is already obliterated in Paul and Luke. A similar problem arises in Jewish prayers, with similarly inconclusive answers.

In view of the later use of sacrificial language in the liturgies, it should be noted that the phrase "the blood of the covenant" refers back to Exodus 24:8, the sacrifice at the foot of Sinai. But in the quotations below from the Epistles, the sacrifices mentioned are "spiritual," and the offerings are of "ourselves" or of "praise," and these senses continue into the earliest liturgical texts, such as Justin Martyr (see below, p. 28).

The prayer in Acts 4 is not explicitly set in the context of a eucharist, though a celebration would be a natural reaction to the release of Peter and John from prison. It may be taken as typical of the kind of prayer that the author of Acts was accustomed to hear. As later in Justin and Hippolytus, it begins with a reference to Creation from Psalm 146 (cf. Nehemiah 9:6 and *St. Mark*, see below, p.53), goes on to an emphatic allusion to the suffering of

Jesus, and ends with a petition for the worshippers, who are "filled with the holy Spirit" (verse 31).

Though absent from the earliest eucharistic prayers, the Sanctus soon becomes an almost invariable feature. It was probably taken over into Christian worship from Jewish prayers, where it occurs in three different contexts. However, a form of the Sanctus already introduces the heavenly worship in Revelation, chapters 4 and 5, which is generally believed to be an idealized presentation of Christian liturgy. In chapter 4 it is followed by the praise of God, first for creating all things, and then for redeeming man by the blood of Christ. These themes appear in the prayer from Acts, are singled out by Justin (q.v.), and continue to appear (with varying degrees of emphasis) in all later eucharistic prayers. The doxology and "Amen" which conclude chapter 5 also set a precedent for later prayers.

BIBLIOGRAPHY
J. Jeremias, *The Eucharistic Words of Jesus* (3rd ed., 1966).
H. Schürmann's three volumes (1953,1955,1957) are conveniently summarized by Vincent Taylor in *The Expository Times*, 74(1962), pp. 77–81.
I. H. Marshall, *Last Supper and Lord's Supper* (1980).
G. A. Mitchell, *Landmarks in Liturgy* (1961), pp. 86–89.
Dix, *The Shape*, pp. 48–102.
L. Ligier, see Bibliography, ch. 1 above (pp.9–10).

Mark 6:41 Taking the five loaves and the two fish, (Jesus) looked up to heaven, and blessed, and broke the loaves, and gave them to the disciples to set before (the people); and he divided the two fish among them all.
=*Matthew 14:18; Luke 9:16.*
Cf. *Mark 8:6–7; Matthew 15:36; John 6:11.*

Mark 14:22–25	*Matthew 26:26–29*
As they were eating, he took bread, and blessed, and broke it, and gave it to them, and said, "Take, this is my body."	As they were eating, *Jesus* took bread, and blessed, and broke it, and gave it to *the disciples*, and said, "Take, *eat*; this is my body."

And he took a cup, and when he had given thanks, he gave it to them, and they all drank of it. And he said to them, "This is my blood of the covenant, which is poured out for many.

Truly, I say to you, I shall not drink again of the fruit of the vine until that day when I drink it new in the kingdom of God."

1 Corinthians 11:23–26
For I received from the Lord what I also delivered to you, that the Lord Jesus on the night when he was betrayed took bread, and when he had given thanks, he broke it, and said, "This is my body which is for you. Do this for my remembrance."

In the same way also the cup, after supper, saying, "This is the new covenant in my blood. Do this, as often as you drink it, for my remembrance."

And he took a cup, and when he had given thanks, he gave it to them, *saying,* "Drink of it, all *of you; for* this is my blood of the covenant, which is poured out for many *for the forgiveness of sins.*

I tell you I shall not drink again of the fruit of *this* vine until that day when I drink it new *with you* in *my Father's* kingdom."

Luke 22:15–20
He said to them *"I have earnestly desired to eat this passover with you before I suffer;* for I tell you that I shall not *eat it* until *it is fulfilled* in the kingdom of God." And he received a cup, and when he had given thanks, he said, *"Take this and divide it among yourselves;* for I tell you that *from now on* I shall not drink of the fruit of the vine until the kingdom of God *comes."* And he took bread, and when he had given thanks, he broke it and *gave it to them,* saying, "This is my body [which is *given* for you. Do this for my remembrance."

And likewise the cup, after supper, saying, "This *cup* is the new covenant in my blood: *it is poured out for you".*]

For as often as you eat this
bread and drink the cup, you
proclaim the Lord's death until
he comes.

Luke 24:30,35 While he was at the table with them, he took the
bread and blessed, and broke it, and gave it to them . . . Then
they told . . . how he was known to them in the breaking of the
bread.

Cf. John 21:13.

Acts 2:42,46,47a They devoted themselves to the apostles' teaching and fellowship*, to the breaking of bread and the prayers . . .
And day by day, attending the Temple together and breaking
bread in their own homes, they partook of food with glad and
generous hearts, praising God and having favor with all the
people.

Acts 20:7,11 On the first day of the week, when we were gathered
together to break bread, Paul talked with them . . . And when
Paul had gone up and had broken bread and eaten, he conversed
with them a long while until daybreak.

Acts 27:35 When he had said this, he took bread and gave thanks
to God in the presence of all, and broke it, and began to eat.

Acts 4:24–30 Sovereign Lord, who "made the heaven and the
earth and the sea and everything in them," you said by the mouth
of our father David your servant[1] through the Holy Spirit, "Why
did the Gentiles rage, and the people imagine vain things? The
kings of the earth set themselves in array, and the rulers were
gathered together against the Lord and against his Anointed."[2]
And in truth both Herod and Pilate were gathered together in this
city with the Gentiles and the peoples of Israel against your holy
servant Jesus, to do whatever your hand and your decree had
foreordained to be done.

Now, Lord, look upon their threats, and grant to your servants to
speak your word with all boldness, while you stretch out your

---

*See footnote 3 below.
1. *Or* child (cf. the *Didache,* below).
2. Psalm 2:1–2.

hand to heal, and signs and wonders are done through the name of your holy servant Jesus.

1 Corinthians 10:16 The cup of blessing which we bless, is it not a participation[3] in the blood of Christ? The bread which we break, is it not a participation in the body of Christ?

Romans 12:1 I appeal to you, brethren, by the mercies of God, to present your bodies as a living sacrifice, holy and acceptable to God, your spiritual[4] worship.

Hebrews 13:15 Through him let us continually offer up to God a sacrifice of praise; that is, the fruit of lips that acknowledge his Name. But do not neglect good works and fellowship,* for such sacrifices are pleasing to God.

1 Peter 2:5 As living stones, be built into a spiritual[5] house, to be a holy priesthood, to offer spiritual sacrifices acceptable to God through Jesus Christ.

Revelation 4:8,11; 5:9,13,14 The four living creatures, each with six wings, are full of eyes all round and within, and day and night they never cease to sing: "Holy, holy, holy is the Lord God almighty, who was and is and is to come" . . . "You are worthy, our Lord and God, to receive glory and honor and power, for you created all things, and by your will they existed and were created" . . . "You are worthy to take the scroll and open its seals, for you were slain, and by your blood you ransomed men for God from every tribe and tongue and people and nation, and you made them a kingdom and priests to our God, and they shall reign on earth" . . . "To him who sits on the throne and to the Lamb be blessing and honor and glory and might for ever and ever." And the four living creatures said, "Amen."

*See footnote 3 below.
3. Greek: *koinōnia.*
4. Greek: *logikēn.*
5. Greek: *pneumatikos.*

3 The *Didache*

This short treatise, whose full title is *The Teaching of the Twelve Apostles*, came to light in 1875, when Archbishop Bryennios discovered the only complete Greek manuscript in Jerusalem. First published in 1883, it evoked a great deal of scholarly argument about its date and place of origin. English and American scholars at first tended to assign it to the second century, but it is now generally accepted as most probably having been written in the first century in Syria. J.-P. Audet suggested that, when the *Didache* quotes sayings of Jesus, its version is earlier than that given in Matthew's gospel, which implies a date of around A.D. 60. The author is unknown, but the claim to apostolic authority is a commonplace in early Christian writing.

The work is the earliest known example of a Church Order (see the Preface, p. vii). It starts with a section entitled "The Two Ways"; then, after chapters on baptism and fasting, follow the prayers printed below. There is still no agreement on the nature of the service concerned. It may be an agape (a meal with a liturgical setting) or a eucharist. Or chapter 9 may be an agape and chapter 10 a eucharist. Chapter 14 is clearly the eucharist.

In favor of both chapters being intended for an agape:
1) The cup is blessed before the bread. This is also the case in the agape described in Hippolytus, ch. 25 (Dix, ch. 26).
2) Ch. 10 begins "After you have had your fill," which suggests that the meal is eaten between the two chapters. There is an emphasis on food and drink in ch. 10 which suggests a meal rather than a service.
3) There is no reference to the Last Supper, or the redemptive power of the Passion, or the Resurrection.

In favor of both chapters being intended for a eucharist:
1) The first words of ch. 9 are: *peri tēs eucharistias*. This may still mean "thanksgiving" in a general sense, but the liturgical sense is possible.

2) The rubric at the end of ch. 9 seems more appropriate to a eucharist.

3) The words translated "had your fill" recur in the *Liturgy of St. Mark* after the communion.

4) The compiler of the *Apostolic Constitutions* clearly thought that they were eucharistic prayers (see below, pp. 101–102).

In any case, in the first century or even later, the dividing line between agape and eucharist must have been very fine. It is perhaps most probable that ch. 9 was originally intended as an agape, but was later understood as a eucharist, while ch. 10 was always a eucharistic prayer. It does not seem possible to reach an unassailable conclusion on the available evidence.

On the other hand, the Jewish element in these prayers is unmistakable, and it has been suggested that they are Christian adaptations of Jewish forms. The thanksgivings even have a *chatimah* (see p.7), here the same for each section: "glory to you for evermore" or a slight expansion of that. The idea of the Church as "the vine" is Jewish, as are the references to the Name of God and Creation; and perhaps the eschatological gathering of the Church into the Kingdom of God. The emphasis on "knowledge" suggests hellenistic Judaism. The Christology of the prayers is archaic, with the use of the word *pais* to describe Jesus. It may mean either "child" or "servant," and occurs several times in the early chapters of Acts.

The image of the broken bread scattered on the mountains may go back to John 6:12 (the feeding of the five thousand) and the "one loaf" of 1 Corinthians 10:17. The quotation at the end of ch. 9 is from Matthew 7:6. The Aramaic words *Marana tha* were interpreted by the early Fathers as meaning "The Lord has come," but they should probably be translated "Come, Lord," as in the parallel passages at the end of 1 Corinthians 16:22 and Revelation 22:20. In all three passages prayer is made for the grace of Christ, and it is possible that a liturgical closing formula is behind all three.

Chapter 14 directs a breaking of bread on Sunday, and stresses that this must be a "pure sacrifice." This requirement is based on a quotation from Malachi which is also used by Justin, Irenaeus, Tertullian, and the *Liturgy of St. Mark* (pp. 27,53 below). They regard it as foretelling the Christian eucharist, which is the only pure sacrifice. W. Rordorf comments that the word "sacrifice" does not necessarily involve "the later idea of eucharistic sacrifice, but more probably means the prayer of thanksgiving, which is frequently evoked in the oldest Christian literature and is rightly opposed to the bloody offerings of antiquity, both Jewish and pagan." The word here makes its first appearance in relation to the eucharist, but nothing is said as yet about what is offered. The requirement of confession may be based on Leviticus 5:5, "when a man is guilty . . . he shall confess the sin which he has committed" before offering a sacrifice; and the requirement of reconciliation on Matthew 5:23–4, "first be reconciled to your brother, and then offer your gift."

The *Didache* evidently had a wide circulation. In a heavily rewritten form, it was incorporated into Book VII of the *Apostolic Constitutions* (see below, p.100), showing that it was still current in Syria in the fourth century. It was very popular in Egypt, where it was translated into Coptic. A papyrus fragment, possibly fourth-century, besides the interesting variant readings mentioned in the notes, adds a blessing of incense which is not in the Greek. Rordorf regards it as a late addition, but it appears in the *Apostolic Constitutions* version, adapted for ointment, so is unlikely to be later than *c.* 300. There are similar prayers in Hippolytus (see p.36) and Sarapion (see p.79). The "broken bread" prayer is quoted in the anaphoras of Sarapion and the Deir Balyzeh papyrus (see pp.77,80). There are also versions in Latin, Ethiopic, and Georgian.

BIBLIOGRAPHY
Prex Eucharistica, pp. 66–8.
F. E. Vokes, (1) *The Riddle of the Didache* (1938). (2) "The Didache still debated," in *Church Quarterly*, 3 (1970), pp. 57–62.
J.-P. Audet, *Le Didaché: Instruction des Apôtres* (1958).
W. Rordorf and A. Tuilier, *La Doctrine des douze Apôtres* (1978).
S. Gero, "The So-called Ointment Prayer in the Coptic Version of the Didache: A Re-evaluation," in *Harvard Theological Review*, 70 (1977), pp. 67–84.

CHAPTERS 1–6: "THE TWO WAYS"
CHAPTER 7: BAPTISM
CHAPTER 8: FASTING
CHAPTER 9
About the thanksgiving: give thanks thus:

First, about the cup:

We give thanks to you, our Father, for the holy vine of your child[1]
David, which you made known to us through your child Jesus;
glory to you for evermore.

And about the broken bread:

We give thanks to you, our Father, for the life and knowledge
which you made known to us through your child Jesus;
glory to you for evermore.

As this broken bread was scattered over the mountains, and
when brought together became one, so let your Church be
brought together from the ends of the earth into your kingdom;
for yours are the glory and the power through Jesus Christ[2] for
evermore.

*But let no one eat or drink of your thanksgiving but those who have been
baptized in the name of the Lord. For about this also the Lord has said,
"Do not give what is holy to the dogs."*

CHAPTER 10
And after you have had your fill, give thanks thus:

We give thanks to you, holy Father, for your holy Name which
you have enshrined in our hearts, and for the knowledge and
faith and immortality which you made known to us through
your child Jesus;
glory to you for evermore.

You, almighty Master, created all things for the sake of your
Name, and gave food and drink to mankind for their enjoyment,
that they might give you thanks; but to us you have granted spiri-

1. *Or* servant; *cf.* Acts 3:13, 4:24–30 (*above*), *etc.*
2. *Coptic omits:* "through Jesus Christ."

tual food and drink and eternal life through your child Jesus. Above all we give you thanks because you are mighty; glory to you for evermore. Amen.

Remember, Lord, your Church, to deliver it from all evil and to perfect it in your love; bring it together from the four winds, now sanctified,[3] into your kingdom which you have prepared for it; for yours are the power and the glory for evermore.

May grace[4] come, and may this world pass away.

Hosanna to the God[5] of David.

If any is holy, let him come; if any is not, let him repent. Marana tha. Amen.

[*But about the words over the sweet savor, give thanks thus, as we say:*[6]

We give thanks to you, Father, for the sweet savor which you made known to us through your Son Jesus; glory to you for evermore. Amen.][6]

CHAPTERS 11–13: PROPHETS
CHAPTER 14

On the Lord's day of the Lord, come together, break bread, and give thanks, having first confessed your transgressions, that your sacrifice may be pure.

But let none who has a quarrel with his companion join with you until they have been reconciled, that your sacrifice may not be defiled.

For this is that which was spoken by the Lord, "In every place, and at every time, offer me a pure sacrifice; for I am a great king, says the Lord, and my Name is wonderful among the nations."[7]

CHAPTER 15: CHURCH DISCIPLINE
CHAPTER 16: THE LAST DAY

3. *Coptic omits:* "now sanctified."
4. *Coptic:* the Lord
5. *Coptic:* house
6. *Only in Coptic:* "[But . . . . Amen]"
7. Malachi 1:11b.

The Didache

4 Justin Martyr

Born in Samaria, Justin was converted to Christianity *c*. A.D. 130. His *Dialogue with Trypho*, a Jew, was written at Ephesus *c*. 135. He later went to Rome, where he wrote his *First Apology c*. 150, and was martyred *c*. 165. In the *Dialogue* he is concerned to show that the eucharist superseded the Jewish sacrifices; in the *Apology*, to show the innocent character of Christian worship.

Chapter 41 of the *Dialogue* opens with a reference to Leviticus 14:10,20 (a cleansed leper "shall take a flour offering . . . of fine flour mixed with oil . . . And the priest shall offer . . . the flour offering on the altar"). This is a type of the Christian thanksgiving: the Christian, cleansed from sin by baptism, brings *his* offering of bread and wine. There follows a brief analysis of the thanksgiving which "Jesus handed down to us to do." It is primarily the remembrance (*anamnesis*) of his Passion, which leads us to thank God "for creating the world . . . and for freeing us from evil," the two themes which we noted as prominent in Jewish prayer, though now closely linked together. There follows the quotation from Malachi already met with in the *Didache*, again taken as a prophecy of the eucharist, which is here described as a sacrifice of the bread and the cup. Chapter 70 adds that the remembrance is also of the Incarnation.

Chapter 117 returns to the theme of sacrifice, now saying that prayers and thanksgiving are the only perfect sacrifices, because they are made at the eucharist. The contradiction with ch. 41 is only apparent, since the offering of the bread and cup was always accompanied by prayer and thanksgiving, as appears below; and the "food" itself is now called *eucharistia*.

In the *Apology* Justin described two eucharists, one following a baptism, and the other the ordinary Sunday morning service. These are the earliest surviving accounts of the eucharist. Putting the two accounts together, this outline is obtained:

1. Readings from the apostles or the prophets.
2. Discourse on the readings by the president.
3. Common prayers (standing).

4. The kiss of peace.
5. Presentation of bread, mixed wine, and water (the last only after a baptism).
6. Prayers and thanksgiving by the president ("praise and glory to God"); the people reply, "Amen."
7. Distribution of the "eucharistized" elements by the deacons.

Justin had no doubt heard accusations against the Christians that they drank blood at their services, and he was anxious to make it clear that the bread and wine over which thanks have been given are no longer "common" bread and wine, but are "the flesh and blood of (the) incarnate Jesus." He then quoted the Institution Narrative in a version drawn from both Paul and Matthew, which suggests a liturgical formula, though accurate scriptural quotation is not to be expected as early as this; but he did not say that the Narrative was actually part of the eucharistic prayer. Possibly Justin was referring to the Institution Narrative when he wrote: "by a word of prayer that is from him" (i.e. Jesus), or this may refer to a tradition of prayer thought to have originated with Jesus (at the Last Supper?). The text can also be translated "by the prayer of the Word, who is from him" (i.e. the Father). But in the passage quoted below from chapter 13, "a word of prayer" is the only possible translation, which makes it likely to be correct in chapter 66 also. Justin made no explanation *how* the bread and wine become the body and blood of Christ, beyond drawing an analogy with the Incarnation. "We have been taught" implies a long-standing tradition.

The leader of the worship is called "the president" (*ho pröestōs;* cf. Romans 12:8). This appears to be the earliest title of the celebrant of the eucharist, and implies the corporate nature of the rite; according to Ignatius, he must be a bishop. The prayer is still left to the president to compose "at some length . . . to the best of his ability." Justin did not mention any breaking of the bread, but it can be safely assumed that it was performed, though no longer giving its name to the service.

BIBLIOGRAPHY
Prex Eucharistica, pp. 68–74.
L. W. Barnard, *Justin Martyr, His Life and Thought* (1967), ch. x, esp. pp. 142–150.

Dix, *The Shape*, pp. 222–224.

J. A. Jungmann, *The Early Liturgy* (1960), pp. 40–44.

G. J. Cuming, "ΔΓΕΥΧΗΣ ΛΟΓΟΥ (Justin, *Apology*, i. 66,2)," in *JTS*, n.s. 31 (1980), pp. 80–2; also critique by A. Gelston, in *JTS*, n.s. 33(1982), pp. 172–175.

B. D. Spinks, "The Cleansed Leper's Thankoffering before the Lord," in B. D. Spinks (ed.), *The Sacrifice of Praise* (1981), pp. 161–178.

Dialogue with Trypho

41.1 The offering of fine flour . . . which was handed down to be offered by those who were cleansed from leprosy, was a type of the bread of the thanksgiving, which our Lord Jesus Christ handed down to us to do for a remembrance of the suffering which he suffered for those who are cleansed in their souls from all wickedness of men, so that we might give thanks to God, both for creating the world with all things that are in it for the sake of man, and for freeing us from the evil in which we were born, and for accomplishing a complete destruction of the principalities and powers through him who suffered according to his will.

2 Hence God speaks about the sacrifices which were then offered by you, as I said before, through Malachi, one of the twelve (prophets):

My will is not in you, says the Lord, and I will not receive your sacrifices from your hands; for, from the rising of the sun to its setting, my name has been glorified among the nations, and in every place incense is offered to my name and a pure sacrifice, for my name is great among the nations, says the Lord, but you profane it. [Malachi 1:10b–12a.]

3 He is prophesying about the sacrifices which are offered in every place by us, the nations, that is the bread of the thanksgiving and likewise the cup of the thanksgiving, saying that we glorify his name, but you profane it.

70.4 This prophecy is about the bread which Christ handed down to us to do for remembrance of his incarnation for the sake of those who believe in him, for whom he suffered; and about the cup, which he handed down for us to do, giving thanks, for remembrance of his blood.

117.1 So God bears witness in advance that he is well pleased with all the sacrifices in his name, which Jesus the Christ handed down to be done, namely in the eucharist of the bread and the cup, and are done in every place in the world by the Christians.

. . . I myself also say that prayers and thanksgivings made by worthy men are the only sacrifices that are perfect and well-pleasing to God.

For these alone have been handed down by Christians to do even for a remembrance of their solid and liquid food, in which also they remember the suffering which the Son of God suffered for them.

First Apology

13.2 . . . We praise him by a word of prayer and thanksgiving, to the best of our ability, over all the things which we offer . . .

65.1 After we have thus baptized him who has believed and has given his assent, we take him to those who are called brethren where they are assembled, to make common prayers earnestly for ourselves and for him who has been enlightened[1] and for all others everywhere, that, having learned the truth, we may be deemed worthy to be found good citizens also in our actions and guardians of the Commandments, so that we may be saved with eternal salvation.

When we have ended the prayers, we greet one another with a kiss.

Then bread and a cup of water and (a cup) of mixed wine[2] are brought to him who presides over the brethren, and he takes them and sends up praise and glory to the Father of all in the name of the Son and of the Holy Spirit, and gives thanks at some length that we have been deemed worthy of these things from him. When he has finished the prayers and the thanksgiving, all the people give their assent by saying "Amen." "Amen" is the Hebrew for "So be it."

1. *i.e. by baptism.*
2. *Justin probably means two cups, as it is a baptismal eucharist.*

And when the president has given thanks and all the people have assented, those whom we call deacons give to each of those present a portion of the bread and wine and water over which thanks have been given, and take them to those who are not present.

66.1 And we call this food "thanksgiving"; and no one may partake of it unless he is convinced of the truth of our teaching, and has been cleansed with the washing for forgiveness of sins and regeneration, and lives as Christ handed down.

For we do not receive these things as common bread or common drink; but just as our Savior Jesus Christ, being incarnate through the word of God, took flesh and blood for our salvation, so too we have been taught that the food over which thanks have been given by a word of prayer which is from him, (the food) from which our flesh and blood are fed by transformation, is both the flesh and blood of that incarnate Jesus.

For the apostles in the records composed by them which are called gospels, have handed down thus what was commanded of them: that Jesus took bread, gave thanks, and said, "Do this for the remembrance of me; this is my body"; and likewise he took the cup, gave thanks, and said "This is my blood"; and gave to them alone.

And the evil demons have imitated this and handed it down to be done also in the mysteries of Mithras. For as you know or may learn, bread and a cup of water are used with certain formulas in their rites of initiation.

67.1 And thereafter we continually remind one another of these things. Those who have the means help all those in need; and we are always together.

And we bless the Maker of all things through his Son Jesus Christ and through the Holy Spirit over all that we offer.

And on the day called Sunday an assembly is held in one place of all who live in town or country, and the records of the apostles or the writings of the prophets are read as time allows.

Then, when the reader has finished, the president in a discourse admonishes and exhorts (us) to imitate these good things.

Then we all stand up together and send up prayers; and as we said before, when we have finished praying, bread and wine and water are brought up, and the president likewise sends up prayers and thanksgivings to the best of his ability, and the people assent, saying the Amen; and the (elements over which) thanks have been given are distributed, and everyone partakes; and they are sent through the deacons to those who are not present.

And the wealthy who so desire give what they wish, as each chooses; and what is collected is deposited with the president.

He helps orphans and widows, and those who through sickness or any other cause are in need, and those in prison, and strangers sojourning among us; in a word, he takes care of all those who are in need.

And we all assemble together on Sunday, because it is the first day, on which God transformed darkness and matter, and made the world; and Jesus Christ our Savior rose from the dead on that day; for they crucified him the day before Saturday; and the day after Saturday, which is Sunday, he appeared to his apostles and disciples, and taught them these things which we have presented to you also for your consideration.

5 Hippolytus: The *Apostolic Tradition*

This work is generally believed to have come down to us in the
form of an anonymous, untitled treatise which in the nineteenth
century was given the name of *The Egyptian Church Order*. This is
extant in Latin, Coptic, Arabic, and Ethiopic versions, and in adaptations such as *The Canons of Hippolytus, The Apostolic Constitutions*,
and the *Testamentum Domini* (q.v.). Its identification was established independently by E. Schwarz in 1910 and R.H. Connolly in
1916, and implies a date of *c.* 215. The work professedly reflects
"the tradition which has remained until now," and so may be
taken as a witness to Roman practice some fifty years earlier. This
brings it close to the time of Justin, with whose account it agrees
quite closely. Hippolytus gives us the earliest surviving text of a
eucharistic prayer, but this should not be regarded as *the* Roman
prayer of its time, being an individual specimen rather than an
invariable form.

Since the original Greek is largely lost, the translation raises problems. Here chapters 4, 5, 6, and 21 are translated from the Latin;
chapter 9, which is lacking from the Latin, from the Sahidic
Coptic version. The numbering follows the editions of Botte and
Cuming: the equivalent chapters in Dix's edition are 4, 5, 6, 10, 22
and 23.

Like Justin, Hippolytus describes two eucharists, one after an ordination, the other after a baptism. Put together, they produce the
following outline:

1. The prayers
2. The kiss of peace
3. The offering (in baptism, with milk and honey, and water)
4. The anaphora (including blessings of produce)
5. Discourse by the bishop, "giving a reason for all these things"
6. The fraction
7. The distribution.

This should be compared with the outline supplied by Justin
(pp.25–26).

The anaphora falls into six sections:

1. The Sursum corda
2. The preface
3. The Institution Narrative
4. The anamnesis
5. The epiclesis
6. The doxology.

There is a danger of imposing later terminology: the distinction between the sections is not as clear-cut as in later anaphoras; but this analysis shows that most of the normal features of a fourth-century anaphora were present, at any rate in embryo, quite early on. The obvious exceptions are the Sanctus, which only entered the anaphora later, and the intercessions, which in Hippolytus' time were made before the peace (see ch. 21). The pattern of ministry is slightly more complex than in Justin: deacons bring up the offering, and presbyters join in the distribution.

The Sursum corda begins as in Egypt and in the Roman Canon; this is its earliest appearance. The preface almost ignores Creation, saying only "through whom you made all things," despite Justin's emphasis on this theme. It is almost entirely devoted to the life of Christ. The language of this section has many parallels in other writings of Hippolytus, and in his individual theology (see Connolly's article listed in the Bibliography). It also contains echoes of Justin and Irenaeus, both of whom were regarded by Hippolytus as authoritative teachers.

The preface runs on without a break into the Institution Narrative. This is given in a very brief form which may be a survival from very early days, or a deliberate shortening of the gospel text for liturgical use. It is placed at the right point chronologically, following the reference to Jesus' ministry and preceding the "remembrance" of his death and resurrection.

The very brief anamnesis is the only part of the anaphora which reappears in the Roman Canon, as it does also in the version of the latter quoted by Ambrose, and in the *Apostolic Constitutions* (see p. 110). It leads into the offering of the bread and the cup, which is an innovation, since Justin only spoke of sending up

Hippolytus: The Apostolic Tradition

prayers and thanksgivings. As in Justin, God is thanked for making us worthy to celebrate the eucharist.

The epiclesis section has aroused a good deal of controversy, partly because of the difficulty of translating the Latin, partly because it has been taken to imply a "higher" doctrine of the Holy Spirit than was current *c.* 215. Various ways of dealing with the first problem have been proposed (see footnote 4 and, in detail, *Essays on Hippolytus* in the Bibliography). The *Testamentum Domini* (see p.140) has a translation which smoothes over the problem, which led Dix to believe that the translator used a better manuscript than the Latin translator. But the smoothness is more probably due to the translator trying to produce a viable piece of liturgy from a corrupt text.

As to the doctrinal problem, the epiclesis has been thought by some scholars to be a fourth-century interpolation. However, the Spirit is not asked to change the elements (as he surely would have been in the fourth century), but only to come upon them for the benefit of the communicants, which is not at all incongruous with early third-century doctrine. The emphasis on the *re*-uniting of the Church recalls the *Didache,* as does the description of Christ as "child" or "servant." In chapter 21 Hippolytus used the terminology of "likeness" (of the body and blood) which remains in the liturgical texts as late as Basil and Ambrose.

E. C. Ratcliff argued that Hippolytus' anaphora originally ended with the Sanctus; though his conclusion has not been widely accepted, the article is still well worth reading for its various insights.

The blessings of oil, cheese, and olives may be intended to follow the doxology, or, as in later years, to be inserted immediately before it.

Hippolytus made it quite clear that this prayer is not to be regarded as mandatory, but simply as a model. The bishop may use his own words or a fixed form. Chapter 9 has survived only in Coptic, Arabic, and Ethiopic: the last two translations clearly date from a time when free composition was a thing of the past, since they omit "not at all" and read "It is necessary"!

Hippolytus: The Apostolic Tradition

An enlarged version of the anaphora has remained in use in Ethiopia under the name of *The Anaphora of the Apostles*. In recent years adaptations have appeared in the Roman rite (prayer 2), the Church of England (prayer 3), and the American Lutheran book (prayer 4).

BIBLIOGRAPHY
G. J. Cuming, (1) *Hippolytus: a text for students* (1976); with bibliography.
(2) "The Eucharist," in G. J. Cuming (ed.), *Essays on Hippolytus* (1978), pp. 39–51; detailed discussion of anaphora.
B. Botte, *La Tradition Apostolique de Saint Hippolyte* (1972).
G. Dix, (1) *The Apostolic Tradition of Saint Hippolytus* ([1]1937; [2]1968, ed. H. Chadwick). (2) *The Shape*, pp. 157–162.
R. H. Connolly, "The Eucharistic Prayer of Hippolytus" in *JTS*, 39(1938), pp. 358–369.
J. A. Jungmann, *The Early Liturgy* (1960), pp. 52–73.
E. C. Ratcliff, "The Sanctus and the pattern of the early Anaphora" in *Journal of Ecclesiastical History*, 1(1950), pp. 29–36, 125–134; reprinted in A. H. Couratin and D. H. Tripp (eds.), *E. C. Ratcliff: Liturgical Studies* (1976), pp. 18–40.

CHAPTER 1: PROLOGUE
CHAPTERS 2,3: ORDINATION OF A BISHOP
CHAPTER 4: THE EUCHARIST
And when he has been made bishop, all shall offer the kiss of peace, greeting him because he has been made worthy.

Then the deacons shall present the offering to him; and he, laying his hands on it with all the presbytery, shall say, giving thanks:

The Lord be with you.[1]

And all shall say:
    And with your spirit.
    Up with your hearts.[2]
    We have (them) with the Lord.
    Let us give thanks to the Lord.
    It is fitting and right.

1. *Coptic adds* all.
2. *The Latin has no verb.*

And then he shall continue thus:

We render thanks to you, O God, through your beloved child[3] Jesus Christ, whom in the last times you sent to us as a savior and redeemer and angel of your will; who is your inseparable Word, through whom you made all things, and in whom you were well pleased. You sent him from heaven into a virgin's womb; and conceived in the womb, he was made flesh and was manifested as your Son, being born of the Holy Spirit and the Virgin. Fulfilling your will and gaining for you a holy people, he stretched out his hands when he should suffer, that he might release from suffering those who have believed in you.

And when he was betrayed to voluntary suffering that he might destroy death, and break the bonds of the devil, and tread down hell, and shine upon the righteous, and fix a term, and manifest the resurrection, he took bread and gave thanks to you, saying, "Take, eat; this is my body, which shall be broken for you." Likewise also the cup, saying, "This is my blood, which is shed for you; when you do this, you make my remembrance."

Remembering therefore his death and resurrection, we offer to you the bread and the cup, giving you thanks because you have held us worthy to stand before you and minister to you.

And we ask that you would send your Holy Spirit upon the offering of your holy Church; that, gathering her into one, you would grant to all who receive the holy things (to receive) for the fullness of the Holy Spirit for the strengthening of faith in truth;[4] that we may praise and glorify you through your child[5] Jesus Christ; through whom be glory and honor to you, to the Father and the Son, with the Holy Spirit,[6] in your holy Church, both now and to the ages of ages. Amen.

---

3. *Or servant (cf. Didache, p.23).*
4. *The Latin is almost untranslatable at this point. Literally translated, "grant" has no object; hence the addition of "to receive." Another possible translation is:* grant to all of us who receive the holy things for the fullness . . . in truth, that we may praise and glorify you . . .
5. *Cf. note 3.*
6. *Not in the Ethiopic:* "to the Father and the Son, with the Holy Spirit."

Hippolytus: The Apostolic Tradition　　　　　　　　　　　　35

CHAPTER 5: THE BLESSING OF OIL

If anyone offers oil, (the bishop) shall render thanks in the same way as for the offering of bread and wine, not saying (it) word for word, but to similar effect, saying:

O God, sanctifier of this oil, as you give health to[7] those who use[8] and receive (that) with which you anointed kings, priests, and prophets, so may it give strength to all those who taste it and health to all who use it.

CHAPTER 6: THE BLESSING OF CHEESE AND OLIVES

Likewise, if anyone offers cheese and olives, he shall say thus: Sanctify this milk which has been coagulated, coagulating us also to your love.

Make this fruit of the olive not to depart from your sweetness, which is an example of your richness which you have poured from the tree of life to those who hope in you.

But in every blessing shall be said:
To you be glory, both to the Father and the Son, with the Holy Spirit, in the holy Church, both now and always and to all the ages of ages. (Amen.)

CHAPTERS 7.1–9.2: PRIESTS, DEACONS, AND CONFESSORS
CHAPTER 9.3–5:

And the bishop shall give thanks according to what we said above. It is not at all necessary for him to utter the same words that we said above, as though reciting them from memory, when giving thanks to God; but let each pray according to his ability. If indeed he is able to pray sufficiently and with a solemn prayer, it is good. But if anyone who prays, recites a prayer according to a fixed form, do not prevent him. Only, he must pray what is sound and orthodox.

---

7. *Dix conjectures:* sanctify (hagiazō *misread as* hugiazō?).
8. *Ethiopic:* are anointed: *the Latin translator has misread* chriomenois ("anointed") *as* chrōmenois ("using").

CHAPTERS 10 – 14: MINOR ORDERS

CHAPTERS 15 – 20: CATECHUMENS

CHAPTER 21: BAPTISM (numbering as in Botte and Cuming; Dix, chs. 21–23)

POST-BAPTISMAL PRAYER; ANOINTING; SEALING.

Then (the newly-baptized) shall pray together with all the people; but they do not pray with the faithful until they have carried out all these things.

And when they have prayed, they shall give the kiss of peace.

THE BAPTISMAL EUCHARIST

And then the offering shall be brought up by the deacons to the bishop: and he shall give thanks over the bread for the representation, which the Greeks call "antitype," of the body of Christ; and after the cup mixed with wine for the antitype, which the Greeks call "likeness",[9] of the blood which was shed for all who believed in him;

(and) over milk and honey mixed together in fulfillment of the promise which was made to the Fathers, in which he said, "a land flowing with milk and honey"; in which also Christ gave his flesh, through which those who believe are nourished like little children, making the bitterness of the heart sweet by the gentleness of his word; and over water, as an offering to signify the washing, that the inner man also, which is the soul, may receive the same thing as the body. And the bishop shall give a reason for all these things to those who receive.

And when he breaks the bread, in distributing fragments to each, he shall say:

The bread of heaven in Christ Jesus.

And he who receives shall answer: Amen.

And if there are not enough presbyters, the deacons also shall hold the cups, and stand by in good order and reverence: first, he who holds the water; second, the milk; third, the wine. And they who receive shall taste of each thrice, he who gives it saying:[10] In God the Father almighty. *And he who receives shall say:* Amen.

9. *Botte conjectures:* for the likeness, which the Greeks call *homoiōma.*
10. *Or* he who gives it saying thrice.

And in the Lord Jesus Christ. (*And he shall say:* Amen.)

And in the Holy Spirit and the holy Church.

And he shall say: Amen.

So shall it be done with each one.

CHAPTERS 22–43: OTHER CHURCH OBSERVANCES

6 The Liturgy of Saints Addai and Mari

This liturgy originated in Edessa, a city of northeastern Syria near the frontier between the Roman Empire and Persia, and one of the earliest centers of Christianity. Judaism remained a strong influence, and this liturgy was, unusually, composed in Syriac. After the Council of Ephesus (A.D. 431), the area became Nestorian, and was later occupied by the Arabs. These two circumstances kept the liturgy relatively free from Byzantine influence.

The anaphora is one of those still in use among Nestorian Christians, the others being *Theodore the Interpreter* and *Nestorius*. The group is variously classified as "Chaldaean" or "East Syrian." Portuguese explorers found *Addai and Mari* still in use in the sixteenth century in south India, and a mission sent by the archbishop of Canterbury in the 1890s found it being used in Iraq. Though known in the West, it was not highly regarded by scholars until E. C. Ratcliff published a seminal article in 1929. Since then, the flow of significant articles has continued unabated at the rate of one about every three years. They are conveniently summarized in the article by E. J. Cutrone (1973) and the edition by B. D. Spinks (1980), which makes it unnecessary to do more here than to comment on the salient points of interest.

Weightier than the conjectures of scholars, however well-founded, is the existence of a closely related anaphora, *The Third Anaphora of St Peter*, also known as *Sharar*, which is printed below on pp. 46–51. This most probably shares a common ancestor with *Addai and Mari*, though the two anaphoras developed differently. *Sharar* has added more to the original, but has sometimes preserved more primitive readings.

It was suggested by R. H. Connolly in 1914 that certain priest's private prayers (not included below) were late additions. Ratcliff concurred, and went on to argue that, although *Addai and Mari* in its present form probably dates from about the sixth century, when apparent later accretions are removed, what remains is a very primitive form of anaphora, to which he gives the name "eucharistia." This would be among the oldest surviving eucharistic prayers.

Ratcliff has won universal support for his deletion of the private prayers, and this was confirmed by the later discovery of the Mar Eshaya manuscript, some five centuries earlier than any known to him in 1929; and almost universal support for his deletion of the Sanctus and its immediate context (though this does appear in the Mar Eshaya manuscript; its addition may have been quite early). More debatable were his deletion of the intercessions and the epiclesis, and the suggestion that the *whole* anaphora was originally addressed to Christ, as the post-Sanctus section still is. What remains after these deletions is:

(a) praise to the Creator and Redeemer;
(b) thanksgiving for redemption;
(c) commemoration of Christ's death and resurrection.

The correspondence with Justin's outline is close.

The sections common to *Addai and Mari* and *Sharar* are: the first three paragraphs, from "Worthy of glory" down to "as you taught us", the prayer for the various orders in the Church, the epiclesis, and the final doxology. Of these, the Sanctus and epiclesis are probably not original, but were early additions. The sixth paragraph of *Addai and Mari*, which has the character of an anamnesis, is absent from *Sharar*.

Conspicuous by its absence from all manuscripts of *Addai and Mari* is the Institution Narrative, which however is found in *Sharar*. As yet, no consensus has been reached on the question whether *Addai and Mari* never had an Institution Narrative, or once had one which was removed before the tenth century. Some scholars have thought that the presence of an anamnesis implies a preceding Institution Narrative. The phrase "we have received through tradition the form which is from you" recalls Justin's "by a word of prayer which is from him," which is involved in a similar uncertainty as to the presence or absence of an Institution Narrative. The whole section may be derived from *Theodore* or *Nestorius*.

Ratcliff regarded the epiclesis as anachronistic, but it is present in *Sharar*, and resembles the epiclesis of the *Apostolic Tradition* in asking the Spirit to come upon the offering for the benefit of the communicants, but not asking him to change the elements (the words "and bless and sanctify it" in *Addai and Mari* are probably a late addition from *Theodore* or *Nestorius*). This is quite acceptable in the second or third century.

Sharar addresses *all* the anaphora after the Sanctus to Christ, which supports Ratcliff's suggestion mentioned above. Several recent scholars see the anaphora as consisting of three *berakoth* and a doxology, very much in the Jewish manner (compare also the *Didache*).

The text translated below is that recently found in the church of Mar Eshaya, Mosul, which was probably written in the tenth or eleventh century. The congregational parts are completed below (in angle-brackets) from other manuscripts.

BIBLIOGRAPHY
B. D. Spinks (ed.), *Addai and Mari—The Anaphora of the Apostles: a text for students* (1980). Full bibliography.
Prex Eucharistica, pp. 375–380.
LEW, pp. 247–305.
W. F. Macomber, "The oldest known text of the Anaphora of the Apostles Addai and Mari," in *Orientalia Christiana Periodica*, 32(1966), pp. 335–337. (Five other articles by Macomber are listed in Spinks.)
E. J. Cutrone, "The Anaphora of the Apostles: Implications of the Mar Esa'ya Text," in *Theological Studies*, 34(1973), pp. 624–642.
Dix, *The Shape*, pp. 78–87.

PRAYERS OF PREPARATION
PSALMS
PRAYERS
TRISAGION
READINGS (OLD TESTAMENT, ACTS)
PSALM
EPISTLE
ALLELUIA
GOSPEL
DISMISSAL OF CATECHUMENS
PRAYERS OF THE FAITHFUL

The Liturgy of Saints Addai and Mari 41

PRAYER OF INCLINATION
TRANSFER OF GIFTS
CREED
PREPARATION FOR ANAPHORA
PEACE

Priest: Peace be with you.
Answer: And with you and your spirit.
Priest: The grace of our Lord ⟨Jesus Christ and the love of God
the Father, and the fellowship of the Holy Spirit be with us all
now and ever world without end⟩.
Answer: Amen.
Priest: Up with your minds.
Answer: They are with you, O God.
Priest: The offering is offered to God, the Lord of all.
Answer: It is fitting and right.

The priest says privately: Worthy of glory from every mouth and
thanksgiving from every tongue is the adorable and glorious
name of the Father and of the Son and of the Holy Spirit. He
created the world through his grace and its inhabitants in his compassion; he saved men through his mercy, and gave great grace to
mortals.

Your majesty, O Lord, a thousand thousand heavenly beings
adore; myriad myriads of angels, and ranks of spiritual beings,
ministers of fire and spirit, together with the holy cherubim and
seraphim, glorify your name, crying out and glorifying
⟨unceasingly calling to one another and saying⟩:

People: Holy, holy, ⟨holy, Lord God almighty; heaven and earth
are full of his praises⟩.

The Priest says privately: And with these heavenly armies we, also
even we, your lowly, weak, and miserable servants, Lord, give
you thanks because you have brought about us a great grace
which cannot be repaid. For you put on our human nature to give
us life through your divine nature; you raised us from our lowly
state; you restored our Fall; you restored our immortality; you forgave our debts; you justified our sinfulness; you enlightened our
intelligence. You, our Lord and our God, conquered our enemies,

and made the lowliness of our weak nature to triumph through
the abundant mercy of your grace.

(*aloud*) And for all ⟨your helps and graces towards us, let us raise
to you praise and honor and thanksgiving and worship, now and
ever and world without end⟩. *People:* Amen.

The priest says privately: You, Lord, through your many mercies
which cannot be told, be graciously mindful of all the pious and
righteous Fathers who were pleasing in your sight, in the commemoration of the body and blood of your Christ, which we offer
to you on the pure and holy altar, as you taught us.

And grant us your tranquillity and your peace for all the days of
this age (*repeat*) *People:* Amen. That all the inhabitants of the earth
may know you, that you alone are the true God and Father, and
you sent our Lord Jesus Christ, your beloved Son, and he, our
Lord and our God, taught us through his life-giving gospel all the
purity and holiness of the prophets, apostles, martyrs, confessors,
bishops, priests, deacons, and all sons of the holy Catholic
Church who have been sealed with the living seal of holy baptism.

And we also, Lord, (*thrice*) your lowly, weak, and miserable servants, who have gathered and stand before you, [and] have received through tradition the form[1] which is from you, rejoicing,
glorifying, exalting, commemorating, and celebrating this great
mystery of the passion, death and resurrection of our Lord Jesus
Christ.[2]

May your Holy Spirit, Lord, come and rest on this offering of
your servants, and bless and sanctify it, that it may be to us,
Lord, for remission of debts, forgiveness of sins, and the great
hope of resurrection from the dead, and new life in the kingdom
of heaven, with all who have been pleasing in your sight.

And because of all your wonderful dispensation towards us, with
open mouths and uncovered faces we give you thanks and glorify
you without ceasing in your Church, which has been redeemed

1. *Or* example *or* pattern.
2. *This sentence has no main verb, except in the Mar Eshaya MS*

The Liturgy of Saints Addai and Mari   43 by the precious blood of your Christ, offering up (praise, honor, thanksgiving and adoration to your living and life-giving name, now and at all times forever and ever). *People:* Amen.

APOLOGIA
FRACTION and SIGNING
LORD'S PRAYER
ELEVATION
The priest proceeds: The holy thing to the holies is fitting in perfection.

People: One holy Father, one holy Son, one holy Spirit. Glory be to the Father and to the Son and to the Holy Spirit to the ages of ages. Amen.

COMMUNION
The body of our Lord for the pardon of offences.
The precious blood for the pardon of offences.

THANKSGIVING FOR COMMUNION
DISMISSAL

7 The Third Anaphora of St. Peter (*Sharar*)

This liturgy originated in the Syriac-speaking hinterland of the patriarchate of Antioch, and is now preserved in the Maronite Church, a Uniat body whose members live chiefly in Lebanon. The anaphora has a close relationship with the anaphora of SS. *Addai and Mari* (q.v.); the two anaphoras are probably derived from a common ancestor, though they developed differently. In the opinion of many scholars, *Sharar* includes various readings which are earlier than the corresponding points in *Addai and Mari*. The name *Sharar* is the first word of a prayer which begins the liturgy in the manuscripts.

The following points in the relationship with *Addai and Mari* are worthy of note: the introductory dialogue is much longer; the new material has probably been derived from a Nestorian anaphora, *Theodore the Interpreter*.

The first three paragraphs (down to "as you taught us") are virtually identical, though the Sanctus looks even more like an insertion, lacking the link "and with these heavenly armies."

The whole anaphora after the Sanctus is addressed to Christ, and the preface also may originally have been, the mention of the persons of the Trinity being a later addition.

After the commemoration of "the Fathers" follows the Institution Narrative, and a lengthy passage of adoration and prayer for propitiation, after which the intercessions are resumed. There is nothing to correspond to the paragraph in *Addai and Mari* starting "and grant us your tranquillity." Both passages look like insertions, interrupting the intercessions.

The intercessions are greatly expanded, but there is no equivalent of the "anamnesis" section of *Addai and Mari*, either after the Institution Narrative, where it would be natural to expect it, or after the intercessions, as in *Addai and Mari*.

The epiclesis is almost identical, but lacks the words "and bless and sanctify it," which suggests an early date for its addition to the anaphora.

The doxology is virtually identical.

The text below is translated from a manuscript dated A.D. 1453 edited by J. M. Sauget (*Anaphorae Syriacae*, 2(1973), pp. 275–323).

BIBLIOGRAPHY
B. D. Spinks, *Addai and Mari—The Anaphora of the Apostles: a text for students* (1980).
Prex Eucharistica, pp. 410–415.
W. F. Macomber, (1) "The Maronite and Chaldaean Versions of the Anaphora of the Apostles," in *Orientalia Christiana Periodica*, 37(1971), pp. 55–84. (2) "A Theory on the origins of the Syrian, Maronite, and Chaldaean Rites," in *Orientalia Christiana Periodica*, 39(1971), pp. 235–242.
M. Hayek, *Liturgie Maronite* (1964).
E. Khoury, "Genesis and Development of the Maronite Divine Liturgy," in J. Madey (ed.), *The Eucharistic Liturgy in the Christian East* (1982).

PREPARATION OF THE GIFTS
PENITENCE
PSALM
EPISTLE
ALLELUIA
GOSPEL
CREED
PEACE
Deacon: Let us stand aright.

Priest: We offer to you, God our Father, Lord of all, an offering and a commemoration and a memorial in the sight of God, living from the beginning and holy from eternity, for the living and for the dead, for the near and for the far, for the poor and for travellers, for the churches and monasteries which are here and in every place and in all regions; and for me, unworthy and a sinner, whom you have made worthy to stand before you (remember me in your heavenly kingdom); and for the souls and spirits whom we commemorate before you, Lord, mighty God, and for this people which is in the true faith and awaits your abundant mercy; and for the sins, faults, and defects of us all, we offer this pure and holy offering.

People: It is fitting and right.

Priest: It is fitting and right, our duty and our salvation, natural and good. Let our minds ever be lifted up to heaven, and all our hearts in purity.

People: To you, Lord, God of Abraham, Isaac, and Israel, O King glorious and holy for ever.

Priest: To you, Lord, God of Abraham, savior of Isaac, strength of Israel, O King glorious and holy forever. The Lord is worthy to be confessed by us and adored and praised.

(Here the priest blesses the people, and says a prayer relating to the incense and a number of commemorations, after which he begins the anaphora.)

Priest (bowing): Glory to you, adorable and praiseworthy name of the Father and of the Son and of the Holy Spirit. You created the world through your grace and all its inhabitants by your mercy and made redemption for mortals by your grace.

Your majesty, O Lord, a thousand thousand heavenly angels adore; myriad myriads of hosts, ministers of fire and spirit, praise you in fear. With the cherubim and the seraphim, who in turn bless, glorify, proclaim, and say, let us also, Lord, become worthy of your grace and mercy, to say with them thrice, "Holy, holy, holy . . ."

(bowing) We give thanks to you, Lord, we your sinful servants, because you have given your grace which cannot be repaid. You put on our human nature to give us life through your divine nature; you raised our lowly state; you restored our Fall; you gave life to our mortality; you justified our sinfulness; you forgave our debts; you enlightened our understanding, conquered our enemies, and made our weak nature to triumph.

(aloud) And for all your grace towards us, let us offer you glory and honor, in your holy Church before your altar of propitiation . . .

(bowing) You, Lord, through your great mercy, be graciously mindful of all the holy and righteous Fathers, when we commemorate your body and blood, which we offer to you on your living and holy altar, as you, our hope, taught us in your holy gospel

The Third Anaphora of St. Peter (Sharar)

and said, "I am the living bread who came down from heaven that mortals may have life in me."

(*aloud*) We make the memorial of your Passion, Lord, as you taught us. In the night in which you were betrayed to the Jews, Lord, you took bread in your pure and holy hands, and lifted your eyes to heaven to your glorious Father; you blessed, sealed, sanctified, Lord, broke, and gave it to your disciples the blessed Apostles, and said to them, "This bread is my body, which is broken and given for the life of the world, and will be to those who take it for forgiveness of debts and pardon of sins; take and eat from it, and it will be to you for eternal life."

(*He takes the cup*) Likewise over the cup, Lord, you praised, glorified, and said, "This cup is my blood of the new covenant, which is shed for many for forgiveness of sins; take and drink from it, all of you, and it will be to you for pardon of debts and forgiveness of sins, and for eternal life." Amen.

"As often as you eat from this holy body, and drink from this cup of life and salvation, you will make the memorial of the death and resurrection of your Lord, until the great day of his coming."

People: We make the memorial, Lord, of your death . . .

Priest: We adore you, only begotten of the Father, firstborn of creation, spiritual Lamb, who descended from heaven to earth, to be a propitiatory sacrifice for all men and to bear their debts voluntarily, and to remit their sins by your blood, and sanctify the unclean through your sacrifice.

Give us life, Lord, through your true life, and purify us through your spiritual expiation; and grant us to gain life through your life-giving death, that we may stand before you in purity and serve you in holiness and offer that sacrifice to your Godhead, that it may be pleasing to the will of your majesty, and that your mercy, Father, may flow over us all. . . .

We ask you, only-begotten of the Father, through whom our peace is established; Son of the Most High, in whom higher things are reconciled with lower; Good Shepherd, who laid down your life for your sheep and delivered them from ravening wolves; merciful Lord, who raised your voice on the cross and gathered us from vain error; God, the God of spirits and of all flesh; may our prayers ascend in your sight, and your mercy descend on our petitions, and let that sacrifice be acceptable before you; we offer it as a memorial of your Passion on your altar of propitiation.

May it please your Godhead, and may your will be fulfilled in it; by it may our guilt be pardoned and our sins forgiven; and in it may our dead be remembered. Let us praise you and adore you, and the Father who sent you for our salvation, and your living and Holy Spirit now. . . .

By it may the glorious Trinity be reconciled, by the thurible and the sacrifice and the cup; by it may the souls be purified and the spirits sanctified of those for whom and on account of whom it was offered and sanctified; and for me, weak and sinful, who offered it, may the mercy of the glorious Trinity arise, Father. . . .

(The priest bows and says a prayer to the Mother of God.)

We offer before you, Lord, this sacrifice in memory of all righteous and pious fathers, of prophets, apostles, martyrs, confessors, and all our patriarchs, and the pope of the city of Rome and metropolitan bishops, area bishops, visitors, priests, deacons, deaconesses, young men, celibates, virgins, and all sons of holy Church who have been sealed with the sign of saving baptism, and whom you have made partakers of your holy body.

(privately) First and especially we commemorate the holy and blessed and saintly Virgin, the Blessed Lady Mary.

Deacon: Remember her, Lord God, and us through her pure prayers.

Priest (bowing): Remember, Lord God, at this time the absent and the present, the dead and the living, the sick and the oppressed, the troubled, the afflicted, and those who are in various difficulties.

Remember, Lord God, at this time, our fathers and brothers in spirit and in body; and forgive their offences and sins.

The Third Anaphora of St. Peter (Sharar) 49

Remember, Lord God, at this time, those who offer sacrifices, vows, firstfruits, memorials; grant to their petitions good things from your abundant store.

Remember, Lord God, at this time, those who join in commemorating your mother and your saints; grant them recompense for all their good works; and for all who communicated in this eucharist which was offered on this holy altar; grant them, Lord God, a reward in your kingdom; and for all who have said to us, "pray for us in your prayers before the Lord." Remember them, Lord God, and purge their iniquities.

Remember, Lord God, at this time, my miserableness, sinfulness, importunity, and lowliness; I have sinned and done evil in your sight consciously or not, voluntarily or not. Lord God, in your grace and mercy pardon me and forgive whatever I have sinned against you; and may this eucharist, Lord, be as a memorial of our dead and for the reconciliation of our souls.

Remember, Lord God, at this time, your weak and sinful servant George, who wrote this, and pardon him and forgive him his offences and sins, and forgive his fathers. Amen.

(*kneeling*) Hear me, Lord (*thrice*), and let your living and Holy Spirit, Lord, come and descend upon this offering of your servants, and may it be to those who partake for remission of debts and forgiveness of sins, for a blessed resurrection from the dead, and for new life in the kingdom of heaven for ever.

(*aloud*) And because of your praiseworthy dispensation towards us, we give thanks to you, we your sinful servants redeemed by your innocent blood, with eloquent mouth in your holy Church before your altar of propitiation, now. . . .

FRACTION and SIGNING
LORD'S PRAYER
PRAYER OF INCLINATION
ELEVATION

Priest: The holy (thing) is given to the holy people in perfection, purity, and holiness; may we have a part and fellowship with them in the kingdom of heaven.

The Third Anaphora of St. Peter (Sharar)

People: One Father only is holy, one Son only is holy, one Spirit only is holy.
Glory to the Father, to the Son, and to the Holy Spirit.

THANKSGIVING FOR COMMUNION
BLESSING

8 The Liturgy of St. Mark

St. Mark was the liturgy of the patriarchate of Alexandria. Our knowledge of the early history of the eucharistic prayer is more detailed for Egypt than for any other area, because of the survival of papyrus and other fragments which have preserved the text in a shorter and simpler form than that of the medieval manuscripts, thus giving us a good idea of the eucharistic prayer as it was in the fourth century and earlier.

In the first two texts translated below, words in brackets have been supplied from the final form of *St. Mark*, and may be taken as certain. Conjectural restorations are followed by a question mark; dots represent a gap which might be filled in more than one way.

A. THE STRASBOURG PAPYRUS

The earliest of the fragments mentioned above are at Strasbourg, and were published in 1928. A number of small pieces all proved to belong to a single leaf, probably written between A.D. 300 and 500, of which the top third is completely lacking. Enough has survived to show that the leaf contained an early version of *St. Mark*, down to the end of the intercessions, then rounded off with a doxology, which in later versions has been replaced by the Sanctus. The presence of the doxology suggests that the prayer was complete on its single leaf.

The prayer begins with a thanksgiving for Creation based on Psalm 146:6, who made heaven and earth, the sea, and all that is in them. Such a thanksgiving also introduces such Jewish prayers as Nehemiah 9:6f (cf. Acts 4:24, above). The lack of any reference to salvation-history is a feature of *St. Mark* which remains constant throughout its existence. The thanksgiving appears to be leading into a doxology, but instead continues with the offering of "the reasonable sacrifice and this bloodless service." The Old and New Testaments, Justin, and Origen all speak of prayer as sacrifice, and this was probably the meaning originally attached to the phrase in this prayer. If so, the presence of an offering in the preface, not exactly paralleled elsewhere, is quite natural. The word "bloodless" is first found in this context in Athenagoras (c. 185), who is thought to have been head of the catechetical school in Alexandria.

Scholars have drawn attention to the similarity of the prayer's structure to Jewish prayers such as the Blessing for food (see p. 10). Originally the prayer may have consisted of three "panels" (cf. the *Didache*): thanksgiving, offering, intercession, rounded off by a *chatimah*. This suggests a very early date, perhaps c. 200, which is supported by the length of the prayer (very much the same as that in the *Apostolic Tradition*) and the quotation from Malachi 1:11, found also in the *Didache*, Justin, Irenaeus, and Tertullian, but not often used by later writers.

BIBLIOGRAPHY
M. Andrieu and P. Collomp, "Fragments sur papyrus de l'anaphore de saint Marc," in *Revue des Sciences Religieuses*, 8(1928), pp. 489–515.
Prex Eucharistica, pp. 116–119.
H. A. J. Wegman, "Une anaphore incomplète?," in R. van den Broek and M. J. Vermaseren (eds.), *Studies in Gnosticism and Hellenistic Religions* (1981).
B.D.Spinks, "A Complete Anaphora? A Note on Strasbourg Gr. 254," in *The Heythrop Journal*, 25 (1984), pp. 51–55.
E. Mazza, "Una Anafora incompleta?," in *Ephemerides Liturgicae*, 99(1985), pp. 425–436.

to bless [you] . . . [night][1] and day . . .

[you who made] heaven [and] all that is in [it, the earth and what is on earth,] seas and rivers and [all that is] in [them]; [you] who made man [according to your] own image and likeness. You made everything through your wisdom, the light [of?] your true Son,[2] our Lord and Savior Jesus Christ; giving thanks through him to you with him and the Holy Spirit, we offer the reasonable[3] sacrifice and this bloodless service, which all the nations offer you,

1. Cf. p. 59f.
2. *Or*, your true light, your Son
3. Greek: *logikēn.*

"from sunrise to sunset," from south to north, [for] your "name is great among all the nations, and in every place incense is offered to your holy name and a pure sacrifice."[4]

Over this sacrifice and offering we pray and beseech you, remember your holy and only Catholic Church, all your peoples and all your flocks. Provide the peace which is from heaven in all our hearts, and grant us also the peace of this life. The . . . of the land peaceful things towards us, and towards your [holy] name, the prefect of the province, the army, the princes, councils . . .
(About one-third of a page is lacking here, and what survives is in places too fragmentary to be restored.)

[for seedtime and] harvest . . . preserve, for the poor of [your] people, for all of us who call upon [your] name, for all who hope in you. Give rest to the souls of those who have fallen asleep; remember those of whom we make mention today, both those whose names we say [and] whose we do not say . . . [Remember] our orthodox fathers and bishops everywhere; and grant us to have a part and lot with the fair . . . of your holy prophets, apostles, and martyrs. Receive(?) [through] their entreaties [these prayers]; grant them through our Lord; through whom be glory to you to the ages of ages.

B. THE BRITISH MUSEUM TABLET

The British Museum possesses a wooden tablet on which has been scratched a Coptic version of the second half of the anaphora of *St. Mark*. Though dating from the eighth century, it presents an earlier form of the text, confirmed by a sixth-century parchment of the same extract in Greek in the John Rylands Library, Manchester, which is much less well-preserved, but goes to the end of the anaphora, whereas the tablet omits the last sentence.

The extract begins with words that imply that the Sanctus has just been sung, picking up the end of the Sanctus (" . . . full of your glory") with the petition "Fill this sacrifice with your blessing

4. Malachi 1:11.

through your Holy Spirit." This is followed immediately by the Institution Narrative, introduced by the word "For", which implies that the Narrative is quoted as a warrant for what is being said and done, rather than as part of the process of consecration. Compared with the Strasbourg fragment, the word "sacrifice" is changing its meaning: its proximity to the Institution Narrative must have caused it here to include the bread and cup. A step has been taken towards the full consecratory epiclesis. Compare the two later fragments (see pp. 79–87).

The Institution Narrative is enlarged by additions and followed by the "Pauline comment" (1 Corinthians 11:26), which has been put into the first person ("you proclaim *my* death"), and is treated as though it were part of the narrative (cf. *Egyptian Basil*, below, p.71). It has also had a reference to the Resurrection added. It is then picked up by the opening of the anamnesis with the word "Proclaiming," rather than the "Remembering" customary elsewhere. The anamnesis leads into an offering, this time quite unequivocal, of the bread and the cup, just as in Hippolytus. Unlike *Egyptian Basil*, the present tense is used, not the aorist.

Next follows an explicitly consecratory epiclesis: the Spirit is to make the elements the body and blood of Christ; and the prayer ends (in the parchment) by specifying the fruits of communion.

It is not easy to date the contents of these fragments: the earlier part seems to imply a more primitive and peculiarly Egyptian theology than the later, which seems to have been influenced by another liturgy, probably *St. James*. A date *c*. 400 would be consistent with the evidence. Taken with the Strasbourg papyrus, these sources provide a fairly complete text of *St. Mark* at an early stage of development.

BIBLIOGRAPHY
H. Quecke, "Ein saïdischer Zeuge der Markusliturgie (Brit. Mus. 54.036)," in *Orientalia Christiana Periodica*, 37(1971), pp. 40–54.
C. H. Roberts, *Catalogue of the Greek and Latin Papyri in the John Rylands Library*, 3(1938), no. 465, pp. 25–28.
Prex Eucharistica, pp. 124–127 (the Rylands fragment).

Full in truth are heaven and earth of your glory through our Lord[4] [and] Savior Jesus Christ: fill, O God, this sacrifice also with the blessing from you through your Holy Spirit.

For our Lord and Savior and King of all, Jesus Christ, in the night when he was betrayed and willingly underwent death, took bread in his holy and undefiled [and] blessed hands, looked up to heaven to you, the Father of all, blessed, gave thanks over it, sanctified, broke [and] gave it to his disciples [and] apostles, saying, "Take and eat of this, all of you; this is my body, which is given for you for the forgiveness of your sins. Do this for my remembrance."

Likewise, after supper, he took a cup, blessed, sanctified, [and] gave it to them, saying, "Take this and drink from it, all of you; this is my blood of the new covenant, which is shed for many for the forgiveness of their sins. Do this for my remembrance.

"For as often as you eat this bread and drink this cup, you proclaim my death [and] confess my Resurrection."

Proclaiming thus, Lord, the death of your only begotten Son, our Lord and Savior Jesus Christ, and confessing his Resurrection and his Ascension into heaven, and looking for his glorious coming, we set before you these gifts from your own, this bread and this cup. We pray and beseech you to send your Holy Spirit and your power on these [your?] [gifts] set before you, on this bread and this cup, and to make the bread the body of Christ and [the cup the blood of the] new [covenant] of our Lord and Savior Jesus Christ.

(The tablet ends here, but the Rylands fragment continues:)
that [they may be to all of us who] receive for faith, for sobriety, [for healing, for joy, for sanctification,] for renewal of soul, body, [and spirit, for sharing in eternal life,] for self-control and of *(sic)* immortality, for . . . [that] in this also as in all [may be glorified and hymned and sanctified your] holy and honored and all- . . . [Name . . .].

4. *Cf. p.64.*

C. THE FINAL FORM

The final thirteenth-century form of the liturgy of Alexandria is preserved in five medieval manuscripts, two far from complete. It is an expansion of the forms contained in the early fragments discussed above. An early edition of this rite appears in a Coptic translation (*the Anaphora of St. Cyril*) made after A.D. 431. This lacks some passages found in the Greek text and includes some which are not in the Greek. But it is possible to construct an almost complete text of *St. Mark* in an early form by piecing together the fragments and other Egyptian sources.

St. Mark retains throughout its history its characteristic structure with the intercessions immediately after the preface, no christological section, and an epiclesis to link the Sanctus to the Institution Narrative based on the word "fill."

The repeated verbs of "acknowledgement" in the preface go back to Jewish usage (see p. 11). The passage between asterisks is absent from the Strasbourg papyrus, and was probably modelled on *St. James*. The word "sacrifice" has disappeared from the preface. The intercessions are enormously enlarged from those in the Strasbourg form, and are significantly longer in MS 1970 than in MS 2281. Their final passage is a traditional formula first found in *1 Clement*, and then in a third-century papyrus at Würzburg.

The pre-Sanctus is noticeably longer than it is in Sarapion or the Deir Balyzeh papyrus (see pp. 78,80). The combination of Daniel and Isaiah is already found in *1 Clement*. The post-Sanctus retains the reticent wording of the British Museum tablet's epiclesis, but the Institution Narrative is considerably expanded. Probably under the influence of *St. Basil* or *St. James*, a second epiclesis is added, with a long list of attributes of the Holy Spirit. There is a similar passage in *St. James*, but *St. Mark's* selection is different and longer, and upsets the syntax.

The relationship of the two epicleses is not wholly clear. The first epiclesis still asks God to "fill this sacrifice with your blessing . . . through the Holy Spirit" without specifying for what purpose. In the second God is asked to send the Spirit "upon us and upon these loaves and these cups to sanctify and perfect them, and to make the bread the body and the cup the blood" of Christ. There seems to have been a definite movement in local Egyptian rites towards developing the post-Sanctus into a consecratory epiclesis, as in the Coptic *St. Mark*, the Deir Balyzeh rite, and the Louvain papyrus (cf. also Cyril's *Catecheses*); whereas the Alexandrian form came under the influence of *St. Basil* and *St. James*, and deferred consecration until the second epiclesis. But the Coptic *St. Mark* goes even further, introducing the word "change" into the second epiclesis (again cf. Cyril).

The offering, however, is still regarded as having been made during the preface, since the anamnesis reads: "we set before you from your own gifts" (aorist). A similar past tense (perfect) is found in the Byzantine form of *St. Basil* (p. 116).

One sign of later date is the tendency throughout the anaphora to add literal quotations from Scripture.

Words in square brackets are absent from the Coptic.

BIBLIOGRAPHY
Prex Eucharistica, pp. 101–115 (Greek), pp. 135–139 (Latin translation of Coptic). *LEW*, pp. 113–143 (Greek), pp. 144–188 (English translation of Coptic).
G. J. Cuming, "The Anaphora of St. Mark: a study in development," in *Le Muséon*, 95 (1982), pp. 115–129.

ENARXIS (THREE PRAYERS)
  THE LITTLE ENTRANCE
PRAYER, MONOGENES, PRAYER, TRISAGION
EPISTLE
ALLELUIA and INCENSE-PRAYER
GOSPEL
SYNAPTE (LITANY) and "THE THREE PRAYERS"
  THE GREAT ENTRANCE
CHERUBIC HYMN (TWO PRAYERS)
PEACE (PRAYER AND INCENSE PRAYER)
CREED
PRAYER OF PROTHESIS

Likewise also after the Creed the bishop[1] seals[2] the people, saying aloud:
The Lord be with all.

People: And with your spirit.
Bishop: Up with your hearts.[3]
People: We have them with the Lord.
Bishop: Let us give thanks to the Lord.
People: It is fitting and right.
Deacon: Spread (the fans?).

The bishop begins the anaphora: It is truly fitting and right, holy and suitable, and profitable to our souls, [I AM,] Master, Lord, God, Father Almighty, to praise you, to hymn you, to give thanks to you, to confess you night[4] and day with unceasing [mouth, unhushed] lips, and unsilenced heart; you who have made heaven and what is in heaven, the earth and what is on earth, seas, springs, rivers, lakes and all that is in them; you who made man according to your own image and likeness, *and granted him the pleasure of paradise. When he transgressed, you did not despise him or abandon him, for you are good, but you called him back through the law, you taught him through the prophets, you reformed and renewed him through this awesome and life-giving and heavenly mystery*. You made everything through your wisdom, the true light, your only Son, our Lord and God and Savior, Jesus Christ, through whom with him and the Holy Spirit we give thanks to you and offer this reasonable and bloodless service, which all the nations offer you [,Lord,] "from sunrise to sunset," from north to south, for your "name is great among all the nations, and in every place incense is offered to your holy name[5] and a pure sacrifice,"[6] a sacrifice and offering.

And we pray and beseech you, for you are good and love mankind: remember, Lord, the holy and only catholic and apostolic

1. Greek: *hiereus.*
2. *i.e., makes the sign of the cross over them.*
3. *The Greek has no verb.*
4. *Cf. p. 53.*
5. *The Coptic reads:* . . . and a pure sacrifice. And over this sacrifice and this offering we pray and beseech you . . . *This is supported by the Strasbourg papyrus (p. 53).*
6. Malachi 1:11; *cf. Didache (p. 24) and Justin (p. 27).*

The Final Form 59

Church from one end of the earth to the other, all your peoples and all your flocks.

Provide the peace from heaven in all our hearts, and grant us also the peace of this life.

Dispose the emperor, the army, the princes, councils, townships, neighborhoods, our goings-out and our comings-in in all peace.

"King of peace,[7] give us your peace, for you have given us everything", possess us, Lord, [in concord and love]; "we know none but you, we name your name." Give life to all our souls, and let not the death of sin prevail against us or all your people.

Visit, Lord, the sick among your people and in mercy and pity heal them. Drive away from them and from us every disease and illness; expel the spirit of weakness [from them]. Raise up those who have lain in lengthy illnesses, heal those that are troubled by unclean spirits. Have mercy on all those who are held in prison, or in the mines, [under accusation or condemnation,] in exile or bitter slavery [or tribute], and free them all. For you, [our God,] are he who looses the bound, who restores the broken, the hope of the hopeless, the help of the helpless, [the raising-up of the fallen,] the harbor of the storm-tossed, [the avenger of the afflicted]. To every afflicted and hard-pressed [Christian] soul give mercy, give relief, give refreshment.[8] And also, Lord, heal the diseases of our souls, and cure our bodily weaknesses, healer of souls and bodies. Overseer of all flesh, oversee [and heal] us through your salvation.[9]

Give a good journey to our brothers who have gone abroad or are about to go abroad in every place, whether by land or by river, on lakes or on roads, or travelling by any means; bring them all back from everywhere to a quiet harbor, to a safe harbor; vouchsafe to sail and to journey with them; return them rejoicing to their rejoicing families, in health to healthy families.[10] And also, Lord, keep our sojourn in this life free from harm and storm until the end.

7. Isaiah 26:12–13.
8. *This passage is not in Vatican MS 2281:* "The avenger . . . refreshment."
9. *This passage is not in Vatican MS 2281:* "and cure our . . . your salvation."
10. *This passage is not in Vatican MS 2281:* "whether by land . . . .to healthy families."

The Final Form

[Send the good rains richly on the places that ask for them and need them; by their falling, gladden and renew the face of the earth, that by their drops it may spring up rejoicing.]

Bring up the waters of the river to their proper measure; [by their rising] gladden [and renew] the face of the earth; water its furrows, multiply its fruits.

[Bless, Lord, the fruits of the earth; keep us safe and unharmed;] grant them to us for seedtime and harvest, [that by their drops it may spring up rejoicing].

Bless, Lord, the crown of the year of your goodness, for the poor of your people, for the widow and the orphan, for the stranger and the proselyte, for all of us who trust in you and call upon your holy name: "for the eyes of all hope for you, and you give them their food in due season."[11] You who give food to all flesh, fill our hearts with joy and gladness, that we may always have all sufficiency and abound in every good work [in Christ Jesus our Lord].

[King of kings and Lord of lords,] guard the kingdom of your servant [our orthodox and Christ-loving emperor, whom you appointed to rule over the land] in peace and bravery and righteousness. Subject to him, O God, every warlike enemy [at home and abroad]. ["Lay hold upon the weapon and buckler, and stand up to help him; bring forth the broadsword and stop the way against them that persecute him; set the fruit of his loins upon his throne;"][12] speak to his heart good things concerning your holy, catholic, and apostolic Church [and all the Christ-loving people], that we may live a quiet and peaceful life in his peace, that we may be found in all godliness and honesty towards you.

Give rest, [Lord our God,] to the souls of our fathers and brothers who have fallen asleep [in the faith of Christ], remembering our forefathers from the beginning, the Fathers, patriarchs, prophets, Apostles, martyrs, confessors, [bishops, holy men,] righteous men, every spirit perfected in the faith [of Christ, and those of

11. Ps. 145:15.
12. Ps. 35:2; Acts 2:30.

whom we make mention today], and [our holy father] Mark the apostle and evangelist, [who showed us the way of salvation].

[Hail, highly favored, the Lord is with you; blessed are you among women, and blessed is the fruit of your womb, for you bore the Savior of our souls.]

(*aloud*) Especially our all-holy, [spotless, blessed Lady] Mary, mother of God and ever-virgin.

[*Deacon:* Bless, Lord.

Bishop: The Lord bless you with his grace, now and always, and to the ages of ages.]

The deacon reads the diptychs.

The bishop bows and prays: Give rest, Master, Lord our God, to the souls of all these [in the tabernacles of your saints in your kingdom], granting them the good things of your promises, "which eye has not seen nor ear heard, neither have entered into the heart of man what God has prepared for those that love your holy name."[13] Refresh their souls and count them worthy of the kingdom of heaven; and grant the ends of our lives to be Christian and well-pleasing [and sinless], and give us to have a part and lot with all your saints.

Receive, O God, the thank-offerings[14] of those who offer the sacrifices, at your [holy and heavenly and] spiritual altar in [the vastnesses of] heaven by the ministry of your archangels, much or little, secretly or openly, willing but unable, and those who offered the offerings today; as you accepted the gifts of your righteous Abel, (*the bishop censes and says:*) the sacrifice of our father Abraham, [the incense of Zachariah, the alms of Cornelius,] and the widow's two mites; [receive also their thank-offerings,] and give them imperishable things for perishable, heavenly things for earthly, eternal for temporal.

Preserve the most holy and blessed pope *N.* [whom you foreknew and foreordained to govern your holy, catholic, and apostolic

13. 1 Corinthians 2:9.
14. Greek: *eucharisteria.*

Church, and our most holy bishop N.]; preserve them for many years to fulfill in peaceful times your holy pontificate, entrusted to them by you according to your holy and blessed will, rightly dividing the word of truth.

Remember also the orthodox bishops, presbyters, deacons, subdeacons, readers, singers, monks, virgins, widows, laymen everywhere.

Remember, Lord, [the holy city of Christ our God, and the imperial city, and] this our city, and every city and land [and those who dwell in them] in the orthodox faith [of Christ, for their peace and safety].

[Remember, Lord, every Christian soul in trials and afflictions, in need of the mercy and help of God, and recovery of the lost.]

[Remember, Lord, those of our brothers who are prisoners of war; grant them to find pity from those who took them prisoner.]

[Remember, Lord, in mercy and pity us sinners also, your unworthy servants, and wipe away our sins, as a good God who loves mankind.]

[Remember, Lord, also me your humble and sinful and unworthy servant, and wipe away my sins as one that loves mankind; and] be present with us who minister to your all-holy name.

Bless our meetings, Lord; root out idolatry altogether from the world; tread down Satan and all his work and wickedness under our feet. Humble now as always, Lord, the enemies of your Church; strip them of their arrogance; show them quickly how weak they are; render harmless their plots and devices and schemings which they contrive against us. "Arise, Lord, and let your enemies be scattered, and all who hate your holy name flee backwards;"[15] but bless your [faithful and orthodox] people who do your [holy] will,[16] to thousands of thousands and myriads of myriads.

Deacon: Those who are seated, stand!

15. Numbers 10:35.
16. *Cf. p. 79.*

The bishop says the prayer: Ransom the prisoners, rescue those in necessity, feed the hungry, comfort the weakhearted, turn back the wanderers, [enlighten those in darkness,] raise the fallen, [strengthen the unstable, heal the sick,] lead all into the way of salvation, and gather them in your holy fold; but save us from our lawbreaking, as our guard and defender in everything.

Deacon: Look eastwards.

The bishop bows and prays: For you are "above every principality and power and virtue and dominion and every name that is named, not only in this age but in the age to come."[17] Beside you stand thousands of thousands and myriads of myriads of [armies of holy] angels and archangels. Beside you stand your two most honorable living creatures, the cherubim with many eyes and the seraphim with six wings, "which cover their faces with two wings, and their feet with two, and fly with two";[18] [and they cry one to the other with unwearying mouths and never-silent doxologies, singing, proclaiming, praising, crying, and saying the triumphal and thrice-holy hymn to your magnificent glory: Holy, holy, holy, Lord of Sabaoth; heaven and earth are full of your holy glory. (*aloud*)] Everything at all times hallows you, but with all that hallow you receive also, Lord and Master, our hallowing, as with them we hymn you and say:

People: Holy, holy, holy, Lord of Sabaoth; heaven and earth are[19] full of your holy glory.

The bishop seals the holy things, saying:[20] Full in truth are heaven and earth of your holy glory through [the appearing of] our Lord and God and Savior Jesus Christ: fill, O God, this sacrifice also with the blessing from you through the descent of your [all-]Holy Spirit.

For our Lord and God and King of all, Jesus the Christ, in the night when he handed himself over for our sins, and underwent death [in the flesh] for all men, [sat down with his holy disciples

17. Ephesians 1:21
18. Isaiah 6:2–3.
19. *Cf. p.81.*
20. *Cf. p.55.*

The Final Form

and apostles, he] took bread in his holy, undefiled, and blameless hands, looked up to heaven to you, his own Father, the God [of us and] of all, gave thanks, blessed, sanctified, broke and gave it to his holy and blessed disciples and apostles, saying: (*aloud*) "Take, eat," [*Deacon:* Stretch forth, presbyters.] "this is my body, which is broken for you and given for forgiveness of sins."

[*People:* Amen.]

[*The bishop says privately:*] Likewise also after supper he took the cup, he mixed wine and water, [looked up to heaven to you, his own Father, the God of us and of all], gave thanks, blessed, and sanctified it, [filled it with Holy Spirit,] and gave it to his holy and blessed disciples and apostles, saying: [*aloud*] "Drink from it, all of you;"

[*Deacon:* Still stretch forth.] "this is my blood of the new covenant, which is shed for you and for many, and given for forgiveness of sins."

People: Amen.

[*The bishop prays thus:*] "Do this for my remembrance. For as often as you eat this bread and drink this cup, you proclaim my death and confess my resurrection [and ascension] until I come."

Proclaiming, [Master,] Lord, almighty, [heavenly King,] the death of your only-begotten Son, our Lord and God and Savior Jesus Christ, and confessing his blessed resurrection [from the dead on the third day] and his ascension into heaven and his session at your right hand, his God and Father, and looking for his second [and dread and awesome] coming, in which he will judge the living and the dead in righteousness and reward each according to his works, [—spare us, Lord our God—] we set[21] before you from your own gifts; and we pray and beseech you, for you are good and love man, send out from your holy height, from your prepared dwelling place, from your unbounded bosom, the Paraclete himself, the Holy Spirit [of truth], the Lord, the life-giver, who spoke through the Law and the prophets and the Apostles, who is present everywhere and fills everything, who on his own au-

21. Greek: *proëthēkamen (aorist)*.

thority and not as a servant works sanctification on whom he wills, in your good pleasure; single in nature, multiple in operation, the fountain of divine endowments, consubstantial with you, sharing the throne of the kingdom with you and your only-begotten Son, our Lord and God and Savior, Jesus Christ; [look] upon us and upon these loaves and these cups; ⟨ ?send › your Holy Spirit to sanctify and perfect them,²² [as almighty God,] (*aloud*) and make the bread the body (*People:* Amen. [*The bishop, aloud:*]) and the cup the blood of the new covenant of our Lord and God and Savior and King of all, Jesus Christ,

[*Deacon:* Descend, deacons; pray, presbyters.] that they may become to all of us who partake of them for faith, for sobriety, for healing, [for temperance, for sanctification,] for renewal of soul, body, and spirit, for fellowship in eternal life and immortality, for the glorifying of your [all-]holy name, for forgiveness of sins; that in this as in everything your all-holy and honorable and glorified name may be glorified and praised and sanctified, with Jesus Christ and the Holy Spirit.

People: As it was and is and shall be, to generation and generation, and to all the ages of ages. Amen.

PRAYER and LORD'S PRAYER
PRAYER OF INCLINATION
PRAYER OF FRACTION AND ELEVATION
The bishop, aloud: The holy things for the holy people.

People: One Father is holy, one Son is holy, one Spirit is holy, [in the unity of the Holy Spirit]. Amen.

COMMUNION
The bishop:
The holy body of our Lord and God and Savior Jesus Christ.
The precious blood of our Lord and God and Savior Jesus Christ.

THANKSGIVING FOR COMMUNION and PRAYER
DISMISSAL (in the sacristy)

22. *Coptic:* that they may be sanctified and changed.

The Final Form

9 The Egyptian Anaphora of St. Basil

The liturgy used in the Coptic Church today consists of the "Coptic Common Order" with a choice of three anaphoras, of which *St. Basil* is that normally used. The anaphora was originally written in Greek, but only one complete manuscript of this version survives. It differs from the Coptic only in a few phrases peculiar to each version. A greatly expanded version (see below, p.116–123) became the official anaphora of Constantinople, and still remains in limited use.

In 1932 Dom Hieronymus Engberding demonstrated that the Egyptian text is an earlier version of the Byzantine, rather than an abbreviation of it, and his conclusions have been universally accepted. His insight was dramatically confirmed in 1960, when a version of the anaphora in Sahidic Coptic came to light (the received text is in Bohairic); this clearly belongs to an even earlier stage of development. Unfortunately, the manuscript lacks the first third of the prayer. This version apparently also underlies the anaphora of *St. James* (see below, pp. 89–99). It may well be dated to the late third century. Of recent years the Egyptian form of the anaphora has been recognized as one of the earliest surviving eucharistic prayers, comparable with the *Apostolic Tradition* and *Addai and Mari*, and has served as a basis for the third prayer in the Roman rite of 1969 and the fourth prayer in Rite II of the American Book of Common Prayer, 1979.

The anaphora is West Syrian in structure, though showing signs of Egyptian influence. Possibly it was brought to Egypt by St. Basil himself in A.D. 357, but at that time he was still a layman, and thus unlikely to give his name to an anaphora. It may have been the rite of Cappadocia, or have originated in Antioch.

The manuscript of the Sahidic version was probably written in the first part of the seventh century (the text refers to Archbishop Benjamin, who died in 662); but the text is clearly at least three hundred years older. This is shown by the sober treatment of the Institution Narrative, with few additions to the biblical text. The "Pauline comment" (1 Corinthians 11:26) is added to the Institution Narrative as part of Jesus' words, but does not have the Resurrection added to it, as in all other anaphoras. There is no request for the Holy Spirit to change the elements, but only "to sanctify them and make them holy of holies." The whole epiclesis is reminiscent of the *Apostolic Tradition*, as is the offering of "this bread and this cup," rather than "this sacrifice."

Among Egyptian features are: the use of Psalm 146:6 ("you made heaven and earth . . ."); "the famous aorist" ("we . . . set forth before you"), implying that the offering has already taken place earlier in the liturgy (this is altered in the Greek and the Bohairic to "we offer"); possibly the addition of the Pauline comment; and the doxology, a very unusual form only paralleled in three other sources, all Coptic and none of the first importance.

As compared with the *Apostolic Tradition*, there are two major additions: first, the Sanctus with its introduction and link, the latter of extreme brevity (nine words), which suggests that the Sanctus itself was a recent innovation. Secondly, the intercessions, which in Hippolytus were not admitted into the anaphora, but were destined to grow steadily in length until finally they reached quite disproportionate size. A comparison of Hippolytus, Sarapion, the Strasbourg papyrus of *St. Mark*, Cyril of Jerusalem, and *Egyptian Basil* shows a gradual acceptance of increasingly specific intercessions into the anaphora, while they still retain their position in the pre-anaphoral part of the liturgy (Justin, Hippolytus, Sarapion, *Apostolic Constitutions*, *St. Mark*, and all later liturgies).

A characteristic of *St. Basil* in all its stages is the brevity of the reference to Creation: "through whom you made all things visible and invisible" (cf. Hippolytus). For the first time there is a reference to the Fall. Curiously, salvation-history is carried right through from the Fall to the Last Judgement *before* the recital of the Institution Narrative, which does not follow on at all naturally, but again looks like an insertion. Consequently, the anamnesis duplicates the mention of the various saving acts, an infelicity which also appears in the *Apostolic Constitutions* (see p. 110).

Another unusual feature is the introduction to the Institution Narrative: "he left us this great mystery of godliness," a quotation from 1 Timothy 3:16, which is altered in the later version of *St. Basil* to: "he left us memorials of his saving passion." It appears in the *Apostolic Constitutions* as: "this is the mystery of the new covenant," put into Jesus' mouth as the beginning of the word over the bread; and reaches the Roman Canon as "the mystery of faith," applied to the cup.

A third feature is the statement: "since, Master, it is a command of your only-begotten Son that we should share in the commemoration of your saints." It is not easy to find such a command in the New Testament.

The text translated here is the Bohairic up to the point where the Sahidic begins, after which the latter is followed to the end of the anaphora.

BIBLIOGRAPHY
J. Doresse and E. Lanne, *Un témoin archaïque de la liturgie copte de saint Basile* (1960), with essay by B. Capelle. The Sahidic version, with Latin translation.
E. Renaudot, *Liturgiarum Orientalium Collectio* (1847), vol. 1, pp. 13–18. Latin translation of the Bohairic text.
Prex Eucharistica, pp. 347–357. The Greek version.
A.Houssiau, "The Alexandrine Anaphora of St. Basil," in L.C.Sheppard (ed.), *The New Liturgy* (1970), pp. 228–243.
L.L.Mitchell, "The Alexandrian Anaphora of St Basil of Caesarea," in *Anglican Theological Review*, 58(1976), pp. 194–206.
J. R. K. Fenwick, *Fourth-century Anaphoral Construction Techniques* (1986).

PRAYERS OF PREPARATION
PRAYER OF THANKSGIVING
PRAYER OF PROTHESIS
PRAYER FOR ABSOLUTION, TO THE SON
INCENSE PRAYER
READING FROM CATHOLIC EPISTLES
PRAYER
EPISTLE
PRAYER
READING FROM ACTS
TRISAGION
PRAYER

The Egyptian Anaphora of St. Basil   69

GOSPEL
PRAYER
SYNAPTE
PRAYERS OF THE VEIL
THE THREE PRAYERS
CREED
PEACE (Three Prayers)

The bishop:[1] The Lord be with you all.
People: And with your spirit.
Bishop: Let us lift up our hearts.
People: We have them with the Lord.
Bishop: Let us give thanks to the Lord.
People: It is fitting and right.
Bishop: It is fitting and right, fitting and right, truly it is fitting and right, I AM, truly Lord God, existing before the ages, reigning until the ages; you dwell on high and regard what is low; you made heaven and earth and the sea and all that is in them. Father of our Lord and God and Savior Jesus Christ, through whom you made all things visible and invisible, you sit on the throne of your glory; you are adored by every holy power. Around you stand angels and archangels, principalities and powers, thrones, dominions, and virtues; around you stand the cherubim with many eyes and the seraphim with six wings, forever singing the hymn of glory and saying:
People: Holy, holy, holy Lord (etc.)
Bishop: Holy, holy, holy you are indeed, Lord our God. You formed us and placed us in the paradise of pleasure; and when we had transgressed your commandment through the deceit of the serpent, and had fallen from eternal life, and had been banished from the paradise of pleasure, you did not cast us off for ever, but continually made promises to us through your holy prophets; and in these last days you manifested to us who sat in darkness and the shadow of death your only-begotten Son, our Lord and God and Savior, Jesus Christ. He was made flesh of the Holy Spirit and of the holy Virgin Mary, and became man; he showed us the ways of salvation, granted us to be reborn from

1. Greek: *hieteus.*

70   *The Egyptian Anaphora of St. Basil*

above by water and the Spirit, and made us a people for our own possession, sanctifying us by his Holy Spirit. He loved his own who were in the world, and gave himself for our salvation to death who reigned over us and held us down because of our sins.

. . . by his blood.[2] From the cross he descended into hell and rose from the dead and the third day, he ascended into heaven and sat at the right hand of the Father; he appointed a day on which to judge the world with justice and render to each according to his works.

And he left us this great mystery of godliness: for when he was about to hand himself over to death for the life of the world, he took bread, blessed, sanctified, broke, and gave it to his holy disciples and apostles, saying, "Take and eat from this, all of you; this is my body, which is given for you and for many for forgiveness of your sins. Do this for my remembrance."

Likewise also the cup after supper: he mixed wine and water, blessed, sanctified, gave thanks, and again gave it to them, saying, "Take and drink from it, all of you; this is my blood which shall be shed for you and for many for forgiveness of your sins. Do this for my remembrance. For as often as you eat this bread and drink this cup, you proclaim my death until I come."

We therefore, remembering his holy sufferings, and his resurrection from the dead, and his ascension into heaven, and his session at the right hand of the Father, and his glorious and fearful coming to us (again), have set forth before you your own from your own gifts, this bread and this cup. And we, sinners and unworthy and wretched, pray you, our God, in adoration that in the good pleasure of your goodness your Holy Spirit may descend upon us and upon these gifts that have been set before you, and may sanctify them and make them holy of holies.

Make us all worthy to partake of your holy things for sanctification of soul and body, that we may become one body and one spirit, and may have a portion with all the saints who have been pleasing to you from eternity.

2. The earliest Coptic text begins here.

Remember, Lord, also your one, holy, catholic, and apostolic Church: give it peace, for you purchased it with the precious blood of Christ; and (remember) all the orthodox bishops in it.

Remember first of all your servant Archbishop Benjamin and his colleague in the ministry holy Bishop Colluthus, and all who with him dispense the word of truth: grant them to feed the holy churches, your orthodox flocks, in peace.

Remember, Lord, the priests and all the deacons who assist, all those in virginity and chastity, and all your faithful people; and have mercy on them all.

Remember, Lord, also this place, and those who live in it in the faith of God.

Remember, Lord, also mildness of climate and the fruits of the earth.

Remember, Lord, those who offer these gifts to you, and those for whom they offered them; and grant them all a heavenly reward.

Since, Master, it is a command of your only-begotten Son that we should share in the commemoration of your saints, vouchsafe to remember, Lord, those of our fathers who have been pleasing to you from eternity: patriarchs, prophets, apostles, martyrs, confessors, preachers, evangelists, and all the righteous perfected in faith; especially at all times the holy and glorious Mary, Mother of God; and by her prayers have mercy on us all, and save us through your holy name which has been invoked upon us.

Remember likewise all those of the priesthood who have already died, and all those of lay rank; and grant them rest in the bosom of Abraham, Isaac, and Jacob, in green pastures, by waters of comfort, in a place whence grief, sorrow, and sighing have fled away.

(*to the deacon*) Read the names. (*The deacon reads the diptychs.*)

Bishop: Give them rest in your presence; preserve in your faith us who live here, guide us to your kingdom, and grant us your peace at all times; through Jesus Christ and the Holy Spirit.

The Father in the Son, the Son in the Father with the Holy Spirit, in your holy, one, catholic, and apostolic Church.

The Egyptian Anaphora of St. Basil

FRACTION (Three Prayers)
LORD'S PRAYER
PRAYER OF INCLINATION
PRAYER FOR ABSOLUTION, TO THE FATHER

The bishop raises the host, saying aloud:
The holy things for the holy people.

People: One Father is holy, one Son is holy, one Spirit is holy.
Amen.

COMMUNION
The holy body and the precious blood of Jesus Christ the Son of
God. Amen.

THANKSGIVING FOR COMMUNION
DISMISSAL

10 Egyptian local rites

A. THE PRAYERS OF SARAPION

The collection of prayers attributed to Sarapion, bishop of Thmuis (a large city in the Nile delta), first published in 1895, was accepted as authentic and therefore dated *c*. 359, until an article by Dom Bernard Botte in 1964 challenged the ascription on the grounds of the presence of Arian language impossible for a friend of Athanasius, as Sarapion was. In fact, the language of the prayers accords with that of Athanasius' letters to Sarapion, and the ascription may be accepted as correct, though the possibility of some later editing cannot be ruled out. At any rate, the collection was first assembled at a time when the intercessions (apart from the memorial of the dead) were placed in an earlier part of the liturgy, as in Justin and Hippolytus, and not in the anaphora.

The beginning of the anaphora implies the customary Sursum corda, but the preface is in quite a different style from those of most other anaphoras, its rhythmic repetition suggesting such Gnostic prayers as have survived. So does the phraseology, which vigorously expands the two words in the preface of the Strasbourg papyrus, "wisdom" and "light." Even at this date, the bishop still retained the right to compose his own thanksgiving, as in Justin's day.

The pre-Sanctus, Sanctus, and post-Sanctus, on the other hand, seem to have been imported from the Liturgy of *St. Mark*, though at an earlier stage than that appearing in the manuscripts. This is probably the earliest version of this section. The use of the word "fill" to connect the Sanctus with what follows has been noticed above (the British Museum tablet, see p. 55).

The treatment of the Institution Narrative is also unusual, each half being preceded and followed by the statement: "we offered the bread/cup," and then a prayer. The past tense must imply that the offering took place before the anaphora. The offering is described as "this living sacrifice, this bloodless offering," language which recalls once more the Strasbourg papyrus, though there, as in the later manuscripts of *St. Mark,* the phrase occurs in the preface. The elements offered are also described as "the likeness" of the body and blood, recalling Tertullian's word *"figura"* and Hippolytus' word "antitype." The words in square brackets are almost certainly a gloss.

The Narrative itself is given in a very simple form, again suggesting an early date; and the same quotation is made from the *Didache* as in the Deir Balyzeh papyrus (see p. 80), though here it is treated less freely. The epiclesis asks for God's holy *Word* to come on the elements, rather than his Spirit.

Botte laid great stress on this as a deliberate depreciation of the Spirit, but Athanasius in his letters to Sarapion often uses language which shows that he still thought of *Logos* and *Pneuma* as inseparable: where one is, there the other is also. Granted the tendency of all liturgies to preserve archaic modes of speech, the use of *Logos* in this context presents no problem, but may be regarded as a genuine archaism.

The only intercession within the anaphora is for the dead and for those who have offered. This is a first step towards repeating all the intercessions within the anaphora, a procedure adopted in all later liturgies. The second half of the doxology is the same as that of *St. Mark,* and was doubtless meant to be said by the people.

It should be noted that the order of the prayers in the manuscript was altered by F. E. Brightman in the edition quoted below, and his order was given numbers by F. X. Funk in his widely used edition. But the order of the manuscript is quite logical, and is followed below, with the original numbering.

BIBLIOGRAPHY
F. E. Brightman, "The Sacramentary of Serapion of Thmuis," in *JTS,* 1(1900), pp. 88–113.
Prex Eucharistica, pp. 128–133.
Dix, *The Shape,* pp. 162–172.
B. Botte, "L'Eucologe de Sérapion est-il authentique?", in *Oriens Christianus,* 48(1964), pp. 50–57.
G. J. Cuming, "Thmuis Revisited: another look at the Prayers of Bishop Sarapion," in *Theological Studies,* 41 (1980). pp. 568–575.

The Prayers of Sarapion   75

PRAYER OF OFFERING OF BISHOP SARAPION (1)

It is fitting and right to praise, to hymn, to glorify you, the un-created Father of the only-begotten Jesus Christ.

We praise you, uncreated God, unsearchable, ineffable, incomprehensible by all created being.

We praise you who are known by the only-begotten Son, who were spoken of through him and interpreted and made known to created nature.

We praise you who know the Son and reveal to the saints the glories about him, who are known by your begotten Word, and seen and interpreted to the saints.

We praise you, unseen Father, provider of immortality: you are the fountain of life, the fountain of light, the fountain of all grace and all truth, lover of man and lover of the poor; you reconcile yourself to all and draw all to yourself through the coming of your beloved Son.

We pray, make us living men.

Give us a spirit of light, that we may know you, the true (God) and him whom you have sent, Jesus Christ.

Give us holy Spirit, that we may be able to speak and expound your unspoken mysteries.

May the Lord Jesus Christ and the Holy Spirit speak in us and hymn you through us.

1. Greek: *cheirothesia* (laying-on of hands).

For[2] you are far above every principality and power and virtue and dominion and every name that is named, not only in this age but in the age to come.

Beside you stand thousands of thousands and myriads of myriads of angels, archangels, thrones, dominions, principalities, and powers. Beside you stand the two most honorable seraphim with six wings, which cover the face with two wings, and the feet with two, and fly with two; and they cry, "Holy." With them receive also our cry of "Holy," as we say: "Holy, holy, holy, Lord of Sabaoth; heaven and earth are full of your glory."

Full is heaven, full also is earth of your excellent glory, Lord of the powers. Fill also this sacrifice with your power and your partaking; for to you we offered[3] this living sacrifice, this bloodless offering.

To you we offered this bread, the likeness of the body of the only-begotten. [This bread is the likeness of the holy body.] For the Lord Jesus Christ, in the night when he was betrayed, took bread, broke it, and gave it to his disciples, saying, "Take and eat; this is my body which is broken for you for forgiveness of sins." Therefore we also offered the bread, making the likeness of the death.

We beseech you through this sacrifice: be reconciled to us all and be merciful, O God of truth. And as this bread was scattered over the mountains, and was gathered together and became one, so gather your holy Church out of every nation and every country and every city and village and house, and make one living catholic Church.[4]

We offered also the cup, the likeness of the blood. For the Lord Jesus Christ after supper took a cup and said to his disciples, "Take, drink; this is the new covenant, which is my blood that is shed for you for forgiveness of sins." Therefore we also offered the cup, presenting the likeness of the blood.

Let your holy Word come on this bread, O God of truth, that the bread may become body of the Word; and on this cup, that the

2. Cf. p. 64.
3. Greek: prosēnegkamen.
4. Cf. The Didache, p. 24.

cup may become blood of the Truth; and make all who partake to receive a medicine of life for the healing of every disease, and for the empowering of all advancement and virtue; not for condemnation, O God of truth, nor for censure and reproach.

For we have called upon you, the uncreated, through the only-begotten in Holy Spirit. Let this people receive mercy; let it be counted worthy of advancement; let angels be sent out to be present among the people for bringing to naught the evil one, and for establishing of the Church.

And we entreat also for all who have fallen asleep, of whom is also the remembrance.

After the recitation of the names: Sanctify these souls, for you know them all; sanctify all (the souls) that are fallen asleep in the Lord and number them among all your holy powers, and give them a place and a mansion in your kingdom.

Receive also the thanksgiving of the people, and bless those who offered the offerings and the thanksgivings,[5] and grant health and soundness and cheerfulness and all advancement of soul and body to all this people.

Through your only-begotten Jesus Christ in Holy Spirit; as it was and is and shall be to generations of generations and to all the ages of ages. Amen.

FRACTION AND PRAYER DURING THE FRACTION (2)
Make us worthy of this communion also, God of truth, and make our bodies receive purity, and our souls insight and knowledge; and make us wise, God of compassion, by participation in the body and the blood; for through the only-begotten are glory and might to you in holy Spirit, now and to all the ages of ages. Amen.

BLESSING[6] OF THE PEOPLE AFTER THE COMMUNION OF THE CLERGY (3)
PRAYER AFTER THE COMMUNION OF THE PEOPLE (4)

5. *i.e. the bread and the wine;* Greek: *eucharisteria.*
6. Greek: *cheirothesia* (laying-on of hands).

PRAYER OVER THE OFFERINGS OF OILS AND WATERS (5)
We bless these created things through the name of your only-begotten Jesus Christ; we name the name of him who suffered, was crucified, rose again, and sits at the right hand of the un-created, on this water and oil. Grant healing power to these created things, that every fever and every demon and every disease may be driven away by drinking and anointing; and the partaking of these created things be a healing medicine and a medicine of wholeness; in the name of your only-begotten Jesus Christ, through whom be glory and might to you in Holy Spirit, to all the ages of ages. Amen.

BLESSING[6] AFTER THE BLESSING[7] OF WATER AND OIL (6)

B. THE DEIR BALYZEH PAPYRUS

This papyrus was probably written in Upper Egypt between A.D. 500 and 700. It is of special interest as presenting a local "use." It includes the pre-Sanctus and Sanctus of *St. Mark*, conveniently filling the gap between the Strasbourg papyrus and the British Museum tablet. More important, it has a definitely consecratory epiclesis immediately after the Sanctus, as in the *Catecheses* of Cyril of Jerusalem (q.v.), thus developing the "fill" link with the Sanctus more explicitly than is done in *St. Mark*. Another point of interest is the free quotation of the "corn prayer" of the *Didache*, as in Sarapion. The Institution Narrative is quite simple, and the anaphora may be dated to the late fourth century.

The last few lines are on a different leaf, and may not be the end of the anaphora at all, but rather of a thanksgiving after communion. Otherwise, it is hard to imagine what was in the missing fifteen lines.

BIBLIOGRAPHY
C. H. Roberts and B. Capelle, *An Early Euchologium* (1949).
Prex Eucharistica, pp. 124–127.

6. Greek: *cheirothesia* (laying-on of hands).
7. Greek: *eulogia*.

PEACE (Three Prayers)

. . . who hate[8] . . . bless (your) people . . . raise the fallen, turn back the wanderers, comfort the weak-hearted.

For you are far above every principality and power and virtue and dominion and every name that is named, not only in this age but also (in the age to come. By you) stand (thousands) of the holy (angels and archangels) unnumbered . . . the . . . stand in a circle . . . (six) wings to one and six to the other, and with two they veiled the face, and with two the feet, and with two they flew. Everything at all times hallows you, but with all that hallow you, receive also our hallowing, as we say to you: Holy, holy, holy, Lord of Sabaoth; heaven and earth are full of your glory.

Fill us also with the glory from (you), and vouchsafe to send down your Holy Spirit upon these creatures (and) make the bread the body of our (Lord and) Savior Jesus Christ, and the cup the blood . . . of our Lord and. . . .

(And)[9] as this bread was scattered on (the mountains) and hills and fields, and was mixed together and became one body . . . so this wine which came from the vine of David and the water from the spotless lamb also mixed together became one mystery, so gather the catholic Church. . . .

For (our Lord Jesus) Christ himself (in the night when) he handed (himself) over . . . his disciples (and) apostles, saying, "Take, (eat) from it; this (is) my body, which is given for you for forgiveness of sins." Likewise after supper he took the cup, blessed, drank, and gave it to them, saying, "Take, drink from it, all of you; this is my blood, which is shed for you for forgiveness of sins. As often as you eat this bread and drink this cup, you proclaim my death, you make my remembrance."

We proclaim your death, we confess your resurrection, and we pray. . . .

(At least fifteen lines are missing here.)

8. *Cf. p. 63.*
9. *Cf. the* Didache, *p. 23.*

The Deir Balyzeh Papyrus

. . .and provide us your servants with the power of the Holy
Spirit, for strengthening and increasing of faith, for the hope of
the eternal life to come; through our Lord Jesus Christ, (through
whom) be glory to you, the Father, with the Holy (Spirit) to the
ages. Amen.

C. THE LOUVAIN COPTIC PAPYRUS

This fragment of an unidentified anaphora has the characteristic
Egyptian "fill" link with the Sanctus; then an anamnesis and offering, followed by a consecratory epiclesis, *before* the Institution Narrative, thus taking a further step in the development of the post-
Sanctus (the Deir Balyzeh papyrus does not have an offering
here). The Greek original of this anaphora has recently been
identified in a papyrus at Barcelona which was written in the
fourth century.

BIBLIOGRAPHY
L. Th. Lefort, "Coptica lovanensia," in *Le Muséon*, 53(1940), pp. 22–24, no. 27.
Prex Eucharistica, p. 140 (Latin translation).

. . . (Full are heaven and)[10] earth of your glory.

Heaven and earth are full of that glory wherewith you glorified us
through your only-begotten Son Jesus Christ, the first-born of all
creation, sitting at the right hand of your majesty in heaven, who
will come to judge the living and the dead. We make the remembrance of his death, offering to you your creatures, this bread and
this cup. We pray and beseech you to send out over them your
Holy Spirit, the Paraclete, from heaven . . . to make(?) the bread
the body of Christ and the cup the blood of Christ of the new
covenant.

Thus the Lord himself, when he was soon to be betrayed, took
bread, gave thanks over it, blessed it, broke it, and gave it to the
disciples, and said to them: "Take, eat, for this is my body which
will be given for you."

Likewise after supper he took the cup also, gave thanks over it,
and gave it to them, saying: "Take, drink, for this is my blood
which will be shed for many for forgiveness (of sins)". . . .

10. *Cf. p. 64.*

11 Cyril of Jerusalem: *Catecheses*

The passages below are taken from the *catecheses* (lectures to candidates for baptism) traditionally ascribed to St. Cyril, bishop of Jerusalem *c.* A.D. 349–386. The last five lectures (*catecheses mystagogicae*) were delivered after the Easter baptism, those on the eucharist on Thursday and Friday of Easter week, in the Anastasis, a church built over the Holy Sepulchre. A Spanish nun, Egeria, who visited Jerusalem *c.* 385, describes the occasion thus: "The bishop stands leaning against the inner screen . . . and interprets all that takes place."

There is some doubt about the authorship of the lectures, since most manuscripts attribute them to Cyril's successor, John II, some to both bishops, but none to Cyril alone. A date of 387 would fit the doctrinal position of the author perfectly, whereas 350 might seem a little early. Both these points may be met by the reasonable assumption that Cyril continued to deliver the lectures throughout his episcopate, during which some doctrinal development would be natural; and that they were then taken over by John. In any case, they give a reliable glimpse of the liturgy of Jerusalem in the late fourth century.

The structure of the Jerusalem anaphora, as far as it can be reconstructed from Cyril's brief comments, is as follows:

Sursum corda—preface—Sanctus—epiclesis—intercessions.
This resembles *St. Mark* in having an epiclesis immediately after the Sanctus, and *Egyptian Basil* and *St. James* in having the intercessions at the end. Whether there was an Institution Narrative remains debatable. Cyril devoted an entire *catechesis* to an exposition of the Narrative, but this may be precisely because it was *not* (yet) in his anaphora. It has been suggested that Cyril confined himself to those parts of the anaphora which were spoken aloud, but it may be questioned whether the practice of private recitation had begun so early.

The Sursum corda appears to lack its first couplet. This may be because an original "The Lord be with you," as in Egypt, was replaced by "the Grace" (2 Corinthians 13:13), as in *St. James*. Cyril would have discarded his comment on the former without replacing it by comment on the latter.

The preface starts out as in *St. Mark*, but confines itself to the heavenly bodies, making an easy transition to the Sanctus, which is first attested in the anaphora in Asterius the Sophist, *c.* 340. After the Sanctus, the phrase "having sanctified ourselves with these spiritual hymns" suggests *St. Mark's* "receive . . . our hallowing" (or "sanctification"). As in *St. Mark*, there is no christological thanksgiving.

The epiclesis is definitely consecratory (compare *Coptic Mark* and, even more explicitly, the Deir Balyzeh and Louvain papyri, pp.80f), "for everything that the Holy Spirit has touched, has been sanctified and changed." The same crucial word "changed" appears in *Coptic Mark*, but not in *Greek Mark* or *St. James*. The words "the spiritual sacrifice, the bloodless service" now quite clearly refer to the offering of the elements, not only to praise and thanksgiving. The phrase is already in the Strasbourg papyrus, but in the preface, while in *St. James* it has moved to the anamnesis. Cyril and *St. Mark* both use the verb "perfect" for the consecration. If there was an Institution Narrative in Cyril's anaphora, it must have come after the epiclesis, as in *St. Mark*. Cyril still speaks of "figure" and "likeness."

The intercessions follow. The link "we beseech God over that sacrifice" again goes back to the Strasbourg papyrus, but it is now a sacrifice of propitiation (*hilasmos*), a concept which becomes increasingly prominent at Jerusalem and Antioch during the later fourth century. The obtaining of forgiveness is not far from becoming the chief purpose of celebrating the eucharist. Cyril even goes so far as to say: "we offer Christ slain for our sins, propitiating God" (section 10).

Another new concept is that of "fear," which appears at the same places at the same period. Only found in *St. Mark* in one very late addition, it occurs several times in *St. James*, and permeates the sermons of John Chrysostom. It may have been evoked by the public nature of the services after the peace of the Church, but it has remained a constant and prominent feature of Eastern liturgy.

Some form of connection between Jerusalem and Alexandria seems clear. If there was originally at Jerusalem some form similar to the Strasbourg papyrus form of *St. Mark*, and if the Sanctus, with epiclesis already attached (as in the British Museum tablet) were inserted between the preface and the intercessions, the result would be exactly as described by Cyril.

BIBLIOGRAPHY

F. L. Cross, *St Cyril of Jerusalem: Lectures* (1951).
E. J. Yarnold, (1) *The Awe-Inspiring Rites of Initiation* (1972), pp. 84–95. (2) "The Authorship of the Mystagogic Catecheses," in *The Heythrop Journal*, 19(1978), pp. 143–161.
G. J. Cuming, "Egyptian Elements in the Jerusalem Liturgy," in *JTS*, n.s.25(1974), pp. 117–124.
E. J. Cutrone, "Cyril's Mystagogical Catecheses and the evolution of the Jerusalem Anaphora," in *Orientalia Christiana Periodica*, 44(1978), pp. 52–64.
B. D. Spinks, "The Jerusalem Liturgy of the *Catecheses Mystagogicae*: Syrian or Egyptian?", in *Studia Patristica*, 18 (in preparation).

CATECHESIS 4, THE BODY AND BLOOD OF CHRIST

1. This teaching of blessed Paul is sufficient to give you full assurance about the divine mysteries of which you have been deemed worthy, so that you have become one body and one blood with Christ. For he has just affirmed, that in the night when he was betrayed our Lord Jesus Christ took bread, gave thanks, broke it, and gave it to his disciples, saying, "Take, eat; this is my body." And taking a cup and giving thanks, he said, "Take, drink; this is my blood."

Since he himself has declared and said of the bread, "This is my body," who will thereafter dare to doubt? And since he has strongly affirmed and said, "This is my blood," who will ever doubt, saying that it is not his blood? . . .

3. So we partake with all assurance as of the body and blood of Christ. For in the figure of bread his body is given to you, and in the figure of wine his blood; that, by partaking of the body and blood of Christ, you may become one body and one blood with him. . . .

5. There was also under the old covenant the shewbread; but, since it was of the old covenant, it came to an end. But under the new covenant there is heavenly bread and a cup of salvation, sanctifying soul and body. For as the bread corresponds to the body, so the word accords with the soul. . . .

7. . . . You see here the cup referred to, which Jesus took in his hands, gave thanks, and said, "This is my blood, which is shed for many for forgiveness of sins."

CATECHESIS 5, (The Eucharist)
2. . . . You saw the deacon giving the *lavabo* to the bishop[1] and to the presbyters who surround the altar of God. . . .

3. Then the deacon cries, "Receive one another" and "Let us greet one another . . ."[2]

4. After this, the bishop cries, "Up with your hearts"[3] Then you answer, "We have them with the Lord". . . .

5. Then the bishop says, "Let us give thanks to the Lord . . ." Then you say, "It is fitting and right. . . ."

6. After this, we call to mind heaven and earth and sea; sun and moon and stars; all Creation, rational and irrational, visible and invisible; angels, archangels, virtues, dominions, principalities, powers, thrones; the cherubim with many faces; saying with full effect the (words) of David, "Magnify the Lord with me." We call to mind also the seraphim, whom Isaiah saw in the Holy Spirit standing in a circle round the throne of God, with two wings veiling the face, and with two the feet, and with two flying, and saying, "Holy, holy, holy (is the) Lord of Sabaoth."

The reason why we say this hymn of praise[4] which has been handed down to us from the seraphim is that we may share with the supernatural armies in their hymnody.

7. Then, having sanctified ourselves with these spiritual hymns, we beseech God, the lover of man, to send forth the Holy Spirit

1. Greek: *hiereus.*
2. *The context implies* "with a holy kiss."
3. *The Greek has no verb.*
4. Reading *doxologian;* other readings are *theologian* and *homologian.*

upon the (gifts) set before him, that he may make the bread the body of Christ, and the wine the blood of Christ; for everything that the Holy Spirit has touched, has been sanctified and changed.

8. Then, after the spiritual sacrifice, the bloodless service, has been perfected, we beseech God over that sacrifice of propitiation, for the common peace of the churches, for the stability of the world, for emperors, for armies and auxiliaries, for the sick, for the oppressed; and, praying in general for all who need help, we all offer this sacrifice.

9. Then we call to mind also those who have fallen asleep; first patriarchs, prophets, apostles, martyrs; that God, through their prayers and advocacy, may receive our supplication. Then also for the holy Fathers and bishops who have fallen asleep before us; for we believe that it will be the greatest profit to the souls for whom supplication is offered in the presence of the holy and most dread sacrifice.

10. . . . In the same way, offering our prayers for those who have fallen asleep, even though they were sinners . . . we offer Christ slain for our sins, propitiating God, the lover of man, for them and for ourselves.

11. Then, after that, we say that prayer which the Savior handed down to his own disciples, with a clear conscience addressing God as Father and saying, "Our Father in heaven. . . ."

18. . . . Then, when the prayer is finished, you say, "Amen," which means "So be it"; thus you set the seal on the contents of this prayer taught us by God.

19. After this, the bishop says, "The holy things for the holy people . . ."
Then you say, "One is holy, one is Lord, Jesus Christ . . ."

20. After this you hear the chanter inviting you with a divine melody to the communion of the holy mysteries, and saying, "Taste and see that the Lord is good." Do not entrust judgement to your bodily palate, but to undoubting faith; for what you taste is not bread and wine, but the likeness of the body and blood of Christ.

Cyril of Jerusalem: Catecheses

21. When you approach . . . hollow your palm and receive the body of Christ, saying after it, "Amen . . ."

22. Then . . . approach also the cup of his blood. Do not stretch out your hands, but, bowing and saying "Amen" in a gesture of adoration and reverence, sanctify yourself by partaking of the blood of Christ also . . . Then wait for the prayer, and give thanks to God who has deemed you worthy of such great mysteries.

23. . . . . To whom be glory to the ages of ages. Amen.

12 The Liturgy of St. James

The anaphora of *St. James*, the liturgy of Jerusalem, has close verbal echoes of the *catecheses* of St. Cyril (see pp. 82f). It appears to be the result of a fusion of the old Jerusalem rite with the anaphora of *St. Basil* in its earliest form (see pp. 67f). Later, it influenced and was influenced by the Byzantine version of *St. Basil* and the Egyptian anaphora of *St. Mark* (see pp. 52, 87). A Syriac translation, made probably soon after the Council of Chalcedon (A.D. 451), presents the text in an earlier stage of development than the Greek, lacking the phrases enclosed in square brackets below, which may be assumed to be later additions. A Georgian version also throws light on the development of the Greek text.

The liturgy was widely used outside Jerusalem until its suppression in the twelfth century: the text translated below is Vatican MS gr 2282, written in the neighborhood of Damascus in the ninth century, while the text printed by Brightman is a fourteenth-century manuscript from Thessalonica. Owing to its ascription to "the brother of the Lord," it was regarded as very ancient, and was much used in controversy during the sixteenth century and as a basis for liturgical revision in England in the eighteenth century.

The Sursum corda begins, as in all Syrian and Byzantine anaphoras, with a version of "the Grace" (2 Corinthians 13:13). The preface is clearly an expansion of that quoted by Cyril, but here the heavenly bodies themselves praise God, instead of being the objects of thanksgiving, thus making the lead into the Sanctus even smoother than it is in Cyril. This procedure has good Jewish precedent, e.g. Psalms 19 and 148 and the *Benedicite*. After the Sanctus *St. James* follows *St. Basil* in going on to the Fall and the process of redemption, whereas Cyril's anaphora went straight on to an epiclesis. The post-Sanctus is introduced by the link word "holy" as in *Egyptian Basil*, rather than the Egyptian word "fill." *St. James* avoids *Basil's* error of going right through to the Last Judgement before the Institution Narrative, and, like the *Apostolic Tradition*, has the latter in its chronological place.

The Liturgy of St. James

The Narrative has been considerably expanded in the medieval manuscripts, including the addition of Jesus filling the cup with Holy Spirit. The rest of the anaphora from the anamnesis to the end is addressed to Christ in the Syriac, which may be original. For the first time in the East, the offering is made in the present tense, as in Hippolytus. The phrase "We set before you . . . this bread and this cup" (past tense) in the earliest form of *St. Basil* has become "We offer to you . . . this awesome and bloodless sacrifice." All these words are in Cyril: "awesome," section 9; "bloodless," section 8; "sacrifice," sections 8 and 9; "bloodless," however, is already in the Strasbourg papyrus of *St. Mark*.

The intercessions are developed by the ninth century to a disproportionate length; in the fourteenth-century manuscript they have been noticeably shortened, an obvious exception to the rule that the shorter text is the later. The Syriac has a different doxology from the Greek, namely the doxology of *St. Mark*, already in the Rylands parchment (see p. 56). This again may be original.

Thus *St. James* has further developed the anaphora known to Cyril by inserting between the Sanctus and the epiclesis an entirely new post-Sanctus section, an Institution Narrative, and an anamnesis. All this solid block is most probably derived from *St. Basil* in its Egyptian form, though greatly expanded in *St. James*.

BIBLIOGRAPHY
Prex Eucharistica, pp. 244–261 (Greek), 269–275 (Latin translation of Syriac).
LEW, pp. 31–68 (Greek), 69–110 (English translation of Syriac).
A. Tarby, *La prière eucharistique de l'église de Jérusalem* (1972).
J. R. K. Fenwick, *Fourth-century Anaphoral Construction Techniques* (1986).
M. H. Shepherd, "Eusebius and the Liturgy of St. James" in *Yearbook of Liturgical Studies*, 4(1963), pp. 109–125.
B. D. Spinks, "The Consecratory Epiclesis in the Anaphora of St. James," in *Studia Liturgica*, 11(1976), pp. 19–32.

PROTHESIS (Three prayers)
ENARXIS (Four prayers)
   THE LITTLE ENTRANCE (*Monogenes* and prayer)
PRAYER, SYNAPTE (Litany), and TRISAGION

The Liturgy of St. James 89

PSALM

EPISTLE

ALLELUIA, PRAYERS, and LITANY

GOSPEL

LITANY (for the catechumens)

  THE GREAT ENTRANCE

CHERUBIC HYMN

FIVE PRAYERS

CREED

PEACE (with prayer)

CATHOLIC SYNAPTE

PRAYERS (of the faithful, of the offertory, and of the veil)

THE ANAPHORA

The bishop.[1] The love of God the Father, the grace of our Lord
[and] God and Savior Jesus Christ, and the fellowship [and the
gift] of the [all-]Holy Spirit be with you all.
People: And with your spirit.
The bishop: Let us lift up our mind and our hearts.
People: We have them with the Lord.
The bishop: Let us give thanks to the Lord.
People: It is fitting and right.

The bishop, bowing, says: It is truly fitting and right, suitable and
profitable, to praise you, [to hymn you,] to bless you, to worship
you, to glorify you, to give thanks to you, the creator of all creation, visible and invisible, [the treasure of eternal good things,
the fountain of life and immortality, the God and Master of all.]
You are hymned by [the heavens and] the heaven of heavens and
all their powers; the sun and moon and all the choir of stars;
earth, sea, and all that is in them; the heavenly Jerusalem, [the
assembly of the elect,] the church of the first-born written in
heaven, [the spirits of righteous men and prophets, the souls of
martyrs and apostles;] angels, archangels, thrones, dominions,
principalities and powers, and awesome virtues. The cherubim
with many eyes and seraphim with six wings, which cover their
own faces with two wings, and their feet with two, and fly with

1. Greek: *hiereus.*

two, cry one to the other with unwearying mouths and never-silent hymns of praise,
(*aloud*) [singing] with clear voice the triumphal hymn of your magnificent glory, proclaiming, praising, crying, and saying:

People. Holy, holy, holy, Lord of Sabaoth; heaven and earth are full of your glory. Hosanna in the highest. Blessed is he that comes[2] and will come in the name of the Lord. Hosanna in the highest.

And the bishop, standing up, seals the gifts, saying privately: Holy you are, King of the ages, and [Lord and] Giver of all holiness; holy too is your only-begotten Son, our Lord Jesus Christ, [through whom you made all things;] and holy too is your [all-]Holy Spirit, who searches out all things, even your depths, O God and Father. (*He bows and says:*) Holy you are, almighty, omnipotent, awesome, good, [compassionate,] with sympathy above all for what you fashioned. You made man from the earth [after your image and likeness,] and granted him the enjoyment of paradise; and when he transgressed your commandment and fell, you did not despise him or abandon him, for you are good, but you chastened him as a kindly father, you called him through the law, you taught him through the prophets.

Later you sent your only-begotten Son, [himself, our Lord Jesus Christ,] into the world to renew [and raise up] your image [by coming himself.] He came down [from heaven] and was made flesh from the Holy Spirit and Mary, the Holy [ever-]Virgin Mother of God. He dwelt among men and ordered everything for the salvation of our race.

And when he was about to endure his voluntary [and life-giving] death [on the cross,] the sinless for us sinners, in the night when he was betrayed,[3] [or rather handed himself over,] for the life and salvation of the world.

(*He stands up, takes the bread, seals it, and says:*) he took bread in his holy, undefiled, blameless [and immortal] hands, [looked up to

2. Syriac: came and comes.
3. Greek: *paredidoto* and *paredidou.*

heaven, and] showed it to you, his God and Father; he gave thanks, blessed, sanctified, and broke it, and gave it to his [holy and blessed] disciples and apostles, saying, (*he puts the bread down, saying aloud:*) "Take, eat; this is my body, which is broken and distributed for you for forgiveness of sins." *People:* Amen.

(*He takes the cup, seals it, and says privately:*) "Likewise after supper [he took] the cup, he mixed wine and water, [he looked up to heaven and showed it to you, his God and Father; he gave thanks,] blessed, and sanctified it, [filled it with the Holy Spirit,] and gave it to his [holy and blessed] disciples and apostles, saying, (*he puts it down, saying aloud:*) "Drink from it, all of you; this is my blood of the new covenant, which is shed and distributed for you and for many for forgiveness of sins." *People:* Amen.

(*Then he stands and says privately:*) "Do this for my remembrance; for as often as you eat this bread and drink this cup, you proclaim the death of the Son of Man and confess his Resurrection, until he comes."[4]

And the deacons present answer: We believe and confess.

People: Your death, Lord, we proclaim and your Resurrection we confess.

Then he makes the sign of the cross, bows, and says:[5] We [sinners,] therefore, [also] remembering [his life–giving sufferings and his saving cross and] his death [and his burial] and his Resurrection from the dead on the third day and his return to heaven and his session at your right hand, his God and Father, and his glorious and awesome second coming, when he [comes with glory to] judge the living and the dead, when he will reward each according to his works [—spare us, Lord our God (*thrice*)—or rather according to his compassion,] we offer you, [Master,] this awesome and bloodless sacrifice, [asking you] that you "deal not with us after our sins nor reward us according to our iniquities," but according to your gentleness and [unspeakable] love for man to [pass over and] blot out [the handwriting that is against us][6] your

4. *Syriac:* my death and confess my Resurrection until I come.
5. *From this point onwards the Syriac version is addressed to Christ.*
6. Syriac: the sins of.

suppliants, [and grant us your heavenly and eternal gifts, "which eye has not seen nor ear heard nor have entered into the heart of man, which you, O God, have prepared for those who love you." And do not set at nought your people on account of me and my sins, O Lord, lover of men (*thrice*),] (*aloud*) for your people and your Church entreats you.

People: Have mercy on us, [Lord, God,] Father, the almighty.

And the bishop stands up and says privately: Have mercy on us, [Lord,] God the Father, almighty; [have mercy on us, God, our Savior. Have mercy on us, O God, according to your great mercy,] and send out upon us and upon these [holy] gifts set before you your [all-]Holy Spirit, (*he bows*) the Lord and giver of life, who shares the throne and the kingdom with you, God the Father and your [only-begotten] Son, consubstantial and co-eternal, who spoke in the law and the prophets and in your new covenant, who descended in the likeness of a dove upon our Lord Jesus Christ in the river Jordan [and remained upon him,] who descended upon your holy apostles in the likeness of fiery tongues [in the Upper Room of the holy and glorious Zion on the day of the holy Pentecost; (*he stands up and says privately:*) send down, Master, your all-Holy Spirit himself upon us and upon these holy gifts set before you,] (*aloud*) that he may descend upon them, [and by his holy and good and glorious coming may sanctify them,] and make this bread[7] the holy body of Christ, (*People:* Amen.) and this cup the precious blood of Christ.[7] (*People:* Amen.)

The bishop stands up and says privately: that they may become to all who partake of them [for forgiveness of sins and for eternal life] for sanctification of souls and bodies, for bringing forth good works, for strengthening your holy, [catholic, and apostolic] Church, which you founded on the rock of faith, that the gates of hell should not prevail against it, rescuing it from every heresy, and from the stumbling-blocks of those who work lawlessness, [and from the enemies who rose and rise up] until the consummation of the age.

The clerics alone answer: Amen.

7. *This passage is greatly enlarged in the Syriac*

The Liturgy of St. James   93

Then he makes the sign of the cross, bows, and says: We offer to you, [Master,] for your holy places also, which you glorified by the theophany of your Christ [and the descent of your all-Holy Spirit;] principally for [holy and glorious] Zion, the mother of all the churches, and for your holy, [catholic, and apostolic] Church throughout all the world: even now, Master, grant it richly the gifts of your [all-]Holy Spirit.

Remember, Lord, also our holy [fathers and] bishops [in the Church,] who [in all the world] divide the word of truth [in orthodoxy]; principally our holy Father N., [all his clergy and priesthood]: grant him an honorable old age; preserve him to shepherd your flock in all piety and gravity for many years.

Remember, Lord, the honorable presbytery here and everywhere, the diaconate in Christ, all the other ministers, every ecclesiastical order, [our brotherhood in Christ, and all the Christ-loving people.

Remember, Lord, the priests who stand around us in this holy hour, before your holy altar, for the offering of the holy and bloodless sacrifice; and give them and us the word in the opening of our mouths to the glory and praise of your all-holy name.]

Remember, Lord, [according to the multitude of your mercy and your pity,] me also [your humble, sinful and unworthy servant, and visit me in mercy and pity; save me and deliver me from those who persecute me, Lord, Lord of hosts;] and since sin abounded in me, your grace shall greatly exceed it.

[Remember, Lord, also the deacons who surround your holy altar, and grant them a blameless life; preserve their ministry[8] unspotted and provide for them good degrees.

Remember, Lord, our God, your holy and royal city, and every city and region, and those who live in them in orthodox faith and reverence for you, for their peace and safety.]

Remember, Lord, our most pious [and Christ-loving] emperor, his pious [and Christ-loving] empress, [all his court and his army, for their help from heaven and their victory:] lay hold upon weapon

8. Greek: *diakonia.*

and buckler, and stand up to help him; subject to him all the warlike and barbarous nations that delight in war,[9] [moderate his counsels,] that we may lead a quiet and peaceful life in all piety and gravity.

Remember, Lord, [Christians at sea, on the road, abroad], our fathers and brothers in chains and prisons, in [captivity and] exile, [in mines and tortures and bitter slavery; for a peaceful return home for each of them.

Remember, Lord, those in old age and infirmity,] those who are sick, ill, or troubled by unclean spirits, [for their speedy healing and salvation by you, their God.

Remember, Lord, every Christian soul in trials and afflictions, in need of your mercy and help, O God, and recovery of the lost.

Remember, Lord, our holy fathers and brothers who live in chastity, piety, and self-discipline, and those who struggle among mountains, dens, and caves of the earth, and the orthodox communities everywhere, and our community in Christ here.

Remember, Lord, our fathers and brothers who labor and serve for your holy name.

Remember, Lord, all men for good; on all have mercy, Master; reconcile us all, bring peace to the multitudes of your people, disperse the scandals, abolish wars, end the divisions of the churches, speedily put down the uprisings of the heresies, cast down the insolence of the heathen, exalt the horn of the Christians, grant us your peace and your love, God our savior, the hope of all the ends of the earth.]

Remember, Lord, mildness of climate, [peaceful] showers, [good] dews, [abundance of] fruit, [a perfect harvest, and] the crown of the year [of your goodness]; for "the eyes of all wait upon you, and you give their food in due season; you open your hand and fill every living thing with blessing." (*Here he nods towards the archdeacon.*) Remember, Lord, [those who have brought and bring forth fruit in your holy churches, O God, those who remember

9. *Syriac:* his enemies.

The Liturgy of St. James   95

the poor, and] those who have bidden us make mention of them in our prayers.

Vouchsafe yet to remember, Lord, those who have offered the offerings today on your holy altar, and those for whom each one offered or whom he has in mind, and those who are now read to you.[10]

And he makes mention of those whom he wishes who are in this present life.

[Remember, Lord, also those our parents and friends and relations and brothers.]

Remember all these, Lord, whom we have remembered and those we have not remembered, [of the orthodox]; give them heavenly things for earthly, imperishable for perishable, eternal for temporal, [according to the promise of your Christ,] since you have authority over life and death.

Vouchsafe yet to remember, Lord, those who have been well-pleasing to you from the beginning, [from generation to generation:] the holy Fathers, patriarchs, prophets, apostles, [martyrs, confessors, holy teachers, and every righteous spirit perfected in the faith of your Christ.

Hail, highly favored; the Lord is with you; blessed are you among women, and blessed is the fruit of your womb, for you bore the Savior of our souls. (*thrice*)]
He says aloud: [Especially our all-] Holy, [Blessed, and spotless Lady] Mary Mother of God [and ever-Virgin. *And the clergy alone answer secretly:* Remember, Lord, our God.] *And the bishop bows down and says:* Holy John, the [prophet,] forerunner and baptist.

[The Holy Apostles Peter, Paul, Andrew, James, John, Philip, Bartholomew, Thomas, Matthew, James, Simon, Jude, Matthias; Mark and Luke, the evangelists.

The holy prophets and patriarchs and righteous men.]

Holy Stephen, the first deacon and first martyr.

[The holy martyrs and confessors, who for Christ our true God witnessed and confessed the good confession.

10. Or *recognized by you.*

The Liturgy of St. James

The infants who were put to death by King Herod.

The holy martyrs Procopius, Theodore, Cyrus, John, George, Leontius, Sergius, Bacchus, Cosmas, Damian, Sabinianus, Paul, Babilas, Agathangelus, Eustratius and his fellow-fighters.

The holy forty, the holy forty-five.

Holy Thecla, the first woman martyr.

The holy women who brought the myrrh.

The holy women martyrs Tatte, Febronia, Anastasia, Euphemia, Sophia, Barbara, Juliana, Irene, Faith, Hope, and Charity.]

Remember, Lord God our holy [Fathers and] archbishops who, from [holy] James the apostle and brother of the Lord and first archbishop down to Leo and Athanasius, have been orthodox archbishops of the holy city of Christ our Lord.[11]

[And those who have been archbishops from the beginning, from our holy and blessed Father Eneas, the apostolic man and first of the bishops down to Sophronius and John.

Remember, Lord, our holy Fathers and teachers Clement, Timothy, Ignatius, Dionysius, Irenaeus, Gregory, Alexander, Eustathius, Athanasius, Basil, Gregory, Gregory,[12] Ambrose, Amphilochius, Liberius, Damasus, John, Epiphanius, Theophilus, Celestinus, Augustine, Cyril, Leo, Proclus, Proterius, Felix, Hormisdas, Eulogius, Ephraem, Anastasius, Theodore, Martin, Agathon, Sophronius.

Remember, Lord, the six holy, great and ecumenical councils: the three hundred and eighteen (Fathers) of Nicaea, and the one hundred and fifty of Constantinople, and the two hundred of the first Ephesus, and the six hundred and thirty of Chalcedon, and the one hundred and sixty-four of the fifth holy council, and the two hundred and eighty-nine of the sixth holy council, and the other holy councils and bishops who in all the world in orthodoxy divided the word of truth.

11. *Syriac:* the present day have preached the word of the orthodox faith in your holy churches.
12. *i.e.* Gregory of Nazianzus *and* Gregory of Nyssa.

Remember, Lord, our holy Fathers and ascetics Paul, Antony, Charito, Paul, Pachomius, Hamoun, Theodore, Hilarion, Arsenius, Macarius, Macarius, Sisoïus, John, Pambo, Poemen, Nilus, Isidore, Ephrem, Symeon, Symeon, Theodosius, Saba, Saba, Euthymius, Theoctistus, Gerasimus, Pantaleon, Maximus, Anastasius, Cosmas, John.

Remember, Lord, our holy Fathers who were put to death by the barbarians in the holy mountain of Sinai and in Raitho, and our other holy Fathers and orthodox ascetics and all the saints; not that we are worthy to make mention of their blessedness, but that they themselves indeed, standing by your awesome and dread judgement-seat, may make mention in turn of our misery.]

Remember, Lord, presbyters, deacons, [deaconesses,] subdeacons, readers, exorcists, interpreters, singers, monks, virgins, [widows, orphans, the continent, those who have been perfected with faith in the fellowship of your holy, catholic, and apostolic Church.

Remember, Lord, the pious and faithful emperors Constantine, Helena, Theodosius the Great, Marcianus, Pulcheria, Leo, Justinian, Constantine, and those who reigned after them in piety and faith,] and all the [Christ-loving] orthodox laymen who now sleep in the faith [and seal] of Christ.

[Remember, Lord, our parents and friends and relations.]

And after them he makes mention of those orthodox whom he wishes.

Remember all [these orthodox], Lord, the God of the spirits and of all flesh, whom we have remembered and whom we have not remembered; give them rest yourself there, [in the land of the living, in your kingdom, in the pleasure of paradise,] in the bosom of Abraham, Isaac and Jacob, [our holy Fathers,] whence pain, sorrow, and sighing have fled away, where the light of your countenance looks on them [and lights them for ever.] Guide the ends of our lives to be Christian [and well-pleasing] and sinless [in peace, Lord]; collect us under the feet of your elect, when you will and as you will, but without shame and transgressions, through your only-begotten Son, our Lord and God and Savior Jesus Christ, for he alone has appeared on earth without sinning.

The Liturgy of St. James

Deacon: And for the peace and stability of the whole world and the holy churches of God; and for those for whom each one has offered or whom he has in mind, and for the people that stand round, for all men and all women.]

The bishop says aloud: Through whom, [as a good God and a Master that loves men,] to us and them (*People:*) remit, forgive, pardon, O God, our transgressions, voluntary and involuntary, witting and unwitting.

The bishop alone says: By the grace and compassion and love for men of your Christ, with whom you are blessed and glorified, with your all-Holy and life-giving Spirit, now and always and to the ages of ages. Amen.[13]

PRAYER and LORD'S PRAYER
PRAYER OF INCLINATION
PRAYER OF ELEVATION and FRACTION

The bishop raises the gift and says aloud: The holy things for the holy people.

People: One is holy, one is Lord, Jesus Christ, to the glory of God the Father, with the Holy Spirit; to him be glory to the ages of ages.[14]

COMMUNION
INCENSE-PRAYERS
PRAYER OF INCLINATION
THANKSGIVING FOR COMMUNION
DISMISSAL
PRAYER (in sacristy)

13. *Syriac:* that in this, as in all things, your all-honored and blessed name may be glorified and extolled, with the name of our Lord Jesus Christ and your holy Spirit, now and ever and to the ages of ages;
  People: as it was, is, and awaits the generations of generations, and to the generations of the ages to come, for ever. Amen.
  Cf. p. 56 and p. 66.
14. *Syriac:* The one Father is holy, the one Son is holy, the one Spirit is holy.
  Cf. p. 66.

13 *The Apostolic Constitutions*

This work belongs to the genus Church Order (cf. the *Didache* and the *Apostolic Tradition*), probably originating in the controversy with the Arian Eunomius (A.D. 360–380). It was edited by the author of the pseudo-Ignatian letters, as was already recognized by Archbishop Üssher in the seventeenth century. Recently the editor has been identified as also the author of a hitherto anonymous commentary on the Book of Job, which in one catena is attributed to "Julian." There was an Eunomian bishop named Julian in Cilicia *c.* 364, which fits the *Apostolic Constitutions* for time, place, and doctrinal position; but more cannot be said. The editor is shown to have had Arian leanings by the best manuscript (Vatican gr 1506), which contains passages which have been omitted from all other manuscripts as heretical (printed below in anglebrackets).

The work includes three liturgies: that in book II is an outline derived from the third-century *Didascalia*, without any text of the anaphora. That in book VII is an expansion of the prayers of the *Didache*; book VII also contains a number of Jewish prayers translated into Greek and adapted for Christian use. Book VIII includes the earliest surviving *complete* text of a liturgy. Since it does not appear to have been used widely (if at all), it can be safely assumed that it has not undergone development, but gives a reliable picture of a fourth-century eucharist in the neighborhood of Antioch, though some details may be idiosyncrasies of the editor. The evidence of the text is confirmed at several points by the sermons of St. John Chrysostom, though hardly at all in the anaphora.

Partly because of its Arian tendencies, partly because of its attribution to the Apostles, who are indicated as contributing the liturgy of book VIII section by section in turn for the benefit of St. Clement of Rome (hence the name "Clementine Liturgy"), the work was highly regarded in eighteenth-century England, where Deism was widespread, and was made the basis of various proposed revisions of the Book of Common Prayer. By the end of the century, both reasons were discredited, but the work continued to be valued as a historical source, and for its relationship to the *Apostolic Tradition*. The editor has incorporated about a third of Hippolytus' text in his anaphora, which is consequently of value for any attempt to restore the original Greek of the *Apostolic Tradition*, though allowance has to be made for the editor's tendency to rewrite his model.

A. BOOK VII

Whatever the original purpose of these prayers, the editor clearly intends his revision for the eucharist, and it is interesting to see how little he thinks it necessary to add. He runs the two thanksgivings of chapter 9 together, with the bread before the cup, and inserts references to Christ's incarnation, passion, and resurrection. The Last Supper is represented simply by the words "he commanded us to proclaim his death." The editor sees no need to add Sanctus, Institution Narrative, anamnesis, offering, epiclesis, or intercessions. It is still a very primitive prayer.

The rubric "after you have had your fill" becomes "after partaking," so that chapter 10 is definitely a thanksgiving after communion. The editor has enlarged it slightly, but without altering its character.

The thanksgiving over the ointment survives in the *Didache* only in the Coptic version (q.v.). It may be compared with similar prayers in the *Apostolic Tradition*, Sarapion, and the Roman rite (see pp. 36, 79, 166).

BIBLIOGRAPHY
F. X. Funk, *Didascalia* . . . (1905), vol. 1, pp. 410–414 (Sections 25–70).
M. Metzger, *Les Constitutions Apostoliques* (1985-7).

Always be thankful, as faithful and well-disposed servants, about the thanksgiving saying thus:

We give thanks to you, our Father, for the life which you made known to us through your child Jesus, through whom also you made everything and take thought for everything. You sent him to become man for our salvation, you granted him to suffer and to die; you also raised him from the dead, you were pleased to glorify him and set him at your right hand, through him you promised us the resurrection of the dead.

Almighty Master, eternal God, as this bread was scattered and when brought together became one, so bring your Church from the ends of the world into your kingdom.

Again we give thanks to you, our Father, for the precious blood of Jesus Christ which was poured out for us, and the precious body of which also we perform these symbols; for he commanded us to proclaim his death. . . . through him be glory to you for evermore. Amen . . .

And after partaking, give thanks thus:

We give thanks to you, God and Father of our Savior Jesus, for your holy name which you have enshrined in us, and for the knowledge and faith and love and immortality which you gave us through your child Jesus. You, almighty Master, the God of all, created the world and the things in it through him, and planted the law in our souls, and made ready beforehand the things for men's partaking; God of our holy and blameless Fathers Abraham, Isaac, and Jacob, your faithful servants, mighty God, faithful and true and not deceitful in your promises, you sent Jesus the Christ to dwell among men as man, being God the Word and man, and to destroy error utterly. Remember now through him your holy Church which you redeemed with the precious blood of your Christ, and deliver it from all evil, and perfect it in your love and your truth, and bring us all into your kingdom, which you prepared for it.

Marana tha.
Hosanna to the son of David.
Blessed is he who comes in the name of the Lord.
God is the Lord, who has appeared to us in the flesh . . .

But about the ointment, give thanks thus:

We give thanks to you, God, creator of all things, for the sweet savor of the ointment, and for the immortal age which you made known to us through your child Jesus;

for yours is the glory and the power for evermore. Amen.

B. BOOK VIII

The Sursum corda begins with "the Grace" (2 Corinthians 13:13), in a slightly different form from that of *St. James*. The preface is of enormous and unparalleled length. Its first section is chiefly concerned with the nature of God, a new theme for the eucharistic prayer. Possibly it ended originally at the end of the third paragraph, which has every appearance of leading into the Sanctus, but instead embarks on the theme of Creation. It has included a phrase which also appears in the anaphora of *St. John Chrysostom:* "you brought all things from non-existence to existence," and two phrases from the *Apostolic Tradition:* "the angel of your [great] purpose" and "you . . . made all things through him."

The next seven paragraphs deal with Creation in great detail, starting with the heavenly bodies and continuing with the four elements of air, fire, earth, and water. Next comes man, "the citizen of the world"; the story of the Fall; and a summary of the Old Testament as far as the fall of Jericho. The first part of this passage recalls Psalm 104; the last part may be compared with the prayer in Nehemiah 9 and with Hebrews 11, both of which also break off with the arrival of the Israelites in Canaan. At the end of the twenty-second paragraph the Sanctus is reached.

Next follows a section on the birth, ministry, and death of Christ, during which quotations from Hippolytus begin to appear once more. These continue in the anamnesis and epiclesis. Here, indeed, it seems that the editor expanded the text of the *Apostolic Tradition*, rather than insert isolated phrases into an already existing prayer. The epiclesis is of the consecratory type which by now has become standard, though the wording is still restrained: the only verb is *"apophaino,"* literally "to reveal as," hence "to make" the bread the body and the cup the blood of Christ.

Compared with those of *St. James*, the intercessions are brief, presumably the typical fourth-century length. They show some kinship with those quoted by St. John Chrysostom in his sermons.

The post-Sanctus contains several examples of a favorite Syriac figure of speech, depending on contrast: "the high priest to be the sacrifice, the shepherd to be a sheep."

The Apostolic Constitutions, *Book VIII* 103

BIBLIOGRAPHY
Prex Eucharistica, pp. 82–95 (lacks the Intercessions and the Arian readings).
LEW, pp. 3–27 (lacks the Arian readings).
M. Metzger, *Les Constitutions Apostoliques* (1985–7).
L. Bouyer, *Eucharist* (1970), pp. 244–268.
C. H. Turner, "Notes on the Apostolic Constitutions: The Compiler an Arian," in *JTS*, 16 (1915), pp. 54–61.
W. E. Pitt, "The Anamneses and Institution Narrative in the Liturgy of Apostolic Constitutions Book VIII," in *Journal of Ecclesiastical History*, 9 (1958), pp. 1–7.

READINGS (LAW, PROPHETS, EPISTLE, GOSPEL)
SERMON
DISMISSALS OF THE CATECHUMENS, THE POSSESSED, AND
   THE PENITENTS (Litanies and Prayers)
PRAYERS OF THE FAITHFUL (Litany and Prayer)
PEACE
OFFERTORY

THE ANAPHORA
Then, after praying privately, the bishop[1] puts on a splendid robe and stands at the altar with the priests, makes the sign of the cross on his forehead with his hands, and says,

The grace of almighty God and the love of our Lord Jesus Christ and the fellowship of the Holy Spirit be with you all.

All say together: And with your spirit.
The bishop: Up with your mind.[2]
All: We have it with the Lord.
The bishop: Let us give thanks to the Lord.
All: It is fitting and right.
The bishop: It is truly fitting and right to praise you before all things, essentially existing God, existing before created things, from whom all fatherhood in heaven and on earth is named, alone unbegotten, without beginning, without lord or master, lacking nothing, provider of all good things, greater than every

1. Greek: *archiereus*.
2. *The Greek has no verb*

cause and origin, always being in one and the same mode, from whom all things came into being as from a starting-point.

For you are knowledge, without beginning, eternal vision, unbegotten hearing, untaught wisdom, first in nature, alone in existence, too great to be numbered. You brought all things from non-existence into existence through your only-begotten Son; and him you begat without an intermediary before all ages by your will and power and goodness, your only-begotten Son, the Word, God, living wisdom, the firstborn of all creation, the angel of your great purpose, your high-priest ⟨and notable worshipper⟩, king and lord of all rational and sentient nature, who was before all, through whom are all.

For you, eternal God, made all things through him, and through him you vouchsafe a fitting providence over everything. Through him you granted existence, through him also a good existence; O God and Father of your only-begotten Son, through him before all things you made ⟨the heavenly powers,⟩ the cherubim and the seraphim, the ages and the hosts, virtues and powers, principalities and thrones, archangels and angels; and through him after all these things you made this visible world and all that is in it.

For you are he who set out heaven as a vault, and stretched it out as a screen, and established the earth on nothing by your sole intent; you fixed the firmament, and arranged night and day; you brought light out of your treasures, and by its contraction you brought on darkness (to give) rest to the living things that move in the world. You appointed the sun in heaven to begin the day and the moon to begin the night, and you inscribed the chorus of the stars in heaven to the praise of your magnificence.

You made water for drinking and cleansing, lifegiving air for breathing in and out, and for the production of sound through the tongue striking the air, and for hearing which is aided by it to receive the speech which falls upon it.

You made fire for comfort in darkness, for supplying our need, that we should be warmed and given light by it.

You divided the ocean from the land, and made the one navigable, the other fit to be trodden by our feet; you filled the one with creatures small and great, the other tame and wild; you wove it a crown of varied plants and herbs, you beautified it with flowers and enriched it with seeds.

You constructed the abyss and set a great covering on it, the piled-up seas of salt water, and surrounded it with gates of finest sand; now you raise it with winds to the height of the mountains, now you level it to a plain; now you drive it to fury with a storm, now you soothe it with a calm, so that it gives an easy journey to travellers in ships.

You girdled the world that was made by you through Christ with rivers and flooded it with torrents, you watered it with ever-flowing springs and bound it round with mountains as an unshakable and most safe seat for the earth.

For you filled the world and adorned it with sweet-smelling and healing herbs, with many different living things, strong and weak, for food and for work, tame and wild, with hissing of reptiles, with the cries of variegated birds, the cycles of the years, the numbers of months and days, the order of the seasons, the course of rain-bearing clouds for the production of fruits and the creation of living things, a stable for the winds that blow at your command, the multitude of plants and herbs.

And not only have you fashioned the world, but you have also made man in it, the citizen of the world, displaying him as the ornament of the world.[3] For you said in your wisdom, "Let us make man in our image and likeness, and let him rule over the fish of the sea and the birds of the air."

So also you made him from an immortal soul and a perishable body, the one from what is not, the other from the four elements. And you gave him in respect of the soul, logical reason, discernment between godliness and ungodliness, observance of right and wrong, and in respect of the body, the five senses and the power of motion.

For you, almighty God, planted by Christ a garden eastward in Eden with adornment of every kind of plant for food, and in it, as

3. Greek: *Kosmou kosmon;* the word *kosmos* has both these meanings.

in a costly home, you placed man; and in making him you gave him an inborn law, that he might have in himself and of himself the seeds of the knowledge of God.

And when you had brought him into the paradise of delight, you allowed him authority to partake of everything, and forbade him the taste of one thing alone, in the hope of better things, that, if he kept the commandment, he should receive immortality as a reward for that.

But when he neglected the commandment and tasted the forbidden fruit, by the deceit of the serpent and the counsel of the woman, you justly drove him out of the paradise; but in your goodness you did not despise him when he was utterly perishing, for he was the work of your hands, but you subjected creation to him, and granted him to provide food for himself by his own sweat and labors, while you caused everything to shoot and grow and ripen. And in time, after putting him to sleep for a short while, you called him to rebirth by an oath; and after destroying the limit of death, you promised him life after resurrection.

Nor was this all, but you poured out his descendants to a countless multitude; you glorified those who remained faithful to you, and punished those who rebelled against you; you accepted the sacrifice of Abel as being a righteous man, and rejected the gift of Cain, who slew his brother, as being a man accursed; and in addition you received Seth and Enosh, and translated Enoch.

For it is you who fashion men and provide life and fill need and give laws and reward those that keep them and punish those who break them; you brought the great Flood upon the earth because of the multitude of the ungodly, and saved righteous Noah from the Flood in the ark with eight souls, the end of those who dwelt there, but the beginning of those who were to be; you kindled the terrible fire against the five cities of Sodom, and turned a fruitful land into salt for the wickedness of those who dwelt in it, and snatched holy Lot from the burning. It was you who rescued Abraham from the godlessness of his forefathers and made him inheritor of the world; and revealed your Christ to him; you chose Melchizedek to be high-priest of your service; you declared your long-suffering servant Job to be the victor over the serpent, the origin of evil; you made Isaac the child of promise; you made Jacob the father of twelve sons, and his descendants to become a multitude, and brought him into Egypt with seventy-five souls.

You, Lord, did not despise Joseph but, as a reward of his chastity for your sake, gave him the rule over the Egyptians. You, Lord, because of your promises to their Fathers, did not despise the Hebrews when they were oppressed by the Egyptians, but you rescued them and punished the Egyptians.

And when men destroyed the law of nature and thought that the Creation had created itself, or honored it more than they should, making it equal to you, God of all, you did not allow them to go astray, but revealed your holy servant Moses and through him gave them the written law in aid of nature, you showed that the Creation was your work and expelled the error of polytheism. You glorified Aaron and his descendants with the honor of priesthood, you punished the Hebrews when they sinned, and received them when they turned back.

You avenged them on the Egyptians with the ten plagues, you divided the sea and led the Israelites through, you drowned and destroyed the pursuing Egyptians. You sweetened the bitter water with wood, you poured water from the precipitous rock, you rained manna from heaven, and quails as food from the air. (You set up) a pillar of fire for light by night and a pillar of cloud for shadow from the heat by day. You declared Joshua to be leader, you destroyed through him the seven nations of Canaanites, you parted Jordan, you dried up the rivers of Etham, you laid walls low without machines or human hands.

For all things glory be to you, almighty Lord. You are worshipped ⟨by every bodiless and holy order, by the Paraclete, and above all by your holy child[4] Jesus the Christ, our Lord and God, your angel and the chief general of your power, and eternal and unending high priest,⟩ by unnumbered[5] armies of angels, archangels, thrones, dominions, principalities, powers, virtues, eternal armies. The cherubim and the six-winged seraphim with two wings

4. *Or* servant (*cf.* Didache, *p. 23*).
5. *Another reading is* orderly.

covering their feet, with two their heads, and with two flying, together with thousands of thousands of archangels and myriads of myriads of angels say unceasingly, never resting their voices:

All the people say: Holy, holy, holy (is the) Lord of Sabaoth; heaven and earth are full of his glory; blessed (is he) for ever. Amen.

The bishop continues: Truly are you holy and all-holy, most high and exalted above all for ever.

Holy also is your only-begotten Son, our Lord and God Jesus the Christ, who ministered to you, his God and Father, in all things, in the varieties of creation, and in appropriate forethought. He did not despise the race of men as it perished; but after the law of nature and the warnings of the Law and the reproofs of the prophets and the guardianship of the angels, when they were violating the natural and the written law, and casting out of memory the Flood, the burning (of Sodom), the plagues of the Egyptians, and the slaughter of the Palestinians, and were all about to perish as never yet, by your counsel it pleased him who was maker of man to become man, the lawgiver to be under the law, the high-priest to be the sacrifice, the shepherd to be a sheep.

And he propitiated you, his own God and Father, and reconciled you to the world, and freed all men from the impending wrath. He was born of a virgin, God the Word made in the flesh, the beloved Son, the firstborn of all Creation, according to the prophecies spoken beforehand by him concerning himself, from the seed of David and Abraham, of the tribe of Judah. He who fashions all who are begotten was made in a virgin's womb; the fleshless became flesh; he who was begotten outside time was begotten in time.

He lived a holy life and taught according to the law; he drove away every disease and every sickness from men; he did signs and wonders among the people; he who feeds those who need food and fills all things living with plenteousness partook of food and drink and sleep; he made known your name to those who did not know it; he put ignorance to flight; he re-kindled piety; he fulfilled your will; he accomplished the work which you gave him.

And when he had achieved all these things, he was seized by the hands of lawless so-called priests and high-priests and a lawless people, by betrayal through one who was diseased with wickedness. He suffered many things at their hands, endured all kinds of indignity by your permission, and was handed over to Pilate the governor. The Judge was judged and the Savior was condemned; he who cannot suffer was nailed to the cross, he who is immortal by nature died, and the giver of life was buried, that he might free from suffering and rescue from death those for whose sake he came, and break the bonds of the devil, and deliver men from his deceit.

And on the third day he rose from the dead, and after spending forty days with his disciples, he was taken up into heaven and sits at your right hand, his God and Father.

Remembering therefore what he endured for us, we give you thanks, almighty God, not as we ought but as we are able, and we fulfil his command.

For in the night he was betrayed, he took bread in his holy and blameless hands and, looking up to you, his God and Father, he broke it and gave it to his disciples, saying, "This is the mystery of the new covenant: take of it, eat; this is my body which is broken for many for forgiveness of sins."

Likewise also he mixed the cup of wine and water and sanctified it and gave it to them, saying, "Drink from this, all of you; this is my blood which is shed for many for forgiveness of sins. Do this for my remembrance; for as often as you eat this bread and drink this cup, you proclaim my death, until I come."

Remembering then his Passion and death and resurrection from the dead, his return to heaven and his future second coming, in which he comes with glory and power to judge the living and the dead, and to reward each according to his works, we offer you, King and God, according to his commandment, this bread and this cup, giving you thanks through him that you have deemed us worthy to stand before you and to serve you as priests.

And we beseech you to look graciously upon these gifts set before you, O God who need nothing, and accept them in honor of your

Christ; and to send down your Holy Spirit upon this sacrifice, the witness of the sufferings of the Lord Jesus, that he may make[6] this bread body of your Christ, and this cup blood of your Christ; that those who partake of it may be strengthened to piety, obtain forgiveness of sins, be delivered from the devil and his deceit, be filled with Holy Spirit, become worthy of your Christ, and obtain eternal life, after reconciliation with you, almighty Master.

Further we pray to you, Lord, for your holy Church from one end of the world to the other, which you redeemed with the precious blood of your Christ, that you would guard it unshaken and sheltered until the consummation of the age; and for all bishops who rightly divide the word of truth.

And we entreat you also for my worthless self who offer to you, and for all the priesthood, for the deacons and all the clergy, that you would instruct them all and fill them with holy Spirit.

And we entreat you, Lord, for the Emperor and those in authority and all the army, that they may be peaceable towards us, that we may live the whole of our life in quietness and concord, and glorify you through Jesus Christ our hope.

And we offer to you also for all those holy men who have been well-pleasing to you from everlasting: patriarchs, prophets, righteous men, apostles, martyrs, confessors, bishops, priests, deacons, subdeacons, readers, singers, virgins, widows, laymen, and all whose names you know.

And we offer to you for this people, that you would make them a royal priesthood, a holy nation, to the praise of your Christ; for those in virginity and chastity, for the widows of the Church, for those in holy marriage and child-bearing, for the infants among your people, that you may make none of us a castaway.

And we ask you on behalf of this city and those who live in it, for those in illnesses, those in bitter slavery, those in exile, those whose goods have been confiscated, for sailors and travellers, that you would become the help of all, their aid and support.

---

6. Greek: *apophēnēi.*

And we entreat you for those that hate and persecute us for the sake of your name, for those who are outside and have gone astray, that you would turn them back to good and soften their hearts.

And we entreat you also for the catechumens of the Church, for those distressed by the Alien, and for those in penitence among our brothers, that you would perfect the first in the faith, and cleanse the second from the works of the devil, and receive the repentance of the third, and forgive them and us our transgressions.

And we offer to you also for a mild climate and an abundant harvest, that we may partake of the good things from you without lack, and unceasingly praise you, who give food to all flesh.

And we entreat you also for those who are absent for good cause, that you would preserve us all in piety, and gather us without change, without blame, without reproach in the kingdom of your Christ, the God of all sentient and rational nature, our King.

For ⟨through him⟩ (is due) to you all glory, worship, and thanksgiving, ⟨and through you and after you to him in⟩[7] the Holy Spirit honor and adoration, now and always and to the ages of ages, unfailing and unending.

And all the people say: Amen.

INCLINATION (Litany and Prayer of blessing)
ELEVATION
The bishop says to the people: The holy things for the holy people.

The people answer: One is holy, one is Lord, Jesus Christ, to the glory of God the Father, blessed to the ages. Amen.
  Glory to God in the highest, and peace on earth, good will among men.
  Hosanna to the Son of David: blessed is he who comes in the name of the Lord.
  God is Lord and has appeared to us: hosanna in the highest.

7. In *was later altered to:* to the Father, the Son, and.

COMMUNION

The bishop gives the offering, saying: The body of Christ.

And he who receives says: Amen,

The deacon takes the cup and gives it, saying: The blood of Christ, the cup of life.

And he who drinks says: Amen.

THANKSGIVING FOR COMMUNION
DISMISSAL (Prayer for protection)

14 The Byzantine Liturgy of St. Basil

This liturgy is still in use in the Orthodox Church, though only on the first five Sundays of Lent, Maundy Thursday, the eves of Easter, Christmas, and Epiphany, and the feast of St. Basil. It seems probable that at some period towards the end of his life St. Basil worked over the anaphora now known as *Egyptian Basil* (see pp. 67–73), expanding it with "theological content clothed in scriptural language" (H. Engberding). Besides the Egyptian version, there are also translations into Syriac and Armenian which show the text in an intermediate state between the Egyptian original and the Byzantine version still in use at the present day. A quotation from Faustus of Byzantium provides a brief glimpse of the text *c.* 385.

The Byzantine text is twice as long as the Egyptian. At several points the wording is very similar to that of the anaphora of *St. John Chrysostom*, which this anaphora has probably influenced. For some centuries *St. Basil* was the principal liturgy of Constantinople, until finally ousted by *St. John Chrysostom*. The text translated here is that of the Barberini manuscript (Vatican MS gr. 336), written *c.* 800, the oldest manuscript of a complete liturgy in existence. Even so, there is a substantial lacuna in the text of *St. Basil*, which in Brightman's edition is supplied from Grottaferrata MS G b vii (ninth or tenth century).

The brief reference to Creation in *Egyptian Basil* is now eliminated, and its place is taken by the sentence "The whole rational and spiritual Creation does you service," a far cry from Justin, let alone Psalm 104. But it is in keeping with Basil's general attitude: in three separate writings he urges that it is more important to give thanks for the work of Jesus Christ than for the glories of Creation.

The appearance of a number of apophatic adjectives ("invisible, incomprehensible, infinite, unchangeable") may be due to the controversy with Eunomius, who held that God is "absolutely intelligible"; but the tradition of their use goes as far back as

Athenagoras (*c.* 180). Dom B. Capelle identified the sentence "who is the image of your goodness . . . the true Light" as a verbatim quotation from a sermon of Athanasius against the Arians. The extent of Basil's use of Scripture to expand the text may be gauged by the fact that in the 29 lines of the anaphora as far as the Sanctus, Brightman has identified 44 scriptural quotations.

The post-Sanctus section is unusually long. The Byzantine text still keeps the past tense "having set forth" (once aorist, once perfect), as in the Egyptian anaphoras; and the bread and the cup are described as "the antitypes of the holy body and blood" of Christ. This preserves an archaic theology of consecration found also in Hippolytus, Tertullian, Sarapion, and the canon quoted by Ambrose, where the relevant word is *"figura."* The literal meaning of the word translated "make" (this bread the precious body) is "show (it) to be," but by this time the stronger meaning is established.

The intercessions are also greatly expanded from the Egyptian version, and altered in order of subject matter, though the expansion may be due to gradual additions over the years, rather than to Basil himself. The transition to the intercessions is headed *"Euchē,"* as though it had once been a separate prayer. In the oldest version of Egyptian Basil it looks quite like one. It is a prayer for the benefits of communion.

Some fairly close parallels have been noted with the writings of Basil, but too much weight should not be put on these, since, as in the case of *St. John Chrysostom,* some may be due to the saint quoting from the liturgy rather than *vice versa.*

In the text below, later additions are in angle-brackets, later omissions in square brackets.

BIBLIOGRAPHY
Prex Eucharistica, pp. 230–243.
LEW, pp. 309–344, 400–411, 521–526.
J. R. K. Fenwick, *Fourth-century Anaphoral Construction Techniques* (1986).
W. E. Pitt, "The Origin of the Anaphora of the Liturgy of St Basil," in *Journal of Ecclesiastical History,* 12(1961), pp. 1–13.

PROTHESIS (Prayer in sacristy)
ENARXIS (Three antiphons and prayers)
PRAYERS OF ENTRANCE AND OF THE TRISAGION
[PRAYER OF THE THRONE (*omitted later*)]
READINGS and CHANTS
EKTENĒ (Litany).
DISMISSAL OF CATECHUMENS, WITH PRAYER
PRAYERS OF THE FAITHFUL 1 and 2
   THE GREAT ENTRANCE
PRAYER and CHERUBIC HYMN
PROSKOMIDE (Prayer of Offering)
PEACE
CREED

THE ANAPHORA

Priest: The grace of our Lord Jesus Christ and the love of the God and Father, and the fellowship of the Holy Spirit be with you all.
People: And with your spirit.
Priest: Let us lift up our hearts.
People: We have them with the Lord.
Priest: Let us give thanks to the Lord.
People: It is fitting and right ⟨to worship the Father, the Son, and the Holy Spirit, the consubstantial and undivided Trinity⟩.

And the priest begins the holy anaphora: I AM, Master, Lord God, Father almighty, reverend, it is truly fitting and right and befitting the magnificence of your holiness to praise you, to hymn you, to bless you, to worship you, to give you thanks, to glorify you, the only truly existing God, and to offer to you with a contrite heart and a humble spirit this our reasonable service. For it is you who granted us the knowledge of your truth; and who is sufficient to declare your powers, to make all your praises to be heard, or to declare all your wonders at all times? [Master,] Master of all, Lord of heaven and earth and all Creation, visible and invisible, you sit on the throne of glory and behold the depths, without beginning, invisible, incomprehensible, infinite, unchangeable, the Father of our Lord Jesus Christ the great God and savior of our hope, who is the image of your goodness, the identical seal, manifesting you

          The Byzantine Liturgy of St. Basil

the Father in himself, living Word, true God, before all ages wisdom, life, sanctification, power, the true Light by whom the Holy Spirit was revealed, the spirit of truth, the grace of sonship, the pledge of the inheritance to come, the first fruits of eternal good things, lifegiving power, the fountain of sanctification, by whose enabling the whole rational and spiritual Creation does you service and renders you the unending doxology; for all things are your servants. For angels, archangels, thrones, dominions, principalities, powers, virtues, and the cherubim with many eyes praise you, the seraphim stand around you, each having six wings, and with two covering their own faces, and with two their feet, and with two flying, and crying one to the other with unwearying mouths and never-silent doxologies, (*aloud*) singing the triumphal hymn, crying aloud and saying:

People: Holy, ⟨holy, holy, Lord of Sabaoth; heaven and earth are full of your glory. Hosanna in the highest. Blessed is he who comes in the name of the Lord. Hosanna in the highest.⟩

The priest says privately: With these blessed powers, Master, lover of men, we sinners also cry and say: you are truly holy and all-holy, and there is no measure of the magnificence of your holiness, and you are holy in all your works, for in righteousness and true judgement you brought all things upon us. For you took dust from the earth and formed man; you honored him with your image, O God, and set him in the paradise of pleasure, and promised him immortality of life and enjoyment of eternal good things in keeping your commandments. But when he had disobeyed you, the true God who created him, and had been led astray by the deceit of the serpent, and had been subjected to death by his own transgressions, you, O God, expelled him in your righteous judgement from paradise into this world, and turned him back to the earth from which he was taken, dispensing to him the salvation by rebirth which is in your Christ. For you did not turn away finally from your creature, O good one, nor forget the works of your hands, but you visited him in many ways through the bowels of your mercy. You sent forth prophets; you performed works of power through your saints who were pleasing to you in every generation; you spoke to us through the mouth of your servants the prophets, foretelling to us the salvation that should come; you gave the Law for our help; you set angels as guards over us.

But when the fullness of the times had come, you spoke to us in your Son himself, through whom also you made the ages, who, being the reflection of your glory and the impress of your substance, and bearing all things by the word of his power, thought it not robbery to be equal with you, the God and Father, but he who was God before the ages was seen on earth and lived among men; he was made flesh from a holy virgin and humbled himself, taking the form of a slave; he was conformed to the body of our humiliation that he might conform us to the image of his glory. For since through man sin had entered into the world, and through sin death, your only-begotten Son, who is in your bosom, O God and Father, being born of a woman, the Holy Mother of God and ever-Virgin Mary, born under the law, was pleased to condemn sin in his flesh, that those who died in Adam should be made alive in him, your Christ. And having become a citizen of this world, he gave us commandments of salvation, turned us away from the error of the idols, and brought us to the knowledge of you, the true God and Father; he gained us for himself, a peculiar people, a royal priesthood, a holy nation; and when he had cleansed us with water and sanctified us by the Holy Spirit, he gave himself as a ransom to death, by which we were held, having been sold under sin. By means of the cross he descended into hell, that he might fill all things with himself, and loosed the pains of death; he rose again on the third day, making a way to resurrection from the dead for all flesh, because it was not possible for the prince of life to be conquered by corruption, and became the firstfruits of those who had fallen asleep, the first-born from the dead, so that he might be first in all ways among all things. And ascending into the heavens, he sat down at the right hand of the[1] majesty in the highest, and will also come to reward each man according to his works. And he left us memorials of his saving passion, these things which we have[2] set forth according[3] to his commandments.

1. *Now your.*
2. *Perfect tense.*
3. *The Barberini MS breaks off here.*

The Byzantine Liturgy of St. Basil

For when he was about to go out to his voluntary and laudable and life-giving death, in the night in which he gave himself up for the life of the world, he took bread in his holy and undefiled hands and showed it to you, the God and Father, gave thanks, blessed, sanctified, and broke it, and gave it to his holy disciples and apostles, saying, "Take, eat; this is my body, which is broken for you for the forgiveness of sins."

People: Amen.

Likewise also he took the cup of the fruit of the vine and mixed it, gave thanks, blessed, sanctified, and gave it to his holy disciples and apostles, saying, "Drink from this, all of you; this is my blood, which is shed for you and for many for the forgiveness of sins. ⟨*People:* Amen.⟩ Do this for my remembrance. For as often as you eat this bread and drink this cup, you proclaim my death, you confess my resurrection."

Therefore, Master, we also, remembering his saving Passion, his lifegiving cross, his three-day burial, his resurrection from the dead, his ascension into heaven, his session at your right hand, God and Father, and his glorious and fearful second coming; (*aloud*) offer[-ing] you your own from your own, in all and through all,

People: we hymn you, ⟨we bless you, we give you thanks, O Lord, and pray to you, our God.⟩

Therefore, Master all-holy, we also, your sinful and unworthy servants, who have been held worthy to minister at your holy altar, not for our righteousness, for we have done nothing good upon earth, but for your mercies and compassions which you have poured out richly upon us, with confidence approach your holy altar. And having[4] set forth the likenesses of the holy body and blood of your Christ, we pray and beseech you, O holy of holies, in the good pleasure of your bounty, that your [all-]Holy Spirit may come upon us and upon these gifts set forth, and bless them and sanctify and make[5] (*he signs the holy gifts with the cross three times, saying:*) this bread the precious body of our Lord and God

4. *Aorist.*
5. Greek: *anadeixai.*

and Savior Jesus Christ. Amen. And this cup the precious blood of our Lord and God and Savior Jesus Christ, [Amen.] which is shed for the life of the world ⟨and salvation⟩ Amen ⟨*thrice*⟩.

Prayer:

Unite with one another all of us who partake of the one bread and the cup into fellowship with the one Holy Spirit; and make none of us to partake of the holy body and blood of your Christ for judgement or for condemnation, but that we may find mercy and grace with all the saints who have been well-pleasing to you from of old, forefathers, Fathers, patriarchs, prophets, apostles, preachers, evangelists, martyrs, confessors, teachers, and every righteous spirit perfected in faith; (*aloud*) especially our all-holy, immaculate, highly blessed ⟨glorious⟩ Lady, Mother of God and ever-Virgin Mary; (*while the diptychs are read by the deacon, the priest says the prayer:*) Saint John the ⟨prophet,⟩ forerunner and Baptist, ⟨the holy and honored apostles,⟩ this saint N. whose memorial we are keeping, and all your saints: at their entreaties, visit us, O God.

And remember all those who have fallen asleep in hope of resurrection to eternal life, and grant them rest where the light of your countenance looks upon them.

Again we pray you, Lord, remember your holy, catholic, and apostolic Church from one end of the world to the other, and grant it the peace which you purchased by the precious blood of your Christ, and stablish this holy house until the consummation of the age, and grant it peace.

Remember, Lord, those who presented these gifts, and those for whom, and through whom, and on account of whom they presented them.

Remember, Lord, those who bring forth fruit and do good work in your holy churches and remember the poor. Reward them with rich and heavenly gifts. Grant them heavenly things for earthly, eternal things for temporal, incorruptible things for corruptible.

Remember, Lord, those in deserts and mountains and in dens and in caves of the earth.

Remember, Lord, those who live in virginity and piety (and self-discipline) and an honest way of life.

Remember, Lord, our most religious and faithful Emperor, whom you thought fit to rule the land: crown him with the weapon of truth, with the weapon of your good pleasure; overshadow his head in the day of war; strengthen his arm, exalt his right hand; make his empire mighty; subject to him all the barbarous people that delight in war; grant him help and peace[6] that cannot be taken away; speak good things to his heart for your Church and all your people, that in his peace we may lead a quiet and peaceful life in all godliness and honesty.

Remember, Lord, all rule and authority, our brothers at court and all the army; preserve the good in their[7] goodness, make the wicked good in your bounty.

Remember, Lord, the people who stand around and those who for good reason are absent, and have mercy on them and on us according to the abundance of your mercy. Fill their storehouses with all good things, preserve their marriages in peace and concord; nourish the infants, instruct the youth, strengthen the old; comfort the fainthearted, gather the scattered, bring back the wanderers and join them to your holy, catholic, and apostolic Church; set free those who are troubled by unclean spirits; sail with those that sail, journey with those that journey; defend the widows, protect the orphans, rescue the captives, heal the sick. Be mindful, O God, of those who face trial, those in the mines, in exile, in bitter slavery, in all tribulation, necessity, and affliction; of all who need your great compassion, those who love us, those who hate us, and those who commanded us, though unworthy, to pray for them.

Remember all your people, O Lord our God, and pour out upon all your rich mercy, granting to all their petitions for salvation. Be mindful yourself of those whom we have not mentioned through ignorance or forgetfulness or the number of the names; O God, you know the age and the title of each, you know every man from

6. *Now* deep peace.
7. *Or* your.

his mother's womb. For you, Lord, are the help of the helpless, the hope of the hopeless, the savior of the tempest-tossed, the haven of sailors, the physician of the sick: yourself be all things to all men, for you know every man and his petition, his house, and his need.

Rescue, Lord, this flock,[8] and every city and country, from famine, plague, earthquake, flood, fire, the sword, invasion by foreigners, and civil war.

⟨aloud⟩ Above all, remember, Lord, our Father and bishop[9] N.: grant him to your holy churches in peace, safety, honor, health, and length of days, rightly dividing the word of your truth.

The diptychs of the living are read.

⟨Deacon: N. the all-holiest metropolitan (or bishop), and him who presents these holy gifts . . . and all men and women. *People:* And all men and women.⟩

Remember, Lord, all the orthodox episcopate who rightly divide[10] the word of your truth.

Remember, Lord, also my unworthiness, according to the multitude of your mercies: forgive me every offence, willing and unwilling; and do not keep back, on account of my sins, the grace of your holy Spirit from the gifts set forth.

Remember, Lord, the priesthood, the diaconate in Christ, and every order of the clergy, and do not put to shame any of us who stand round your holy altar.

Look upon us, Lord, in your goodness; appear to us in your rich mercies; grant us temperate and favorable weather; give kindly showers to the land for bearing fruit; bless the crown of the year of your goodness, Lord. End the divisions of the churches; quench the ragings of the nations; quickly destroy the uprising of heresies by the power of your Holy Spirit. Receive us all into your kingdom, making us sons of light and sons of the day; grant us

---

8. *Now* city or *this monastery.*
9. *Now* archbishop.
10. *The Barberini MS resumes here.*

your peace and your love, Lord our God, for you have given us all things;

(*aloud*) and grant us with one mouth and one heart to glorify and hymn your all-honorable and magnificent name, the Father and the Son and the Holy Spirit, now (and always and to the ages of ages.)

People: Amen.

PRAYER and LORD'S PRAYER
PRAYER OF INCLINATION
PRAYER OF ELEVATION
The priest raises the holy bread and says: The holy things for the holy people.

People: One is holy, one is Lord, Jesus Christ, to the glory of God the Father.

COMMUNION
THANKSGIVING FOR COMMUNION
PRAYER BEHIND THE AMBO and DISMISSAL.

15 The Anaphora of the Twelve Apostles

This anaphora, which is extant only in Syriac, has much of its material in common with the anaphora of *St. John Chrysostom* (see pp. 129–134). Since the publication in 1937 of an article by Dom H. Engberding, it has been generally accepted that the two anaphoras share a common source of considerable antiquity. Recently, however, Bishop G. Wagner has argued that *Twelve Apostles* is a late abridgement of *St. John Chrysostom* by the Syriac translator. The remainder of *Twelve Apostles* is derived from *St. James*, and both its date and origin must be regarded as still open to debate.

Some scholars have suggested that the preface constitutes a complete prayer in itself, including references to Creation, redemption, and the parousia. If it existed in this form on its own, it must be of great antiquity. It would be comparable in length and content to the prayers in the *Didache*. In any case, it lacks the negative adjectives found in the preface of *St. John Chrysostom*, which suggests a date no later than 350; and the references to the persons of the Trinity have the appearance of later insertions, so that the preface may go back even to the third century or earlier. An early date is also suggested by the comparative lack of attention to the Holy Spirit.

The two anaphoras are largely the same up to the end of the Institution Narrative. From that point, *Twelve Apostles* is based on *St. James*, taking the "Pauline comment" and the people's acclamation from the Syriac version. The anamnesis and epiclesis share phrases with *St. John Chrysostom*, but the language of these sections tends to be stereotyped, and some of it may equally come from *St. James*, which is certainly the source of the remainder of the anaphora, except for two passages which are peculiar to *Twelve Apostles*. Two phrases from *St. James* occur only in the Greek, not the Syriac, which suggests that the conflation had already been carried out before the Syriac translation was made, though the translator may have added passages which are only found in the Syriac, not the Greek. The intercessions seem to go back behind *St. James* to the earliest version of *Egyptian Basil*.

BIBLIOGRAPHY

Prex Eucharistica, pp. 265–268 (Latin translation of British Museum MS Add. 14.493, 10th century).

G. J. Cuming, review article in *Eastern Churches Review*, 7(1975), pp. 95–97 (with references to the previous literature).

PEACE
PRAYER OF INCLINATION
PRAYER OF THE VEIL

Priest: The love of God the Father ⟨and the grace of the only-begotten Son and our Lord and great God and Savior Jesus Christ, and the fellowship of the Holy Spirit be with you all⟩.
People: And with ⟨your spirit⟩.
Priest: Up with ⟨your hearts⟩.[1]
People: We have them with the Lord.
Priest: Let us give thanks to the Lord.
People: It is fitting and right.
Priest: It is fitting and right that we should adore you and glorify you, who are truly God, and your only-begotten Son and the Holy Spirit. For you brought us out of non-existence into existence; and when we had fallen, you recalled us, and did not cease to work until you brought us up to heaven and granted us the kingdom that is to come. For all these things we give thanks to you and to your only-begotten Son and to the Holy Spirit. For around you stand the cherubim with four faces and the seraphim with six wings with all the heavenly powers, glorifying with never-silent mouths and voices the praise of your majesty, proclaiming, crying, and saying,

People: Holy, holy, holy . . .

Priest (*bowing*): Holy you are and all-holy, and your only-begotten Son, and the Holy Spirit. Holy are you and all-holy, and magnifi-

1. *The Syriac has no verb.*

The Anaphora of the Twelve Apostles   **125**

cent is your glory, for you so loved the world that you gave your only-begotten Son for it, that all who believe in him may not perish but have eternal life.

(*aloud*) When he had come and fulfilled all the dispensation which is for us, on the night in which he was betrayed, he took bread in his holy hands, and after he had raised them to heaven, he blessed, sanctified, broke, and gave it to his disciples the Apostles, saying, "Take, eat from it, all of you; this is my body, which is broken for you and for many, and is given for forgiveness of sins and for eternal life."

Likewise the cup also after supper, mixing wine and water; he gave thanks, blessed, sanctified, and after he had tasted it, gave it to his disciples the Apostles, saying, "Take, drink from it, all of you; this is the blood of the new covenant, which is shed for you and for many, and is given for forgiveness of sins and for eternal life. Do this for my remembrance. For as often as you eat this bread and drink this cup, you will proclaim my death and confess my resurrection, until I come."

People: Your death, Lord, ⟨we commemorate, your resurrection we confess, and your second coming we await. We seek from you mercy and pardon, and we pray for forgiveness of sins. May your mercy be on us all⟩.

Priest: While therefore we remember, Lord, your saying command and all your dispensation which was for us, your cross, your resurrection from the dead on the third day, your ascension into heaven and your session at the right hand of the Father, and your glorious second coming, in which you will come in glory to judge the living and the dead, and to repay all men according to their works in your love for man—for your Church and your flock beseech you, saying through you and with you to your Father, "have mercy on me,"

People: Have mercy ⟨on us, O God, almighty Father, have mercy on us⟩—

Priest: we also, Lord, give thanks and confess you on behalf of all men for all things

People: We praise you, ⟨we bless you, we give thanks to you, Lord, and we ask you, our God, "be gracious, for you are good, and have mercy on us"⟩.

Deacon: ⟨Stand and pray⟩ in silence and awe. ⟨Pray, "peace be with us and tranquillity with us all."⟩

Priest: We ask you therefore, almighty Lord and God of the holy powers, falling on our faces before you, that you send your Holy Spirit upon these offerings set before you, (*aloud*) and show this bread to be the venerated body of our Lord Jesus Christ, and this cup the blood of our Lord Jesus Christ, that they may be to all who partake of them for life and resurrection, for forgiveness of sins, and health of soul and body, and enlightenment of mind, and defence before the dread judgement-seat of your Christ; and let no one of your people perish, Lord, but make us all worthy that, serving without disturbance and ministering before you at all times of our life, we may enjoy your heavenly and immortal and life-giving mysteries, through your grace and mercy and love for man, now ⟨and to the ages of ages⟩.

People: Amen.

Priest (bowing): We therefore offer to you, almighty Lord, this reasonable sacrifice for all men, for your catholic Church, for the bishops in it who rightly divide the word of truth, for my insignificance, and for the priests and deacons, for the orthodox of every land, for all your faithful people, for the safekeeping of your flock, for this holy church, for every town and district of the faithful, for good weather and the fruits of the earth, for faithful brethren who are in misery, for those who offered these offerings, for all who are named in your holy churches: grant help to them all; and for our fathers and brothers who have died before us in the true faith: set them in divine glory on the day of judgement, not entering into judgement with them, for in your sight no man living is innocent.

(*aloud*) For there is one who was seen on earth without sin, your only-begotten Son our Lord Jesus Christ, who is the great propitiation of our race, through whom we hope to find mercy and forgiveness of sins; on account of whom to them also . . .

The Anaphora of the Twelve Apostles   127

People: Remit, forgive, ⟨Lord, our offences which we have committed willingly, unwillingly, wittingly or unwittingly⟩.

Priest: Especially therefore let us make the memorial of the holy Mother of God and ever-Virgin Mary, the divine Apostles, the holy prophets, the martyrs glorious in victory, and all your saints who have pleased you, by whose prayers and supplications may we be preserved from evil, and may mercy be upon us in either world; that in this also, as in all things, your blessed name may be greatly glorified with (the name) of Jesus Christ and your Holy Spirit.

People: As it was ⟨in the beginning, so now and for ever. Amen⟩.

LORD'S PRAYER
PRAYER OF INCLINATION
THANKSGIVING
LAST PRAYER.

The Anaphora of the Twelve Apostles

16 The Liturgy of St. John Chrysostom

This liturgy became, and has remained, the principal and normal rite of the Orthodox Church, having ousted *St. Basil* from that position by A.D. 1000. The structure of the anaphora has become regarded as the norm, being identical with that of the *Apostolic Constitutions*, *St. Basil*, *St. James*, and upwards of eighty West Syrian anaphoras. It may well have preserved the form used in Antioch during Chrysostom's episcopate (370–398).

It is a short anaphora, less than half the length of *St. Basil*, which is no doubt the reason why it supplanted the latter. The preface makes only the briefest reference to Creation (the phrase "you brought us out of non-existence into existence," which appears also in the *Apostolic Constitutions*); and the post-Sanctus, usually an opportunity for setting forth Christ's redeeming work in some detail, is here confined to the quotation of John 3:16 ("God so loved the world . . ."). The link-word from the Sanctus is "holy," as is customary outside Egypt. The words "Do this in remembrance of me" are inexplicably omitted, though implied by the following phrase "We *therefore*, remembering this saving command . . ."

The ancient phrase "this reasonable and bloodless service" is prominent in the anamnesis and the intercessions, which it links closely with the offering, which is in the present tense. The work of the Holy Spirit is specified as "changing" the elements, a verb which is otherwise only found in Cyril of Jerusalem and Coptic *Mark*.

Much of the latter half of the prayer is closely related to the Byzantine form of *St. Basil*, especially the intercessions. The anaphora shares a certain austerity and reticence with the historic Roman Canon and the consecration prayer of the 1662 Book of Common Prayer. Two problems need to be discussed: the relationship between this anaphora and that of *The Twelve Apostles*, and the authenticity of the ascription of authorship to St. John Chrysostom.

The Twelve Apostles (see pp. 124–8) is an anaphora originally written in Greek, but extant only in Syriac, which has much material in common with *St. John Chrysostom*. This had been noticed in the eighteenth century, but was finally demonstrated in 1937 by Dom H. Engberding, who concluded that the two anaphoras were descended from a common source. Later scholars assumed that *Twelve Apostles* was an ancestor of *St. John Chrysostom*, and therefore of a very early date. The preface is certainly much older than the late fourth century. In 1973 Georg Wagner, himself an Orthodox bishop, proposed a contrary theory, that *Twelve Apostles* is a sixth-century abridgement of *St. John Chrysostom* made by the Syriac translator, who also added some material of his own. Wagner's theory has not received much support.

The question of authorship is probably impossible to answer finally. Undoubtedly, there are several linguistic parallels between the anaphora and the saint's sermons. But in some cases, if not all, the saint may be quoting from the liturgy, as he often explicitly does: "You heard the deacon proclaim . . ." Preachers from churches which use fixed forms of service tend to quote from them almost unconsciously. Wagner produces a list of theological subjects common to liturgy and sermons: this is more convincing, but equally they may have been suggested by the anaphora. The most likely to have been contributed by the saint are the negative adjectives in the preface and the idea of God's secret benefits.

In any case, by that date the anaphora was rapidly becoming standardized, and opportunities for fresh composition were limited to certain sections within an already established framework. Chrysostom may have done no more than touch up a liturgy already existing at Antioch which acquired his name when he was transferred to Constantinople.

The text translated below is that of the Barberini manuscript, written at the end of the eighth century, with the people's part supplied from modern editions. As far as the anaphora is concerned, the contemporary form differs from the Barberini text only in a few additions and completions (here in angle-brackets) and the omission of two phrases (here in square brackets).

BIBLIOGRAPHY
Prex Eucharistica, pp. 223–229.
LEW, pp. 309–399 (Barberini text), 470–481 (modern text).
T. Ware, *The Orthodox Church* (1980), pp. 269–295.

The literature about this anaphora is abundant, but largely concerned with the theological or devotional exposition of the current text, rather than with its historical development. See also the Bibliography for *The Twelve Apostles* (above).

PROTHESIS (Prayer in vestry)
SYNAPTE (Litany)
ENARXIS (Three antiphons and prayers)
   THE LITTLE ENTRANCE
PRAYERS OF ENTRANCE AND OF THE TRISAGION [PRAYER OF
   THE THRONE[1]]
FOUR HYMNS (including *Trisagion*)
PSALM, EPISTLE, ALLELUIA, PRAYER, GOSPEL
EKTENE (Prayer of supplication)
DISMISSAL OF CATECHUMENS, with PRAYER
PRAYERS OF THE FAITHFUL 1 and 2
   THE GREAT ENTRANCE
CHERUBIC HYMN
PROSKOMIDE (Prayer of offering) and LITANY
PEACE
CREED

THE ANAPHORA
The priest says: The grace of our Lord Jesus Christ, and the love of the God and Father, and the fellowship of the Holy Spirit be with you all.
People: And with your spirit.
Priest: Let us lift up our hearts.
People: We have them with the Lord.
Priest: Let us give thanks to the Lord.
People: It is fitting and right ⟨to worship the Father, the Son, and the Holy Spirit, the consubstantial and undivided Trinity⟩.

1. *Later omitted.*

The Liturgy of St. John Chrysostom   131

The priest begins the holy anaphora: It is fitting and right to hymn you, ⟨to bless you, to praise you,⟩ to give you thanks, to worship you in all places of your dominion. For you are God, ineffable, inconceivable, invisible, incomprehensible, existing always and in the same way, you and your only-begotten Son and Your Holy Spirit. You brought us out of non-existence into existence; and when we had fallen, you raised us up again, and did not cease to do everything until you had brought us up to heaven, and granted us the kingdom that is to come. For all these things we give thanks to you and to your only-begotten Son and to your Holy Spirit, for all that we know and do not know, your seen and unseen benefits that have come upon us.

We give you thanks also for this ministry; vouchsafe to receive it from our hands, even though thousands of archangels and ten thousands of angels stand before you, cherubim and seraphim, with six wings and many eyes, flying on high,
(*aloud*) singing the triumphal hymn ⟨proclaiming, crying, and saying⟩:

People: Holy, ⟨holy, holy, Lord of Sabaoth; heaven and earth are full of your glory. Hosanna in the highest. Blessed is he who comes in the name of the Lord. Hosanna in the highest⟩.

The priest, privately: With these powers, Master, lover of man, we also cry and say: holy are you and all-holy, and your only-begotten Son, and your Holy Spirit; holy are you and all-holy and magnificent is your glory; for you so loved the world that you gave your only-begotten Son that all who believe in him may not perish, but have eternal life.

When he had come and fulfilled all the dispensation for us, on the night in which he handed himself over, he took bread in his holy and undefiled and blameless hands, gave thanks, blessed, broke, and gave it to his holy disciples and apostles, saying, (*aloud*) "Take, eat; this is my body, which is ⟨broken⟩ for you ⟨for forgiveness of sins." *People:* Amen⟩. ⟨*privately*⟩ Likewise the cup also after supper, saying, (*aloud*) "Drink from this, all of you; this is my blood of the new covenant, which is shed for you and for many for the forgiveness of sins."
People: Amen.

The priest, privately: We therefore, remembering this saving commandment and all the things that were done for us: the cross, the tomb, the resurrection on the third day, the ascension into heaven, the session at the right hand, the second and glorious coming again; *(aloud)* offering you your own from your own, in all and for all,

People: we hymn you, ⟨we bless you, we give you thanks, Lord, and pray to you, our God⟩.

The priest says privately: We offer you also this reasonable and bloodless service, and we pray and beseech and entreat you, send down your Holy Spirit on us and on these gifts set forth; and make this bread the precious body of your Christ, [changing it by your Holy Spirit,] Amen; and that which is in this cup the precious blood of your Christ, changing it by your Holy Spirit, Amen; so that they may become to those who partake for vigilance of soul, for fellowship with the Holy Spirit, for the fullness of the kingdom ⟨of heaven⟩, for boldness toward you, not for judgement or condemnation.

We offer you this reasonable service also for those who rest in faith, ⟨forefathers,⟩ Fathers, patriarchs, prophets, apostles, preachers, evangelists, martyrs, confessors, ascetics, and all the righteous ⟨spirits⟩ perfected in faith;
(aloud) especially our all-holy, immaculate, highly glorious, Blessed Lady, Mother of God and ever-Virgin Mary; ⟨*diptychs of the dead;*⟩ Saint John the ⟨prophet,⟩ forerunner, and Baptist, and the holy, ⟨glorious,⟩ and honored Apostles; and this saint whose memorial we are keeping; and all your saints: at their entreaties, look on us, O God.

And remember all those who have fallen asleep in hope of resurrection to eternal life, ⟨*he remembers them by name*⟩ and grant them rest where the light of your own countenance looks upon them.

Again we beseech you, remember, Lord, all the orthodox episcopate who rightly divide the word of your truth, all the priesthood, the diaconate in Christ, and every order of the clergy

We offer you this reasonable service also for the (whole) world, for the holy, catholic, and apostolic Church, for those who live in

The Liturgy of St. John Chrysostom   133

a chaste and reverend state, [for those in mountains and in dens and in caves of the earth,] for the most faithful Emperor, the Christ-loving Empress, and all their court and army: grant them, Lord, a peaceful reign, that in their peace we may live a quiet and peaceful life in all godliness and honesty.

Remember, Lord, the city in which we dwell, and all cities and lands, and all who dwell in them in faith.
(*aloud*) Above all, remember, Lord, our Archbishop *N*.

⟨*Diptychs of the living.*⟩

Remember, Lord, those at sea, travellers, the sick, those in adversity, prisoners, and their salvation.

Remember, Lord, those who bring forth fruit and do good works in your holy churches and remember the poor; and send out your mercies upon us all, (*aloud*) and grant us with one mouth and one heart to glorify and hymn your all-honorable and magnificent name, the Father, the Son, and the Holy Spirit, ⟨now and always and to the ages of ages⟩.
People: Amen.

PRAYER and LORD'S PRAYER
PRAYER OF INCLINATION
PRAYER OF ELEVATION and FRACTION
The priest raises the holy bread and says aloud: The holy things for the holy people.
People: One is holy, one is Lord, Jesus Christ, to the glory of God the Father.

COMMUNION
THANKSGIVING FOR COMMUNION
PRAYER (behind the ambo)
DISMISSAL.

17 Theodore of Mopsuestia: *Catecheses*

Theodore, a fellow student with John Chrysostom, after a ministry in Antioch became bishop of Mopsuestia in southeast Asia Minor in A.D. 392. His baptismal *catecheses* resemble those of Cyril of Jerusalem, but are much longer. Though delivered in Greek, they have survived only in Syriac. They were probably first delivered in Antioch. From scattered sentences in them it is possible to piece together the structure and some of the wording of the liturgy Theodore used, which must not be confused with the Nestorian anaphora of *Theodore*. It clearly belongs to the Syrian family. The structure exactly matches that of *St. John Chrysostom*, but the wording appears to have been independent, including, for instance, a quotation of Philippians 2:6–7.

The text below is translated from the French rendering by R. Tonneau, and the numbers refer to the pages in his edition.

BIBLIOGRAPHY
R. Tonneau and R. Devréesse, *Les homélies catéchétiques de Theodore de Mopsueste* (1949), pp. 513–605.
E. J. Yarnold, *The Awe-Inspiring Rites of Initiation* (1972), pp. 230–256.
Dix, *The Shape*, passim.

CATECHESIS 15

513 PROTHESIS (Prayer and thanksgiving)
521 PEACE
527 LAVABO
527 DIPTYCHS OF THE LIVING AND THE DEAD

CATECHESIS 16

529 *Deacon:* Behold the offering.
531 *Bishop:* The grace of our Lord Jesus Christ and the love of God the Father and the communion of the Holy Spirit be with you all.
People: And with your spirit.

Bishop: Up with your spirits.[1]

People: To you, O Lord.

Bishop: Let us give thanks to the Lord.

People: It is fitting and right.

541 The bishop proclaims that all praise and glory are fitting for God, and that it is right for us to give him adoration and worship.

543 He speaks of the greatness of the Father and of the Son and of the Holy Spirit.

545 *Bishop:* Praise and adoration be offered to the divine nature by all Creation,

548 and by the invisible powers (among them the seraphim), and we say with them,

People: Holy, holy, holy, Lord of Sabaoth; heaven and earth are full of your praises.

549 *Bishop:* Holy is the Father, holy also the Son, holy also the Holy Spirit.

He speaks of the ineffable compassion which God showed in the dispensation through Christ, who though he was in the form of God, was willing to accept the form of a servant, and put on perfect and complete man for the redemption of the whole human race.

551 Our Lord, when he was about to go to his Passion, handed down to his disciples the immortal and spiritual food that we might receive it.

Bishop: But now our Lord Christ must rise from the dead by virtue of these actions and spread his grace over us.

553 The bishop must ask and beseech God that the Holy Spirit should come, and that grace should come thence upon the bread and wine offered, that they may be known to be truly the body and blood of our Lord, the memorial of immortality.

555 He prays that the grace of the Holy Spirit may come upon all gathered together, that they may be united as into one body by partaking of the body of our Lord . . . and that they may be one in concord, peace, and well-doing.

He ends the liturgy by offering prayer for all whom it is our

---

1. *The Syriac has no verb.*

rule to mention in church at all times. Then he goes on to the commemoration of those who have died.

557 FRACTION
563 PRAYER FOR ACCEPTANCE OF THE SACRIFICE

565 *Bishop:* That which is holy for the holy people.
569 *People:* One Father alone is holy; one Son alone is holy; one Spirit alone is holy.
Glory to the Father, to the Son, and to the Holy Spirit, to the ages of ages. Amen.

557 COMMUNION
579 *Bishop:* The body of Christ.
People: Amen.

581 THANKSGIVING FOR COMMUNION.

18 Adaptations of Hippolytus

A. THE *TESTAMENTUM DOMINI*

This work is a greatly expanded version of the *Apostolic Tradition* of Hippolytus, and has received much, perhaps too much, attention from editors of that text. Extant only in Syriac, it is uncertain where or when the original Greek was written, though most scholars would accept the first half of the fifth century in Syria or Asia Minor. Its treatment of Hippolytus should be compared with that of the *Apostolic Constitutions:* the latter work seems to have amalgamated Hippolytus with another anaphora, whereas the *Testamentum* has simply expanded Hippolytus to double the original length by inserting two lengthy new passages.

The most interesting feature of this anaphora is that no attempt was made in expanding Hippolytus to incorporate the Sanctus, although the inclusion of the latter had become well-nigh universal in the East during the fourth century; or to introduce more than the briefest of intercessions. Modern adaptations of Hippolytus have been less respectful of the original. The only place where the redactor has departed significantly from Hippolytus' text is at the epiclesis, where he has produced a smoothly running paraphrase which avoids the difficulties evident in the Latin version. Like Hippolytus, he speaks of the cup as a "type" of the blood of Christ.

The translation below is based on the English version of A. J. Maclean and the Latin of I. E. Rahmani, and, for the sentence marked * *, the French of B. Botte.

BIBLIOGRAPHY
Prex Eucharistica, pp. 219–222 (Latin translation by I. E. Rahmani).
J. Cooper and A. J. Maclean, *The Testament of the Lord* (1902; Eng. trans. and commentary).

PROPHETS

APOSTLES

DISMISSAL OF CATECHUMENS

HOMILY
PEACE
OFFERTORY
ADMONITION BY DEACON

The bishop: Our Lord be with you.
People: And with your spirit.
Bishop: Up with your hearts.
People: We have them with the Lord.
Bishop: Let us give thanks to the Lord.
People: It is fitting and right.
Bishop: The holy things for the holy people.
People: In heaven and on earth unceasingly.
Bishop: We render thanks to you, holy God, strengthener of your souls, giver of our life, treasure of incorruptibility, Father of your only-begotten, our Savior, whom in the last times you sent to us as Savior and proclaimer of your will. For it is your purpose that we should be saved through you. Our heart, mind, and soul, with all its thinking, gives thanks to you, Lord, that your grace may come upon us, Lord, that we may continually praise you and your only-begotten Son and your Holy Spirit, now and always and to the ages of ages.

O power of the Father, grace of the nations, knowledge, true wisdom, the exaltation of the meek, the medicine of souls, the confidence of us who believe, you are the strength of the righteous, the hope of the persecuted, the haven of the buffeted, the illuminator of the perfect, the Son of the living God. Make to arise on us, out of your unsearchable gift, courage, might, reliance, wisdom, strength, unlapsing faith, unshaken hope, the knowledge of your Spirit, meekness, uprightness, so what we your servants and all your people may always praise you purely, bless you, give thanks to you, Lord, and entreat you at all times.

Lord, the founder of the heights, king of the treasuries of light, visitor of the heavenly Zion, king of the orders of archangels, of dominions, praises, thrones, vestures, lights, joys, and delights, father of kings, you hold all things in your hand and guide them by your counsel, through your only-begotten Son, who was crucified for our sins. You sent your Word, Lord, the sharer of your counsel and covenant, through whom you made all things, and in

The Testamentum Domini   139

whom you were well-pleased, into a virgin's womb. When he was conceived and made flesh, he was manifested as your Son, being born of the Holy Spirit and the Virgin. Fulfilling your will and gaining a holy people, he stretched out his hands to suffering, that he might release from suffering and the corruption of death those who have hoped in you.

When he was betrayed to voluntary suffering that he might set upright those who had stumbled, and find the lost, and give life to the dead, and destroy death, and break the bonds of the devil, and fulfill the counsel of the Father, and tread down hell, and open the way of life, and guide the righteous to light, and fix a limit, and lighten the darkness, and nurture babes, and manifest the Resurrection, he took bread and gave it to his disciples, saying, "Take, eat; this is my body, which is broken for you for forgiveness of sins. When you shall do this, you shall make my resurrection." Also the cup of wine which he mixed, he gave for a type of the blood which was shed for us.

Remembering therefore your death and resurrection, we offer you bread and the cup, giving thanks to you who alone are God for ever and our Savior, because you have held us worthy to stand before you and serve you as priests. Therefore, we your servants, Lord, render thanks to you. (*The people say likewise.*) We offer you this thanksgiving, eternal Trinity, Lord Jesus Christ, Lord the Father, before whom all creation and all nature trembles, fleeing into itself; *Lord, send the Holy Spirit upon this drink and this your holy food;* cause them to be to us, not for condemnation nor reproach nor destruction, but for the healing and strengthening of our Spirit.

Yea, O God, grant us that by your Name every thought of things displeasing to you may flee away. Grant, O God, that every proud conception may be driven away from us by your Name, which is written within the veils of your sanctuaries, those high ones. When Sheol hears that Name, it is amazed, the depth is rent, the spirits are driven away, the dragon is bruised, unbelief is cast out, disobedience is subdued, anger is appeased, envy works not, pride is reproved, avarice rooted out, boasting taken away, arrogance humbled, every root of bitterness destroyed.

Grant therefore, Lord, to our innermost eyes to see you, praising you and glorifying you, commemorating you, serving you, having a portion in you alone, Son and Word of God, to whom all things are subdued. Sustain to the end those who have gifts of revelations; confirm those who have a gift of healing; make those who have the gift of tongues courageous. Keep those who have the word of doctrine upright; care for those who do your will always. Visit the widows; help the orphans; remember those who have fallen asleep in the faith; and grant us an inheritance with your saints, and bestow the power to please you as they also pleased you. Feed the people in uprightness; sanctify us all, O God; but grant that all who partake and receive of your holy things may be united to you so that they may be filled with the Holy Spirit for the strengthening of faith in truth; that they may always lift up a doxology to you and your beloved Son Jesus Christ, through whom be glory and might to you with your holy Spirit to the ages of ages. (*People.* Amen.)

COMMUNION
Let each, when he receives the thanksgiving, say before partaking: Amen. *When he receives the cup, let him say twice:* Amen, *for a complete symbol of the body and blood.*

THANKSGIVING FOR COMMUNION.

B. THE ANAPHORA OF EPIPHANIUS OF SALAMIS

This fragmentary anaphora, presumably written in Greek but recovered from the Armenian, was published in 1960. Several phrases suggest a date later than the Council of Chalcedon (A.D. 451). But when these are removed, what remains is a brief and probably early anaphora. Indeed, the first paragraph seems to be based on the *Apostolic Tradition:* "you sent . . . from heaven your . . . child . . . in the last times . . . made flesh . . . through the Holy Spirit." Yet, as in the case of *Testamentum Domini* above, although the prayer was vigorously updated, the opportunity was not taken to include the Sanctus. Note the use of the word "changed" in relation to the bread.

BIBLIOGRAPHY
Prex Eucharistica, pp. 262–263.
G. Garitte, "Un opuscule grec traduit de l'arménien sur l'addition d'eau au vin eucharistique," in *Le Muséon*, 73(1960), pp. 297–310.

It is fitting and right, our God, to give you thanks unceasingly for all your benefits which you have bestowed on us; above all, because you sent to us from heaven your holy child, who is seated with you on the throne of your kingdom, your co-eternal Son, God the Word, who came in the last times and took our humanity; the Word made flesh, suffering no change, receiving through the Holy Spirit the flesh and rational mind of a man and all that belongs to a man except sin, not as it were dwelling in some man, but in all ways perfect God the Word, perfectly incarnate, not changing humanity, nor becoming two, but one King, one Christ, one Lord in divinity and in humanity, without confusion or division, confirming his divine and human nature by divine signs and human feelings.

When he had come to a voluntary and glorious and life-giving death for us, after he took bread in his holy and unspotted hands and showed it to you, God and Father, he gave thanks, blessed, sanctified, (and) gave to his disciples, the holy apostles, saying, "Take, eat; this is my body which is broken for you for forgiveness of sins."

Likewise after supper, after he took the cup and mixed it from two elements, the fruit of the vine and water, he sealed the cup of immortality and gave to his disciples, saying, "Drink from this, all of you; this is my blood of the new covenant, which is shed for you and for many for forgiveness of sins". . . .

. . . that this bread may be changed and become the body of Christ, the divine body, the body of salvation for souls and bodies; and that what is mixed in this cup (may become) the very blood of Christ, the blood of the new covenant, the blood of salvation for us, that we may all be partakers of your holy mysteries, in newness of spirit and not in the oldness of the letter.

19 Ambrose: *On the Sacraments*

After the *Apostolic Tradition* of Hippolytus, no evidence has survived about the eucharistic prayer at Rome until the end of the fourth century, and then only in fragments and quotations. The earliest text of the Roman canon is found in the sacramentaries written in the eighth century, which also contain collects and prefaces for every occasion in the church year. It appears that a rite had developed at Rome which was also used in North Africa, while a similar but by no means identical rite developed in northern Italy, Gaul, and Spain. Each of these areas had its own peculiarities, but they formed a recognizable non-Roman family, owing more than Rome did to the Eastern liturgies.

The use of Milan at the end of the fourth century is known from quotations in the *De Sacramentis* of St. Ambrose. This treatise, whose authenticity was once suspect, is now generally held to contain "the actual words of the addresses of Ambrose to the newly-baptized, taken down at the time by a *notarius*."[1] These addresses were delivered in Milan, where Ambrose was bishop from A.D. 374 until his death in 397. He was thus contemporary with John Chrysostom. The canon from which Ambrose quotes is significantly different from the Roman. It should not be confused with the (later) canon of the Ambrosian rite, which is closer to the Roman, and is still in use in Milan.

Ambrose's reference to the "earlier parts" (of the service) may possibly be rather to the earlier parts of the canon, though this seems less likely. The words "reasonable" and "acceptable" come from Romans 12:1, used also in the Greek anaphoras (e.g. the Strasbourg papyrus of *St. Mark,* and *St. John Chrysostom*). The Milanese canon speaks of the *"figura"* of the body and blood, as Tertullian did; it asks God to make the offering acceptable *"because it is the figure of the body . . ."*; at Rome the request is *"that it may become* to us the body . . ."* But this is still before consecration: "when the words of Christ are added, it is the body of Christ . . . a sacrament whose likeness has come first." Thus consecration is

1. Srawley, *Early History*, p. 155.

effected by the words of Christ, which are added to the elements and accomplish the sacrament. "The word of Christ has power to *change* everything."

The words of Christ are, of course, the Institution Narrative, which has already been considerably expanded from the biblical text, with "until I come again" added from the Pauline comment (1 Corinthians 11:26) in Eastern fashion. This is followed by an anamnesis of Eastern type, still in an early stage of development; here the canon comes closest to the *Apostolic Tradition*. The idea of the heavenly altar and the sacrifices of Abel and Abraham may be derived from *St. Mark*, though there they appear in a passage of the intercessions which is among the later strata and does not include Melchizedek. *St. James* also has them, but only in a late incense prayer. "Angels" is in the plural, as in *St. Mark;* in the Roman canon there is only one angel.

BIBLIOGRAPHY
H. Chadwick (ed.), *Saint Ambrose on the Sacraments* (1960); Latin text.
J. H. Srawley (ed.), *Saint Ambrose on the Sacraments and on the Mysteries* (1950); English translation.
J. H. Srawley, *The Early History of the Liturgy* (1949), pp. 150–164.
E. J. Yarnold, (1) *The Awe-Inspiring Rites of Initiation* (1972), pp. 133–141.
(2) "Did St. Ambrose know the Mystagogical Catecheses of St. Cyril of Jerusalem?", in *Studia Patristica*, 12 (1971), pp. 185–189.

BOOK 4
13. Who therefore is the author of the sacraments, if not Jesus? Those sacraments came from heaven, for all counsel is from heaven. It was a great and divine miracle that God rained manna on the people from heaven, and the people ate without working for it.

14. Perhaps you will say, "My bread is common (bread)." But that bread is bread before the words of the sacraments; when consecration has been applied, from (being) bread it becomes the flesh of Christ. So let us explain how that which is bread can be the body of Christ. And by what words and by whose sayings does consecration take place? The Lord Jesus'. For all the other things which are said in the earlier parts are said by the

bishop[2]: praise is offered to God; prayer is made for the people, for kings, for others; when the time comes for the venerated sacrament to be accomplished, the bishop no longer uses his own words, but uses the words of Christ. So the word of Christ accomplishes this sacrament . . .

21. Do you wish to know how consecration is done with heavenly words? Hear what the words are. The bishop says:

Make for us this offering approved, reasonable, acceptable, because it is the figure of the body and blood of our Lord Jesus Christ; who, the day before he suffered, took bread in his holy hands, looked up to heaven to you, holy Father, almighty, eternal God, gave thanks, blessed, and broke it, and handed it when broken to his apostles and disciples, saying, "Take and eat from this, all of you; for this is my body, which will be broken for many."

22. Notice this. *Likewise after supper, the day before he suffered, he took the cup, looked up to heaven to you, holy Father, almighty, eternal God, gave thanks, blessed, and handed it to his apostles and disciples, saying, "Take and drink from this, all of you; for this is my blood."*

See, all those words up to *"Take,"* whether the body or the blood, are the evangelist's; then they are Christ's words, *"Take and drink from this, all of you; for this is my blood."*

23. Notice these points. He says, *"Who, the day before he suffered, took bread in his holy hands."* Before it is consecrated, it is bread; but when the words of Christ are added, it is the body of Christ. Then hear his words: *"Take and eat from this, all of you; for this is my body."* And before the words of Christ, the cup is full of wine and water; when the words of Christ have been employed, the blood is created which redeems his people. So you see in what ways the word of Christ has power to change everything. Our Lord Jesus himself therefore bore witness that we should receive his body and blood. Ought we to doubt his faith and witness? . . .

25. So you do not say *"Amen"* to no purpose: you confess in spirit that you are receiving the body of Christ. When you seek it, the bishop says to you, *"The body of Christ,"* and you say, *"Amen,"*

2. Latin: *sacerdos.*

which means *"It is true."* What your tongue confesses, let your feelings retain, so that you may know that this is a sacrament whose likeness has come first.

26. Next, you must learn how great a sacrament it is. See what he says: *"As often as you do this, so often you will make remembrance of me until I come again."*

27. And the bishop says:

Therefore, remembering his most glorious Passion and resurrection from the dead, and ascension into heaven, we offer to you this spotless victim, reasonable victim, bloodless victim, this holy bread and this cup of eternal life; and we pray and beseech you to receive this offering on your altar on high by the hands of your angels, as you vouchsafed to receive the gifts of your righteous servant Abel, and the sacrifice of our patriarch Abraham, and that which the high priest Melchizedek offered to you.

BOOK 5

18. Now what is left but the (Lord's) Prayer? . . .

BOOK 6

24. . . . What follows? Hear what the bishop says:

Through our Lord Jesus Christ, in whom and with whom honor, praise, glory, magnificence, and power are yours, with the Holy Spirit, from the ages, and now, and always, and to all the ages of ages. Amen.

Ambrose: On the Sacraments

20 The Gallican Rite

The name "Gallican" strictly applies to the rite used in France until its supersession by the Roman rite completed by Charlemagne c. 800; but it is also used in a wider sense to include the Ambrosian rite used in northern Italy and the Mozarabic rite used in Spain, forming a family of non-Roman Latin rites. All these rites tend to show more traces of Eastern influence than does the native Roman rite. They are written in a florid style quite unlike the Roman, often at greater, sometimes considerable length. Some of the prayers are clearly of great antiquity, predating the Roman canon in its historic form.

The rites are organized in sets of variable prayers known as "masses." As far as the eucharistic prayer is concerned, they differ in organization both from the Eastern anaphoras and from the Roman canon. Whereas the typical Eastern anaphora is completely invariable, remaining the same all the year round, even at great festivals, the Roman canon has a variable preface according to the season of the church year. The Gallican eucharistic prayer is organized on a basis of four fixed points: Sursum corda, Sanctus, Institution Narrative, and Doxology, between which are inserted three passages varying from Sunday to Sunday.

In the Gallican rite these passages are known as *contestatio* or *immolatio* (the equivalent of the preface), *post-Sanctus*, and *post-secreta* or *post-mysterium* (the Institution Narrative being known as *secreta*). The content, especially of the *post-secreta*, is less stereotyped than that of the Eastern and Roman prayers. Where the Eastern anaphora will have a sequence of anamnesis, offering, epiclesis, and intercessions, any or all of these elements may be absent from the *post-secreta*. The inclusion of an epiclesis is quite frequent, one of the Eastern features noted above. The prayers are often addressed to Christ rather than to the Father, a sign of early date, and possibly of Syrian origin.

The example below is for general Sunday use, and comes from a manuscript at Reichenau first published by F. J. Mone, and hence often referred to in older writers as "the masses of Mone." Its *contestatio* displays an Eastern emphasis on Creation, and a very brief treatment of redemption, while the *post-secreta* has no anamnesis, epiclesis, or intercessions.

BIBLIOGRAPHY
Prex Eucharistica, pp. 467–468 (bibliography, p. 462).
A. A. King, *Liturgies of the Past* (1959), ch. 3, "Gallican Rite", pp. 77–185.
W. S. Porter, *The Gallican Rite* (1958).
Dix, *The Shape*, pp. 552–554 (text of two other masses).
E. G. P. Wyatt, *The Eucharistic Prayer* (1914), pp. 33–39 (table of Ambrosian, Gallican, and Mozarabic prayers).
L. Bouyer, *Eucharist* (1970), pp. 315–337.

SALUTATIONS
PROPHETIA (BENEDICTUS)
COLLECT POST PROPHETIAM
OLD TESTAMENT LESSON and EPISTLE
BENEDICITE
GOSPEL
SERMON
DISMISSAL OF CATECHUMENS AND PENITENTS
PRAYERS OF THE FAITHFUL
OFFERTORY
PRAEFATIO (Admonition to earnest prayer)
COLLECTIO (Prayer for acceptance of prayers)
NAMES AND PRAYER POST NOMINA (Offertory prayer)
PRAYER AD PACEM and PEACE
SURSUM CORDA

CONTESTATIO *or* IMMOLATIO (PREFACE)
(*Priest:*) It is fitting and right, just and right, here and everywhere to give you thanks, Lord, holy Father, eternal God; you snatched us from perpetual death and the last darkness of hell, and gave mortal matter, put together from the liquid mud, to your Son and to eternity. Who is acceptable to tell your praises, who can make a full declaration of your works? Every tongue marvels at you, all priests extol your glory.

When you had overcome chaos and the confused elements and the darkness in which things swam, you gave wonderful forms to the amazed elements: the tender world blushed at the fires of the sun, and the rude earth wondered at the dealings of the moon. And lest no inhabitant should adorn all this, and the sun's orb shine on emptiness, your hands made from clay a more excellent likeness, which a holy fire quickened within, and a lively soul brought to life throughout its idle parts. We may not look, Father, into the inner mysteries. To you alone is known the majesty of your work: what there is in man, that the blood held in the veins washes the fearful limbs and the living earth; that the loose appearances of bodies are held together by tightening nerves, and the individual bones gain strength from the organs within.

But whence comes so great a bounty to miserable men, that we should be formed in the likeness of you and your Son, that an earthly thing should be eternal? We abandoned the commandments of your blessed majesty; we were plunged, mortal once more, into the earth from which we came, and mourned the loss of the eternal comfort of your gift. But your manifold goodness and inestimable majesty sent the saving Word from heaven, that he should be made flesh by taking a human body, and should care for that which the age had lost and the ancient wounds. Therefore all the angels, with the manifold multitude of the saints, praise him with unceasing voice, saying:

SANCTUS
(*People:*) Holy, holy, [holy, lord God of Sabaoth; heaven and earth are full of your glory. Hosanna in the highest. Blessed is he who comes in the name of the Lord. Hosanna in the highest].

POST-SANCTUS
(*Priest:*) As the supernal creatures resound on high the praise of your glory, your goodness wished that it should be made known also to your servants; and this proclamation, made in the starry realms, was revealed to your servants by the gift of your magnificence,[1] not only to be known but also to be imitated.

SECRETA (INSTITUTION NARRATIVE)
(*privately*) Who, the day before he suffered for the salvation of us all, standing in the midst of his disciples the apostles, took bread

1. *Or:* This proclamation of your magnificence, made in the starry realms, was revealed to your servants by a gift,

in his holy hands, looked up to heaven to you, God the Father almighty, gave thanks, blessed, and broke it, and gave it to his apostles, saying, "Take, eat from this, all of you; for this is my body, which shall be broken for the life of the age." Likewise after supper he took the cup in his hands, looked up to heaven to you, God the Father almighty, gave thanks, blessed, and handed it to his apostles, saying, "Take, drink from this, all of you; for this is the cup of my holy blood, of the new and eternal covenant, which is shed for you and for many for forgiveness of sins." In addition to these words he said to them, "As often as you eat from this bread and drink from this cup, you will do it for my remembrance, showing my Passion to all, (and) you will look for my coming until I come."

POST-SECRETA *or* POST-MYSTERIUM
(*aloud*) Therefore, most merciful Father, look upon the commandments of your Son, the mysteries of the Church, (your) gifts to those who believe: they are offered by suppliants, and for suppliants they are to be sought;

DOXOLOGY
through [Jesus Christ your Son, our God and Lord and Savior, who, with you, Lord, and the Holy Spirit, reigns for ever, eternal Godhead, to the ages of ages].
(*People:*) Amen.

FRACTION
LORD'S PRAYER
BLESSING
COMMUNION
THANKSGIVING FOR COMMUNION
COLLECT and DISMISSAL

The Gallican Rite

21 The Mozarabic Rite

A liturgy of the Gallican family was developed in Spain quite early: some of the masses may be dated *c.* 400. From 470 Spain was occupied by the Visigoths, who recognized the liturgy as the official rite in 633. The country was occupied by the Arabs from 711 to 1085; hence the name "Mozarabic." The liturgy thus remained in use much later than the Gallican, and is still celebrated in Toledo.

The comments in the previous chapter on the Gallican liturgy apply largely to the Mozarabic, though the Spanish style is more restrained. The Mozarabic names for the variable portions of the eucharistic prayer are *illatio*, *post-Sanctus*, and *post-pridie*, respectively.

The example below is for daily use, which probably accounts for its brevity. The *illatio* omits Creation altogether, and is entirely devoted to redemption, making good use of the Epistle to the Hebrews. The offering is already described as a "victim," a term which the Roman canon uses only after the Institution Narrative. The *post-Sanctus* prays for the acceptance of the offering just as the Roman canon does at the point, but then goes on to an epiclesis in similar terms to the post-Sanctus of *St. Mark* (see pp. 55f., 64f.). Notice the characteristic Mozarabic link, "Truly holy, truly blessed."

The Pauline comment is kept in the third person ("until he comes"); and the people respond to the Institution Narrative with "So we believe," as in the Coptic anaphoras. The doxology implies the offering of other gifts ("all these truly good things"), a practice which goes back to Hippolytus (see p. 36) and is also implied by the Roman canon (see p. 166). Creation thus makes a belated appearance.

BIBLIOGRAPHY
Prex Eucharistica, pp. 497–498 (bibliography p. 495).
A. A. King, *Liturgies of the Primatial Sees* (1957), ch. 4, "Rite of Toledo," pp. 457–631.

W. S. Porter, *The Gallican Rite* (1958).

Dix, *The Shape*, pp. 554–555 (mass for St. James).

C. Vagaggini, *The Canon of the Mass and Liturgical Reform* (1967), pp. 41–49 (text of mass for Easter III).

W. C. Bishop, *The Mozarabic and Ambrosian Rites* (1924), ch. 2, "The Mass in Spain," pp. 18–54 (text of another mass, pp. 37–40).

L. Bouyer, *Eucharist* (1970), pp. 315–337.

INTROIT

SALUTATION

GLORIA IN EXCELSIS

COLLECT POST GLORIAM

OLD TESTAMENT LESSON

BENEDICITE

EPISTLE

PSALM

GOSPEL

SERMON

DISMISSAL OF CATECHUMENS AND PENITENTS

OFFERTORY

MISSA (Admonition to earnest prayer)

PRAYERS OF THE FAITHFUL

ALIA (Prayer for acceptance of prayers)

NAMES and PRAYER POST NOMINA

PRAYER AD PACEM, THE GRACE, THE PEACE, ANTIPHON AD
    PACEM

SURSUM CORDA

Priest: I will go to the altar of God:
People: To the God of my joy and gladness.
Priest: Ears to the Lord.[1]
People: We have them with the Lord.
Priest: Up with your hearts.[2]
People: Let us lift them to the Lord
Priest: To our God and Lord Jesus Christ, Son of God, who is in heaven, let us offer fitting praise and fitting thanks.
People: It is fitting and right.

1. and 2. *The Latin has no verb.*

ILLATIO (PREFACE)

(*Priest*): It is fitting and right, almighty Father, that we should give you thanks through your Son Jesus Christ, the true and eternal high priest forever, the only priest without spot of sin; for by his blood, which cleanses the hearts of all, we sacrifice to you the propitiatory victim, not only for the sins of the people, but also for our offences, that by the intercession of our high priest for us, every sin committed by the weakness of the flesh may be forgiven; to him rightly all angels cry unceasingly and say,

SANCTUS

(*People:*) Holy, holy, holy, Lord God of Sabaoth. Heaven and earth are full of the glory of your majesty. Hosanna to the Son of David. Blessed is he who comes in the name of the Lord. Hosanna in the highest.

POST-SANCTUS

(*Priest:*) Truly holy, truly blessed is your Son, Jesus Christ our Lord, in whose name we offer to you, Lord, these holy offerings, praying that you will be pleased to accept what we offer, and bless it by the outpouring of your Holy Spirit.

SECRETA (INSTITUTION NARRATIVE)

God the Lord and eternal redeemer, who, the day before he suffered, took bread, gave thanks, blessed, and broke it, and gave it to his disciples, saying, "Take and eat; this is my body, which shall be betrayed for you. As often as you eat it, do this for my remembrance."

(*People:* Amen.) Likewise the cup also, after supper, saying, "This is the cup of the new covenant in my blood, which shall be shed for you and for many for forgiveness of sins. As often as you drink it, do this for my remembrance."

(*People:* Amen.)

"As often as you eat this bread and drink this cup, you will proclaim the death of the Lord, until he comes in glory from heaven."

(*People:*) So we believe, Lord Jesus

The Mozarabic Rite   153

POST-PRIDIE

(*Priest*): Bless, Lord, this victim that is offered to you in honor of your name, and sanctify the minds and purify the wills of those who partake of it. (*People:*) Amen.

By your gift, holy Lord, for you create, sanctify, quicken, bless, and provide for us your unworthy servants all these truly good things, that they may be blessed by you, our God, to the ages of ages. (*People:*) Amen.

FRACTION

CREED

LORD'S PRAYER

BLESSING

COMMUNION

The body of our Lord Jesus Christ be your salvation.
The blood of Christ remain with you as true redemption.

ANTIPHON and **COLLECT**

DISMISSAL

The Mozarabic Rite

22 Non-Roman Versions of the Canon

These five fragments, when put together, make up a complete canon. Each of the first three overlaps with the next fragment, which authenticates the sequence. It is not suggested that a canon ever existed anywhere in exactly this form, but that this is the sort of canon which was widely current until superseded by the Roman form. Note that it does not include the Sanctus, which only reached Rome *c.* 450, and has only the briefest of intercessions, but does include an epiclesis.

1. An anonymous Arian in the early fourth century quotes this extract from an otherwise unknown canon which he must have found in an orthodox sacramentary. It makes no reference to Creation, but proceeds straight to redemption. There was clearly no Sanctus, but the prayer for acceptance of the offering follows without a break. The offering is in the present tense.

2. A Mozarabic prayer entitled *post-pridie* in the manuscript, but which must originally have been a *post-Sanctus*. It appears with little alteration and some expansion in the first two paragraphs of the Roman Canon (see pp. 163–164). The petition for the Church has a decidedly Eastern flavor. Pope Gelasius (492–496) writes of the "*imago et similitudo corporis et sanguinis,*" although this phraseology must have seemed archaic by then.

3. These paragraphs are from Ambrose (see above, pp. 145–6).

4. A Mozarabic *post-pridie,* this time in its right place. It includes an epiclesis upon the "solemn things," which the Spirit is asked only to sanctify, not to transform; and upon the people, "that they may receive healing for their souls." Gelasius also writes of "the heavenly Spirit who is invoked for the consecration of the divine mystery."

5. From Ambrose.

The order in which the five framgents arrange themselves closely resembles that of the sections of the Roman Canon, as follows:

1. Sursum corda—Preface—*Te igitur*
2. *Te igitur—Memento Domine—Quam oblationem*

3. *Quam oblationem—Qui pridie—Unde et memores—Supplices te—*
   Supra quae
4. *Supra quae*—epiclesis
5. Doxology

All the paragraphs from the Roman Canon not included above
(Sanctus, *Communicantes, Hanc igitur, Memento etiam, Nobis quoque*)
are thought on other grounds to be later additions. Thus the hypo-
thetical canon, as well as being a possible prayer in its own right,
may also indicate a stage in the development of the Roman
Canon.

C. Vagaggini offers a reconstruction by M. Righetti based on fragments 1–3, to which Righetti appended an epiclesis which he
"put together . . . out of fragments of the *Missale Gothicum* and
Fulgentius" of Ruspe.

BIBLIOGRAPHY
1. *Prex Eucharistica,* p. 422. Dix, *The Shape,* pp. 539–541.
2. *Prex Eucharistica,* p. 428, note 1 (*Liber Ordinum,* p. 321). L. Eizenhöfer,
Canon Missae Romanae, vol. II (1966), p. 41 (no. 179). B. Botte and C.
Mohrmann, *L'Ordinaire de la Messe* (1953), p. 21.
3. *Prex Eucharistica,* pp. 421–422. H.Chadwick (ed.), *St. Ambrose on the
Sacraments* (1960), pp. 34–36.
4. *Prex Eucharistica,* p. 433, note 1 (*Liber Ordinum,* p. 265). L. Eizenhöfer,
Canon Missae Romanae, vol. II (1966), p. 149 (no. 1020). B. Botte and C.
Mohrmann, *L'Ordinaire de la Messe* (1953), pp. 19–20.
5. H. Chadwick (ed.), *St. Ambrose on the Sacraments* (1960), p. 53.
C. Vagaggini, *The Canon of the Mass and Liturgical Reform* (1967), pp.28–34.

1.

It is fitting and right, it is just and right, that we should give you
thanks for all things, O Lord, holy Father, almighty eternal God,
for you deigned in the incomparable splendor of your goodness
that light should shine in darkness, by sending us Jesus Christ as
savior of our souls. For our salvation he humbled himself and
subjected himself even unto death that, when we had been restored to that immortality which Adam lost, he might make us
heirs and sons to himself.

Neither can we be sufficient to give thanks to your great generosity for this loving kindness with any praises; but we ask (you) of your great and merciful goodness to hold accepted this sacrifice which we offer to you, standing before the face of your divine goodness; through Jesus Christ our Lord and God, [through whom we pray and beseech . . .

2.

Through him we pray and beseech] you, almighty Father, vouchsafe to accept and bless these offerings and these unblemished sacrifices; above all, those which we offer to you for your holy Catholic Church: vouchsafe to grant it peace, spread through the whole world in your peace.

Remember, Lord, also, we pray, your servants who in honor of your Saints NN. pay their vows to the living and true God, for the forgiveness of all their sins. [Vouchsafe to make their offering blessed, ratified, and reasonable; it is the image and likeness of the body and blood of Jesus Christ, your Son and our Redeemer.

3.

. . . Make for us this offering approved, reasonable, acceptable, because it is the figure of the body and blood of our Lord Jesus Christ;] who, the day before he suffered, took bread in his holy hands, looked up to heaven to you, holy Father, almighty eternal God, gave thanks, blessed and broke it, and handed it when broken to his apostles and disciples, saying, "Take and eat from this, all of you; for this is my body, which will be broken for many." Likewise after supper, the day before he suffered, he took the cup, looked up to heaven to you, holy Father, almighty eternal God, gave thanks, blessed, and handed it to his apostles and disciples, saying, "Take and drink from this, all of you, for this is my blood. As often as you do this, so often you will make remembrance of me until I come again."

Therefore, remembering his most glorious Passion, and resurrection from the dead, and ascension into heaven, we offer to you this spotless victim, reasonable victim, bloodless victim, this holy bread and cup of eternal life: [and we pray and beseech you to receive this offering on your altar on high by the hands of your angels, as you vouchsafed to receive the gifts of your righteous servant Abel, and the sacrifice of our patriarch Abraham, and that which the high priest Melchizedek offered to you.

4.

We beseech and entreat you to accept and bless this offering also, as you accepted the gifts of your righteous servant Abel, and the sacrifice of the patriarch Abraham our father, and that which your high priest Melchizedek offered to you.] Let your blessing, I pray, descend here invisibly, as once it used to descend on the victims of the Fathers. Let a sweet-smelling savor ascend to the sight of your divine majesty by the hands of your angel. And let your Holy Spirit be borne down upon those solemn things, to sanctify both the offerings and the prayers alike of the people who stand here and offer, that all we who taste of this body may receive healing for our souls.

5.

Through our Lord Jesus Christ, in whom and with whom honor, praise, glory, magnificence, and power are yours, with the Holy Spirit, from the ages, and now, and always, and to all the ages of ages. Amen.

23 The Mass of the Roman Rite

The Roman Canon cannot be dated with any precision. Quotations and parallels begin to appear towards the end of the fourth century in such writers as Ambrose and Ambrosiaster, and in the letter of Pope Innocent I to Bishop Decentius (416). The oldest manuscripts are no older than the eighth century. The canon has very little in common with the anaphora of Hippolytus, or any Eastern prayer, with the possible exception of *St. Mark*.

The canon gives the impression of having been assembled from a number of independent prayers. Scholars seem fairly well agreed that Sursum corda, *Te igitur*,* *Memento Domine, Quam oblationem, Qui pridie, Unde et memores, Supra quae,* and the doxology constitute an earlier stratum, the other sections being later additions which all end "through Christ our Lord," to which "Amen" was added during the Middle Ages. (*Communicantes* and *Nobis quoque* are attributed to Pope Gelasius, part of *Hanc igitur* to Gregory the Great.) This is strikingly confirmed by the non-Roman fragments (see pp. 155–8).

The Sursum corda is in the same words as in Hippolytus and *St. Mark,* but instead of the invariable preface found in those anaphoras, the Roman Canon implies the insertion of proper prefaces, so that salvation-history is spread over a whole year instead of being rapidly traversed every Sunday. The Sanctus only appears in Rome *c.* 450, and soon becomes detached from the rest of the canon, which thus loses the idea of consecration by thanksgiving. During the Middle Ages the canon was regarded as beginning at *Te igitur*.

Te igitur and *Memento Domine* should be compared with the Mozarabic prayer on p. 157, which has been expanded in the canon by the inclusion of prayer for those *for* whom the offering is made. A new idea appears, that the offerer makes the offering for himself *or others*, to obtain "redemption for their souls, for the hope of their salvation and safety." The giving of thanks, so

---

* *The various sections of the canon are always referred to by the opening Latin words.*

prominent in Hippolytus, is replaced by a plea for acceptance of the offering, the first of four such pleas.

Communicantes, a further expansion of the Mozarabic prayer, consists of prayer for the saints, especially the Twelve Apostles, eight popes, and four martyrs, the help of whose prayers is invoked. *Hanc igitur* may be varied on occasion. *Quam oblationem* brings back the last sentence of the Mozarabic prayer. The language of "image and likeness" is now replaced by "that it may become to us the body and blood." A change in the elements is suggested by the use of "become" rather than "be," which in connection with "to us" might detract from the reality of the presence.

There is little to say about the Institution Narrative (*Qui pridie*), which has received the customary embellishments. An anamnesis (*Unde et memores*) follows, which is a developed version of that in Hippolytus; *Supra quae* makes the last of the four pleas for acceptance of the offering. The references to Abel and Abraham, found also in Ambrose and the second Mozarabic prayer on p.158, seem ultimately to derive from *St. Mark*. Melchizedek is only found in the Western sources. The words "a holy sacrifice, an unblemished victim" are attributed to Leo the Great. The word "victim" (*hostia*) only appears after the Institution Narrative; previously the elements have been referred to as "gifts, offerings, and sacrifices" (*dona, munera, sacrificia*). This seems to locate the offering of the sacrifice in *Qui pridie*.

Memento etiam, though reminiscent in tone of Eastern liturgies such as *St. James*, seems in fact to have originated in Rome. It does not appear in the manuscripts until the ninth century, and may originally have been a diaconal bidding. Similarly, *Nobis quoque* may have been a priest's private prayer referring to the celebrant and his assistants. The doxology contains passing mentions of Creation and the Holy Spirit (otherwise conspicuous by their absence).

The absence of any epiclesis has been the subject of much scholarly discussion. Certainly the phrase "that they may become to us the body and blood" (*Quam oblationem*) looks like part of a consecratory epiclesis, and "that all of us who have received . . .

by partaking" (*Supplices te*) like part of an epiclesis on the worshippers. The difficulty is to account for the removal of any mention of the Spirit, unless it was done to confine the power of consecration to *Qui pridie*. Even so, it is very odd that it should have left no trace in the writings of the Fathers.

Two important doctrinal points should be noticed. First, stress is laid on the participation of the people in offering: "we . . . your holy people . . . offer," and "may be *to us*" mentioned above. Even in one of the medieval offertory prayers, the priest speaks of "my sacrifice *and yours*." Secondly, the medieval doctrine of transubstantiation may be implicit in the words of the canon, but it is nowhere explicit.

A selection is included of the priest's private prayers from the 1571 Missal, all later than 800. Those for the offertory pre-empt the consecration in the canon, and indeed came to be known as *canon minor*.

The blessings on p. 166 are to be inserted before the doxology (*Per quem*). They are taken from the Gregorian ("*Hadrianum*") and Leonine ("*Veronense*") Sacramentaries respectively. They have obvious affinities with those of the *Apostolic Tradition* (see p. 36).

The literature about the canon is enormous, and the following bibliography is only a starting point.

BIBLIOGRAPHY
Prex Eucharistica, pp. 424–426 (with bibliography).
B. Botte, *Le canon de la messe romaine* (1935, reprinted 1962).
B. Botte and C. Mohrmann, *L'Ordinaire de la messe* (1953); includes the private prayers.
L. Eizenhöfer, *Canon Missae Romanae* (I, 1954; II, 1966); sources.
Dix, *The Shape*, pp. 434–612 (NB p. 557, note 1).
J. A. Jungmann, *The Mass of the Roman Rite* (1951), vol. I, pp.49–59; vol. II, pp. 101–274.
G. G. Willis, (1) *Essays in Early Roman Liturgy* (1964). (2) *Further Essays in Early Roman Liturgy* (1968). Excellent bibliographies.
C. Vagaggini, *The Canon of the Mass and Liturgical Reform* (1967).
R. A. Keifer, "The Unity of the Roman Canon," in *Studia Liturgica*, 11(1976), pp. 39–58.

PSALM 43

CONFESSION and ABSOLUTION

INTROIT PSALM

KYRIE

GLORIA IN EXCELSIS

COLLECT OF THE DAY

EPISTLE

GRADUAL and SEQUENCE

GOSPEL

SERMON

CREED

OFFERTORY PRAYERS

Receive, holy Father, almighty eternal God, this unblemished offering which I, your unworthy servant, offer to you, my living
and true God, for my innumerable sins, offences, and
negligences; for all who stand round, and for all faithful Christians, alive and dead; that it may avail for my salvation and theirs
to eternal life.

O God, who in a wonderful way created human nature in its dignity, and more wonderfully restored it; grant us through the mystery of this water and wine, to share his divinity who vouchsafed
to share our humanity, Jesus Christ, your Son, our Lord; who is
alive and reigns with you as God in the unity of the Holy Spirit
through all the ages of ages.

We offer you, Lord, the cup of salvation, and pray that of your
kindness it may ascend in the sight of your divine majesty for our
salvation and that of the whole world, in a sweet smelling savor.

Receive, Lord, our humble spirits and contrite hearts; and may
our sacrifice be performed today in your sight so as to please you,
Lord God.

Come, Sanctifier, almighty, eternal God, and bless this sacrifice
prepared for your holy name.

Through the intercession of blessed Michael the archangel, who
stands at the right of the altar of incense, and of all the elect, may
the Lord vouchsafe to bless this incense and receive it as a sweet
smelling savor; through Christ our Lord.

(Psalm 142:2–4; Psalm 25:6–12.)

Receive, Holy Trinity, this offering which we offer to you as a memorial of the Passion, Resurrection, and Ascension of our Lord Jesus Christ; and in honor of the Blessed ever-Virgin Mary, and Blessed John the Baptist, and the holy Apostles Peter and Paul, and of NN. and all the saints; that it may avail to their honor and our salvation. May they vouchsafe to intercede for us in heaven, whose memory we celebrate on earth, through the same Jesus Christ our Lord.

Pray, brothers, that my sacrifice and yours may be acceptable to God, the almighty Father.

People: May God receive the sacrifice from your hands to the praise and glory of his name, and to our benefit, and that of all his holy Church, through all the ages of ages. Amen.

THE CANON

Priest: The Lord be with you.
People: And with your spirit.
Priest: Up with your hearts.[1]
People: We have them with the Lord.
Priest: Let us give thanks to the Lord our God.
People: It is fitting and right.

Priest: Vere dignum—It is truly fitting and right, our duty and our salvation, that we should always and everywhere give you thanks, O Lord, holy Father, almighty eternal God, through Christ our Lord;[2]

through whom angels praise your majesty, dominions adore, powers fear, the heavens and the heavenly hosts and the blessed seraphim, joining together in exultant celebration. We pray you, bid our voices also to be admitted with theirs, beseeching you, confessing, and saying:

People: Holy, holy, holy, Lord God of Sabaoth. Heaven and earth are full of your glory. Hosanna in the highest.

1. The Latin has no verb.
2. Here a passage proper to the occasion may be inserted

Blessed is he who comes in the name of the Lord. Hosanna in the highest.

Priest: Te igitur—We therefore pray and beseech you, most merciful Father, through your Son Jesus Christ our Lord, to accept and bless these gifts, these offerings, these holy and unblemished sacrifices; above all, those which we offer to you for your holy catholic Church; vouchsafe to grant it peace, protection, unity, and guidance throughout the world, together with your servant N. our pope, and N. our bishop, and all orthodox upholders of the catholic and apostolic faith.

Memento Domine—Remember, Lord, your servants, men and women, and all who stand around, whose faith and devotion are known to you, for whom we offer to you, or who offer to you this sacrifice of praise for themselves and for all their own, for the redemption of their souls, for the hope of their salvation and safety, and pay their vows to you, the living, true, and eternal God.

Communicantes—In fellowship with (*here a seasonal clause may follow*) and venerating above all the memory of the glorious ever-Virgin Mary, mother of God and our Lord Jesus Christ, and also of your blessed apostles and martyrs Peter, Paul, Andrew, James, John, Thomas, Philip, Bartholomew, Matthew, Simon and Thaddaeus, Linus, Cletus, Clement, Xystus, Cornelius, Cyprian, Laurence, Chrysogonus, John and Paul, Cosmas and Damian, and all your saints; by their merits and prayers grant us to be defended in all things by the help of your protection; through Christ our Lord.

Hanc igitur—Therefore, Lord, we pray you graciously to accept this offering made by us your servants, and also by your whole family; and to order our days in peace; and to command that we are snatched from eternal damnation and numbered among the flock of your elect; through Christ our Lord.[3]

Quam oblationem—Vouchsafe, we beseech you, O God, to make this offering wholly blessed, approved, ratified, reasonable, and

[3]This paragraph varies according to the occasion.

The Mass of the Roman Rite

acceptable; that it may become to us the body and blood of your dearly beloved Son Jesus Christ our Lord;

Qui pridie—who, on the day before he suffered, took bread in his holy and reverend hands, lifted up his eyes to heaven to you, O God, his almighty father, gave thanks to you, blessed, broke, and gave it to his disciples, saying, "Take and eat from this, all of you; for this is my body." Likewise after supper, taking also this glorious cup in his holy and reverend hands, again he gave thanks to you, blessed and gave it to his disciples, saying, "Take and drink from it, all of you; for this is the cup of my blood, of the new and eternal covenant, the mystery of faith, which will be shed for you and for many for forgiveness of sins. As often as you do this, you will do it for my remembrance."

Unde et memores—Therefore also, Lord, we your servants, and also your holy people, having in remembrance the blessed Passion of your Son Christ our Lord, likewise his resurrection from the dead, and also his glorious ascension into heaven, do offer to your excellent majesty from your gifts and bounty a pure victim, a holy victim, an unspotted victim, the holy bread of eternal life and the cup of everlasting salvation.

Supra quae—Vouchsafe to look upon them with a favorable and kindly countenance, and accept them as you vouchsafed to accept the gifts of your righteous servant Abel, and the sacrifice of our patriarch Abraham, and that which your high priest Melchizedek offered to you, a holy sacrifice, an unblemished victim.

Supplices te—We humbly beseech you, almighty God, bid these things be borne by the hands of your angel to your altar on high, in the sight of your divine majesty, that all of us who have received the most holy body and blood of your Son by partaking at this altar may be filled with all heavenly blessing and grace; through Christ our Lord.

Memento etiam—Remember also, Lord, the names of those who have gone before us with the sign of faith, and sleep in the sleep of peace. We beseech you to grant to them and to all who rest in Christ a place of restoration, light, and peace; through Christ our Lord.

Nobis quoque—To us sinners your servants also, who trust in the multitude of your mercies, vouchsafe to grant some part and fellowship with your holy Apostles and martyrs, with John, Stephen, Matthias, Barnabas, Ignatius, Alexander, Marcellinus, Peter, Felicity, Perpetua, Agatha, Lucy, Agnes, Cecilia, Anastasia, and all your saints: into whose company we ask that you will admit us, not weighing our merit, but bounteously forgiving; through Christ our Lord.[4]

Per quem—Through him, Lord, you ever create, sanctify, quicken, bless, and bestow all these good things upon us. Through him and with him and in him all honor and glory is yours, O God the Father almighty, in the unity of the Holy Spirit, through all the ages of ages. Amen.

SELECTED BLESSINGS

Blessing of chrism on Maundy Thursday:

Send forth, Lord, your Holy Spirit the Paraclete from heaven upon this richness of the olive, which you vouchsafed to bring forth from the green tree for the healing of the body; that by your holy blessing it may be to all who anoint and touch a protection to mind and body, to drive out all pains and all infirmities, all sickness of body; your perfect chrism, with which you anointed priests, kings, prophets, and martyrs, blessed by you, Lord, remaining in our reins, in the name of Jesus Christ our Lord.

Through him, Lord, you ever create . . . (*as above*).

Blessing of water and milk and honey at Pentecost:

Bless, Lord, also these your creatures of water, honey, and milk; and give your servants to drink from this fountain of the water of eternal life, which is the Spirit of truth, and nourish them with this milk and honey, as you promised to our fathers Abraham, Isaac, and Jacob to bring them into the Promised Land, a land flowing with milk and honey. Unite your servants therefore, Lord, to the Holy Spirit, as this milk and honey was united,

4. Here a blessing may follow.

The Mass of the Roman Rite

thereby signifying the union of heavenly and earthly substance in Christ Jesus our Lord.

Through him, Lord, you ever create . . . (*as above*).

LORD'S PRAYER with EMBOLISM and FRACTION
PEACE

COMMUNION PRAYERS
May this sacramental mixing of the body and blood of our Lord Jesus Christ bring eternal life to us who receive it.

Lamb of God, you take away the sins of the world: have mercy on us.

Lamb of God, you take away the sins of the world: have mercy on us.

Lamb of God, you take away the sins of the world: give us peace.

Lord Jesus Christ, Son of the Living God, who by the Father's will and the Holy Spirit's help, gave life to the world through your death: by this your most holy body and blood, free me from all my wickedness and every evil; make me always cleave to your commandments, and let me never be separated from you; for you are alive and reign as God with the same God the Father and the Holy Spirit, to the ages of ages.

May the receiving of your body, Lord Jesus Christ, which in my unworthiness I dare to take, bring on me neither judgement nor condemnation; but in your mercy may it be to me protection of mind and body, and receiving of a remedy; for you are alive and reign as God with God the Father, in the unity of the Holy Spirit, for all the ages of ages.

COMMUNION
The body of our Lord Jesus Christ keep your soul in eternal life.

The blood of our Lord Jesus Christ keep your soul in eternal life.

POSTCOMMUNION PRAYER
DISMISSAL.

24 Ordo Romanus Primus

This document does not contain the text of a eucharistic prayer, but is included to provide the background of the Roman Canon. It describes the ceremonial used when the Pope visited one of the churches in Rome for a stational mass. Internal evidence suggests that it was compiled about A.D. 700 by someone with an intimate knowledge of the organization of the papal court. As such, it may be regarded as thoroughly reliable. The text translated below is that of the oldest manuscript, Saint-Gall 614, written about 850. Later manuscripts make numerous additions to the text, which reflect minor developments of the ceremonial.

BIBLIOGRAPHY
M. Andrieu, *Les Ordines Romani du Haut-Moyen Age*, vol. 2(1948), pp. 74–108.
E. G. C. F. Atchley, *Ordo Romanus Primus* (1905), pp. 132–145 (full commentary).
J. A. Jungmann, *The Mass of the Roman Rite* (1951), vol. 1, pp. 67–74.

PRELIMINARIES TO THE SERVICE
INTROIT
KYRIES
GLORIA IN EXCELSIS
COLLECT
EPISTLE
GRADUAL and ALLELUIA
GOSPEL
SALUTATION and OREMUS (but no prayer)

12. Then as the deacon goes to the altar, an acolyte comes with a chalice and a corporal over (it), raises the chalice in his left hand and hands the corporal to the deacon. He takes it off the chalice and lays it on the right side of the altar, throwing the other end to the second deacon so that they can spread it out . . .

A subdeacon with the empty chalice follows the archdeacon.

The pope, after saying *Let us pray*, goes down at once to the senatorial area, the chancellor holding his right hand and the chief counsellor his left, and receives the offerings of the princes in the order of their authorities. After him the archdeacon receives the flasks and pours them into a larger chalice held by a district subdeacon. He is followed by an acolyte with a bowl outside his cope into which the chalice is poured when it is full. The district subdeacon receives the offerings from the pope and hands them to the subdeacon in attendance, and he puts them in a linen cloth held by two acolytes. After the pope, the bishop on duty that week receives the rest of the offerings, so that he may put them with his own hand into the linen cloth which follows him. After him the deacon who follows the archdeacon receives (the flasks) and pours them into the bowl with his own hand.

The pope, before crossing to the women's side, goes down before the *confessio* and receives the offerings of the chancellor, the secretary, and the chief counsellor; for on festivals they offer at the altar after the deacons. Likewise the pope goes up to the women's side and carries out the above order. Likewise the presbyters do also, if need be, after him or in the presbytery.

After this the pope, with the chancellor and the secretary holding his hands, returns to his seat and washes his hands. The archdeacon, standing before the altar, when the collection is completed, washes his hands; then he looks towards the pope, who nods to him; and thus saluted he goes to the altar.

Then the district subdeacons, taking the offerings from the subdeacon in attendance, hand them to the archdeacon, and he arranges them on the altar; the subdeacons hand them on each side. When the altar is ready, the archdeacon takes a flask from the oblationary subdeacon and pours it through a strainer into the chalice, and then the deacons' (flasks). Then the subdeacon in attendance goes down to the choir, takes a ewer from the chief singer and brings it to the archdeacon, who pours it into the chalice, making the sign of the cross. Then the deacons go up to the pope. When they see them, the chancellor, the secretary, and the chief district counsellor and the district notaries and the district counsellors come down from their ranks to stand in their proper places.

Then the pope rises from his seat, goes down to the altar, salutes it, and receives the offerings from the presbyter of the week and the deacons. Then the archdeacon receives the pope's offerings from the oblationary and gives them to the pope. When the pope has placed them on the altar, the archdeacon takes the chalice from the district subdeacon and puts it on the altar near the pope's offering with the offertory-veil twisted round its handles. He lays the veil on the corner of the altar, and stands behind the pope. The pope, bowing slightly to the altar, looks at the choir and nods to them to be silent.

The offertory finished, the bishops are standing behind the pope, the senior in the middle, then in order; and the archdeacon on the right of the bishops, the second deacon on the left, and the others in order arranged in a line. And the district subdeacons go behind the altar when the offertory is finished, and look at the pope, so that, when he says *For ever and ever* or *The Lord be with you* or *Lift up your hearts* or *Let us give thanks*, they may be ready to answer, standing upright until they begin to say the angelic hymn, that is *Holy, holy, holy*.

And when they have finished, the pope alone rises for the canon, but the bishops, priests, deacons, and subdeacons remain bowed. And when he has said *To us sinners also*, the subdeacons rise; when he has said *Through whom all these things, O Lord*, the arch-deacon rises alone; when he has said *Through him and with him* (the archdeacon) lifts up the chalice by the handles with the offertory-veil and holds it, raising it towards the pope. The pope touches the side of the chalice with the offerings, saying *Through him and with him* up to *For all the ages of ages*, and puts the offerings in their place, and the archdeacon puts the chalice near them.

We have left out something about the paten: when (the pope) begins the canon, an acolyte comes to his side with a linen cloth tied round his neck and holds the paten before his breast on the right side until the middle of the canon. Then the subdeacon in attendance receives it outside his chasuble and comes before the altar, and waits for a district subdeacon to receive it.

When the canon is finished, the district subdeacon stands with the paten behind the archdeacon. When he has said *and safe from all distress*, the archdeacon turns, kisses the paten, and gives it to the second deacon to hold. When he has said *The peace of the Lord be always with you*, he makes the sign of the cross over the chalice with his hand three times, (and puts a consecrated fragment into it). The archdeacon gives the peace to the chief bishop, then the rest in order and the people likewise.

Then the pope breaks the offering on the right and leaves the fragment which he has broken off on the altar; but he puts his other offerings on the paten which a deacon is holding. Then at once he goes up to his seat.

The archdeacon takes the chalice from above the altar, gives it to a district subdeacon, and he holds it near the right corner of the altar until the offerings are broken. The subdeacons in attendance with the acolytes, who carry little bags, come on the right and on the left; the acolytes hold out their arms with the little bags, and the subdeacons in attendance stand at each corner of the altar. They make ready the openings of the little bags for the archdeacon to put the offerings in them, first on the right, then on the left. Then the acolytes go to the right and left through the bishops round the altar; the rest go down to the presbyters, for them to break the hosts. Two district subdeacons proceed to the seat, carrying the paten to the deacons, for the fraction. They look at the pope, so that he may nod to them to do the fraction; and when he nods to them, they return the pope's salutation and do the fraction.

When the altar has been cleared of the offerings, except for the fragment which the pope broke off his own offering and left on the altar—they do it thus so that the altar should not be without the sacrifice while the solemnities of Mass are celebrated—the archdeacon looks at the choir and nods to them to say *O Lamb of God*, and goes to the paten with the rest.

When the fraction has been completed, the second deacon takes the paten from the subdeacon and takes it to the seat, in order that the pope may communicate. When he has communicated, he makes the sign of the cross three times over the fragment from which he has bitten, and puts it in the chalice in the hands of the archdeacon. And he is communicated thus by the archdeacon.

Then the archdeacon comes with the chalice to the corner of the altar, and announces the (next) station. When he has poured a little from the chalice into the bowl held by an acolyte, the bishops come up first to the seat, that they may communicate from the hand of the pope in order. The presbyters also come up to communicate. The chief bishop receives the chalice from the archdeacon, and stands at the corner of the altar; he communicates the remaining ranks down to the chief counsellor. Then the archdeacon receives the chalice from him, and pours it into the above-mentioned bowl, and hands the chalice to a district subdeacon, who gives him the reed with which he communicates the people. The subdeacon in attendance receives the chalice and gives it to an acolyte, who replaces it in the sacristy.

When (the archdeacon) has administered to those whom the pope communicated, the pope comes down from his seat with the chancellor and the chief counsellor, to administer to those who are in the senatorial area, after which the archdeacon communicates them. After the archdeacon the bishops give the communion, the deacons administering after them. For (when) the pope came to give the communion, an acolyte went before him with a linen cloth hanging round his neck, with which he held the paten with the host. Likewise they go after the deacons also with ewers and bowls, pouring the wine into gemellions for the communion to the people. When they do this, they cross from right to left. When the chancellor nods, the presbyters, by command of the pope, communicate the people in both kinds.

Now as soon as the pope begins to give the communion in the senatorial area, the choir at once begins the communion antiphon by turns with the subdeacons, and sings until all the people have been communicated, and the pope nods for them to say *Glory be to the Father*; and then, when they have repeated the verse, they fall silent.

The pope, as soon as he has communicated those on the women's side, returns to his seat and communicates the district officials in order as they stand in line. When the station has been announced, they go up to the altar. The archdeacon gives them the communion after the pope. When all have communicated, the pope sits down, and washes his hands.

COLLECT
DISMISSAL
BLESSING

PART II

Reformed Prayers of the Eucharist

THE STUDY OF REFORMED LITURGY

The fact that Zwingli follows Ordo Romanus Primus in this volume implies in no way that there is some close historical link between the two. In fact a period of some eight hundred years separated them—a period longer than that covered by all the early liturgical texts. Nor does it imply that no liturgical changes of any kind took place during that period. It is true that the actual texts of the two great rites in East and West—St. John Chrysostom and the Roman rite—underwent no significant change, and the former remains unchanged still: but in the West the way in which that Roman text was used and the meanings which gathered around it changed considerably. For example, the active participation of the laity virtually disappeared, the eucharist becoming a spectacle, overlaid with ceremonies and symbolism unknown to the early Church: communion itself became a rare occurrence, being supplanted by the elevation and adoration of the consecrated elements: and the Mass was regarded as a sacrifice in itself, additional to that offered by Jesus Christ on Calvary. Dom Gregory Dix described it aptly and succinctly: the Reformers "looked upon a Church plagued with a multitude of real superstitions, some gross and wholly evil in their effects, some merely quaint and fanciful, but all equally irrelevant to the Christian religion" (*The Shape of the Liturgy*, 1945, p. 627): and these errors and misconceptions had been gradually accumulating over the centuries.

The Renaissance and the Reformation heralded new attitudes towards the liturgy, not only through new thinking, but through its important adjuncts. There was, for example, the invention of printing. The days when both worshipper and scholar were restricted by the rare and expensive handwritten volume on vellum were over. Significantly the first major book to be printed and published was John Gutenberg's Bible at Mainz in 1456. Presses were established throughout Europe and the Church became the new invention's best customer. Service books, increasingly in the vernacular, were obvious material; and they became widely accessible and in an established form, both for worshippers and for scholars. The Byzantine service books began to be printed in Venice and in Rome in the first part of the sixteenth century, and Cranmer certainly made use of the 1528 Venice edition of the liturgy of St. John Chrysostom in his work on the Prayer Book. He was also indebted, over and above Hermann, to a number of the German Church Orders, and in particular that of Brandenburg-Nürnberg. Or again, there was the case of the English refugees from the Marian persecution at Frankfurt in 1554: the fact that Calvin's Genevan Service Book was available to them in an English translation by William Huycke, which had been printed and published in London in 1550, was of enormous help: and Knox had no problem in consulting communities at Strasbourg, Emden, Zürich,and elsewhere as to its use. Gone were the days of the handwritten service book, which could vary from copy to copy. Nor was it long before the printing of early theological and liturgical texts opened up new fields of study for an increasing number of students. The first edition of *The Apostolic Constitutions*, containing the so-called Clementine Liturgy, on which seventeenth- and eighteenth-century scholars set so much store, appeared in 1563, while Pamelius produced a collection of Latin texts including the Gregorian Sacramentary in *Liturgicon Ecclesiae Latinae* in 1571.

Men's horizons were widening both physically and intellectually. The old traditional theological disputations of the universities became outmoded. The Bible was rediscovered: and the study of eucharistic theology took on a new impetus. Men came to realize the need, not only for a revitalized and purified proclamation of the Christian faith but also for new ways of worship. Sadly the early sixteenth-century popes—Alexander VI, Julius II, and Leo X—were not the kind of men capable of understanding or meeting the spiritual needs of their day. Frankly, they did not look like Vicars of Christ but were more concerned with the reestablishment of the monarchical rule and territorial power of the Papacy. The impetus for change came therefore not from within the Roman Church but from men who had broken away from it. Zwingli, Luther, Bucer, Calvin, Hermann, Knox, Cranmer—all had held office of some kind at some stage but eventually were excommunicated or left of their own free will. But many of them did not find it easy to free themselves overnight from the influences of late medieval scholastic and devotional practice. Liturgi-

The Study of Reformed Liturgy

cal change came to them gradually, and sometimes they discarded what was good as well as what was bad. In that respect Cranmer could be regarded as rather more cautious and conservative than Zwingli and Luther: and it is interesting to note that in the seventeenth and eighteenth centuries, when early texts were more readily available and the comparative study of liturgy more developed, a readiness to return to primitive patterns of eucharistic prayer was more marked in Anglicanism than in other Protestant Churches. But clearly in the first generation of Continental reformed liturgies there was strong reaction against any idea that the eucharist was in itself a sacrifice: there was only one sacrifice—that of Jesus Christ on Calvary; although the views on the relationship of that sacrifice to the eucharist and the presence of Christ in the eucharist varied. Certainly, with the exception of Cranmer and to a lesser extent Petri, the Reformers would have nothing to do with the traditional Roman eucharistic canon and its concept of offering, for this was contrary to their great doctrine of justification by faith: while Calvin's and Zwingli's views on *sola scriptura* resulted in rites which were brief and bare in the extreme.

Three permanent groups of liturgies emerged from the Reformation—Lutheran, Anglican and Calvinist. All three became worldwide; and by the inclusion of some eighteenth-century texts it has now been possible to indicate in this volume a little of this international influence and the variety of eucharistic patterns. But what has remained constant has been the original shape laid down by Jesus Christ himself. "At the heart of it all is the eucharistic action, a thing of absolute simplicity—the taking, blessing, breaking and giving of bread and the taking, blessing and giving of a cup of wine and water, as these were first done with their new meaning by a young Jew before and after supper with his friends on the night before he died. Soon it was simplified still further, by leaving out the supper and combining the double grouping before and after it into a single rite. So the four-action shape of the Liturgy was found by the end of the first century. He had told his friends to do this henceforward with the new meaning 'for the *anamnesis*' of him, and they have done it always since. Was ever another command so obeyed? For century after century, spreading slowly to every continent and country and among every race on earth, this action has been done, in every conceivable human circumstance, for every conceivable need from infancy and before it to extreme old age and after it, from the pinnacles of earthly greatness to the refuge of fugitives in the caves and dens of the earth. . . . One could fill many pages with the reasons why men have done this, and not tell a hundredth part of them. And best of all, week by week and month by month, on a hundred thousand successive Sundays, faithfully, unfailingly, across all the parishes of Christendom, the pastors have done this just to *make* the *plebs sancta Dei*—the holy common people of God. . . . The sheer stupendous *quantity* of the love of God which this ever repeated action has drawn from the obscure Christian multitudes through the centuries is in itself an overwhelming thought." (Dix, *The Shape of the Liturgy*, pp. 743–745).

25 Ulrich Zwingli:
a. *Epicheiresis* 1523 and
b. *Action oder Brauch des Nachtmahls* 1525

Zwingli, the papal chaplain and professional soldier turned Reformer, produced his *De Canone Missae Epicheiresis* (*An Attack upon the Canon of the Mass*) in 1523, which proved to be a fairly conservative revision of the Roman rite. Vestments were permitted, it was still in Latin (except for the lessons), and there was little up to the Sanctus that was changed, save for a simplification of the lectionary, and the removal of the propers for Saints' Days and the Offertory. It was a transitional rite, produced "for the sake of the weaker brethren." Zwingli attacked the canon, however, both for its theology and for its poor literary quality: he opposed its teaching on sacrifice and the real presence, and considered it incoherent and full of contradictions. The Sursum corda, Preface and Sanctus remained, but these were now followed by four Latin prayers of his own composition, of roughly the same length as the canon, and incorporating some elements expected in a eucharistic prayer.

The first prayer, recounting the history of salvation in a style not unlike that of an ancient anaphora, culminated in the Lord's Prayer. The second prayer prayed that the faithful might be fed with spiritual food and quickened by the Spirit—a hint perhaps of an epiclesis. But here the important point was that for Zwingli this spiritual food was the Word of God, not the sacrament: unlike Luther, he could not believe that Christ could be both in heaven and in the eucharistic bread and wine: for him Christ was in heaven and not in the elements, and the eucharist was simply a memorial of Christ's death—an aid to the worshipper but not a means of grace. The third prayer—with a suggestion of an anamnesis—began with a confession of faith in Jesus Christ's sacrifice on the Cross and went on to pray that the faithful might have grace to follow his example and have unity and fellowship in him. The fourth prayer was a prayer of humble access with the *Agnus Dei* leading into the Institution Narrative from 1 Corinthians 11, but lengthened by one verse to include, "For as often as you eat this bread and drink this cup, you proclaim the death of the Lord, until he comes." This was followed by our Lord's invitation, "Come, all you who labor," and communion. The rite ended with the *Nunc Dimittis*, a brief thanksgiving and dismissal.

This rite satisfied no one—neither conservatives nor radicals. Just before Easter 1525 the radicals approached the Council of Zurich, demanding that the traditional Mass be replaced by one agreeable to the Scriptures. Zwingli promptly submitted *Action oder Brauch des Nachtmahls*, which he had recently published in German. This was accepted, coming into use on Maundy Thursday. It was the first German rite in Zurich and was much more radical than its predecessor. Ceremonies and ritual were reduced to the barest minimum: it was no longer "the Mass," but "The Lord's Supper": and its celebration was limited to four times a year—Easter, Whitsun, Autumn, and Christmas. It was simply a fellowship meal, with the faithful sitting around the Table, commemorating the great fact of their redemption. The Epistle and Gospel were unchanging—1 Corinthians 11:20–29 and John 6:47–63: and the Sursum corda, Preface, Sanctus and the four prayers of *Epicheiresis* had all disappeared. All that remained was an exhortation to devout communion, the Lord's Prayer, a Prayer of Humble Access, and the Institution Narrative. The administration followed in silence, the bread and wine being brought by deacons to the faithful, who remained sitting in their places around the Table. The rite ended with an antiphonal recitation of Psalm 113:1–9, a thanksgiving, and a dismissal.

As a eucharistic rite it was brief and bare with little attempt to secure its avowed purpose of expressing the sense of fellowship. Certainly it conveyed no idea of communion with the rest of the Church on earth or in heaven. The direct influence of *Action oder Brauch* was limited mainly to Zurich, Bern, and Basel: but this may have been due in some measure to Zwingli's early and untimely death in battle at Cappel in 1531.

BIBLIOGRAPHY
Coena Domini I (1983), pp. 185–198.
A. Barclay, *The Protestant Doctrine of the Lord's Supper* (1927), pp. 41–106.

Bouyer, pp. 391–394.
Y. Brilioth, *Eucharistic Faith and Practice Evangelical and Catholic* (1930), pp.153–164.
W. D. Maxwell, *An Outline of Christian Worship* (1945), pp. 81–87.
N. Micklem (ed.), *Christian Worship* (1938), pp. 137–153.
Bard Thompson, pp. 141–156.

a. An Attack on the Canon of the Mass (1523)

INTROIT

KYRIES

GLORIA IN EXCELSIS

COLLECT ⎫

EPISTLE ⎬ but none for Saints' Days

GRADUAL ⎪

GOSPEL ⎭

NICENE CREED, during which there is
PREPARATION OF THE ELEMENTS

The Lord be with you.
(℟. And with your spirit.)
Up with your hearts.
(℟. We have them with the Lord.)
Let us give thanks to the Lord our God.
(℟. It is fitting and right.)
It is fitting and right, our duty and our salvation, that we should always and everywhere give you thanks, O Lord, holy Father, almighty eternal God, through Christ our Lord; through whom angels praise, dominions adore, powers fear, the heavens and the heavenly hosts and the blessed seraphim, joining together in exultation celebrate your majesty.
We pray you, bid our voices to be admitted with theirs, beseeching you, confessing you, and saying:
℟. Holy, holy, holy, Lord God of Sabaoth. Heaven and earth are full of your glory. Hosanna in the highest.
Blessed is he who comes in the name of the Lord. Hosanna in the highest.

After we have hymned thrice-holy, almighty God with the heavenly souls, let us at length begin thus with prayer:

Ulrich Zwingli 183

The Canon is then replaced by the four following prayers:

I. Most merciful and thrice holy Father, you created man in the beginning to enjoy paradise here and then afterwards to enjoy yourself. From this state of grace man fell through his own fault and was deemed worthy of death: he tainted all those who came after him; and then there was simply no hope of life, unless you, who alone are good, decided to relieve man's distress. You promised his seed that he would bruise the head of the evil seducer, so that wretched man would not waste away in perpetual despair. In accordance with this promise, when the appointed time was fulfilled, you offered your Son, our Lord Jesus Christ, who took our flesh through the pure and ever-Virgin Mary, that he might become for us perfect priest and perfect victim, unique among the human race. He gave himself to be the sacrifice for those who were lost: and not content with this, so that we might lack for nothing, he gave himself to be our food and drink. So, most blessed Father, we pray that your goodness may be constantly on our lips: and, although our deepest gratitude can never match your kindness, we pray that in your constant and unfailing goodness you will make us worthy to sing your praises continually with our hearts and lips and in our deeds, and to ask for nothing that would be alien to you. In confidence, therefore, we shall offer you prayer and praise in accordance with your will, as we have been taught by your most dearly beloved Son, Jesus Christ our Lord. Guided therefore by his precepts, we are bold to say:

Our Father . . .

2. O God, you fed not only man from his youth but also every living creature. Feed our hungry souls, we pray, with heavenly food: for you are he who fills the hungry with good things. Our souls are spiritual, made in your image; therefore they can only be refreshed with spiritual food, and that food can only be given by your word. Your word is truth: for you are truth, and from you nothing can come save that which is genuine, holy, steadfast and unspotted. Never deprive us of the food of your word, but ever feed us in your goodness. That is the true bread, which gives life to the world. We would eat the flesh and drink the blood of your Son in vain, if we did not firmly believe above all things through

the faith of your word, that your Son our Lord Jesus Christ was crucified for us and atoned for the sins of the whole world. He himself said that the flesh profits nothing, but it is the Spirit which gives life. Quicken us, therefore, by your Spirit and never deprive us of your word; for your word is the vehicle of your Spirit, and assuredly it will never return to you empty. By that one thing, and that alone, is the human mind set free, for it is the truth; and you have promised through your Son that if the truth sets us free, then indeed we shall be truly free. So we pray that we may never lack the food of your word, for by that one thing we are granted the freedom and security of salvation. Through your Son, Jesus Christ our Lord, who is alive and reigns with you in the unity of the Holy Spirit, God through all the ages of ages. Amen.

3. Therefore, O Lord, as you have taught us by your word that heaven and earth shall pass away rather than your word, so we firmly believe that not even the least particle will ever fall. And as we believe that your Son, once offered for us, made reconciliation to the Father, so we also firmly believe that he offered himself to be the food of our souls under the forms of bread and wine; so that the memory of his generous deed may never be abolished. Increase our faith, if it falters in any way; and grant that as your Son brought us back into your grace through the shame and bitterness of the cross and provided us with everlasting delights, so with him as leader and protector may we overcome the hardships and afflictions of this world, while we eat his body and drink his blood. For he gave himself to us as food, so that just as he himself vanquished the world, we, nourished by him, might hope to vanquish it in turn. In vain do we say that we make remembrance of him and what he did, if we do it by word alone. Grant us, therefore, merciful Father, through Christ your Son our Lord, through whom you give life to all things, and through whom you renew and sustain all things, that we may show him forth in our lives; so that the likeness which we lost in Adam may be restored. And in order that this may take place in us the more effectively and surely, grant that all we who partake of the body and blood of your Son may have one hope and purpose, and be ourselves one in him, as he is one with you. Through the same Christ our Lord.

4. O God, among those born of women none has arisen greater than your Son, and you have deigned to reveal that he is the Lamb to take away our sins. Through him be ready to hear our cry, "O Lamb of God, you take away the sins of the world, have mercy on us." In our kindness forgive all our faults. For he suffered, that through him we might have perpetual access to you: he wished to be clothed with our weakness, that in him we might have strength: he gave himself as food, that we might be nourished by him and grow into the fullness of his perfect life. O Lord, draw our hearts by your gracious light, that we may worthily and faithfully join in the sacred banquet of your Son, of which he himself is both our host and our most delectable food.

For on the night on which he was betrayed, he took bread, and giving thanks, he blessed and broke it, and gave it to his disciples, and said:

Take and eat. This is my body, which is given for you. Do this in remembrance of me.

Likewise the cup, after they had eaten; he took it, offered thanks, and gave it to them, saying:

Drink of this, all of you. For this is my blood of the new testament which is shed for you in the remission of sins. Do this, as often as you drink it, in remembrance of me.

For as often as you eat this bread and drink this cup, you proclaim the death of the Lord, until he comes.

Therefore come to me, all you who labor and are heavy laden, and I will give you rest.

COMMUNION
The body of our Lord Jesus Christ preserve you to everlasting life. The blood of our Lord Jesus Christ preserve you to everlasting life.

BRIEF THANKSGIVING
NUNC DIMITTIS
BLESSING

Ulrich Zwingli

b. *Action or Use of the Lord's Supper* (1525)

PREFACE

PRAYERS AND INTERCESSIONS

SERMON

CONFESSION OF SINS

PRAYER FOR PARDON

PREPARATION OF THE ELEMENTS

COLLECT

EPISTLE (1 Corinthians 11:20–29)

GLORIA IN EXCELSIS (said antiphonally: omitted in the 1529 edition)

GOSPEL (John 6:47–63)

APOSTLES' CREED (said antiphonally: omitted in the 1529 edition)

EXHORTATION

LORD'S PRAYER

PRAYER OF HUMBLE ACCESS

THE WAY CHRIST INSTITUTED THIS SUPPER
The pastor reads as follows:

On the night when he was betrayed and given up to death, Jesus took bread; and when he had given thanks he broke it, and said, "Take, eat; this is my body: do this in remembrance of me." In the same manner also, he took the cup after supper, said thanks, and gave it to them, saying, "Drink this, all of you: this cup is the new testament in my blood. Do this as often as you drink it, in remembrance of me. For as often as you eat this bread and drink this cup, you proclaim and glorify the Lord's death."

Then the designated ministers carry around the unleavened bread, from which each one of the faithful takes a morsel or mouthful with his hand, or has it offered to him by the minister who carries the bread around. And when those with the bread have proceeded so far that everyone has eaten his small piece, the other ministers then follow with the cup, and in the same manner give it to each person to drink. And all of this takes place with such honor and propriety as well becomes the Church of God and the Supper of Christ.

Ulrich Zwingli

Afterwards, the people having eaten and drunk, thanks is given according to the example of Christ, by the use of Psalm 113:1–9.

BRIEF THANKSGIVING
DISMISSAL

26 Martin Luther:
a. *Formula Missae* 1523 and
b. *Deutsche Messe* 1526

Luther's first major statement on liturgical matters appeared in
1520 in his *Babylonian Captivity of the Church*, where he urged the
need for a vernacular liturgy, declared the Last Supper to be the
standard of every eucharist, and attacked the Roman rite for its
denial of the chalice to the laity and its doctrines of transubstantiation and the sacrifice of the Mass. His attempt to give practical
expression to these views came three years later in *Formula Missae
et Communionis*, which displayed a remarkable blend of conservatism and radicalism. On the one hand he had a deep sense of
continuity with the traditional forms of worship, showing no desire for a completely new service which might be regarded as a
symbol of a particular person. What was needed was purification,
removing from the historic Mass "the wretched accretions which
corrupt it" and ensuring that it expressed the mind of the New
Testament and early Christianity. There was therefore little to
which he objected in the first part of the rite, and traditional
Latin, vestments, and ceremonial were retained. On the other
hand after the Nicene Creed there was significant change.

The Offertory disappeared, because "from here on almost everything smacks and savors of sacrifice." The bread and wine were
prepared after the Creed or sermon, followed by a new and
shorter eucharistic prayer of Sursum corda, brief preface and Institution Narrative, now chanted audibly by the priest. The Sanctus
and Benedictus no longer concluded the preface but came after
the Narrative; and during the Benedictus there was an elevation,
retained "for the benefit of the weak in faith" as a dramatic proclamation of the Gospel—the seal and sign of the Testament. The
Pax was also retained as a declaration of the forgiveness of sins—
"the one and most worthy preparation for the Lord's Table." Communion was administered in both kinds: but Luther made the provision that if so desired the Narrative could be split into two, and
the bread and wine administered separately as a literal following

of Christ's example. He admitted that this raised problems with the Sanctus and other ensuing devotions, but he offered no solution to the difficulty. In this eucharistic pattern Luther believed that he had secured the right emphasis: attention was focussed on the Narrative—the heart of the Gospel. The eucharist was a testament, conveying God's gracious gift to men: whereas the Roman rite had done the opposite, expressing a sacrifice offered by men to God.

Formula Missae seems to have had little immediate effect. Instead more radical rites appeared, to Luther's anger and dismay: "some have the best intentions, but others have no more than an itch to produce something novel so that they might shine before men as leading lights." After experiment, therefore, and with help from Johann Bugenhagen and Justus Jonas, two other young reformers, he published his *Deutsche Messe* in 1526, intended as a rite for "unlearned lay folk" with both German words and German music. Once again there was little change in the first part of the rite save for the omission of the Gloria in excelsis. But in the eucharistic action itself there was more revision. The Institution Narrative was still central, but the Sursum corda and the preface were replaced by a paraphrase of the Lord's Prayer and an Exhortation to Communion. This form, however, beginning with the injunction to "lift up your hearts" and including intercessions, together with a request to use a prescribed form of words, leading into the Institution Narrative, suggested a further development in Luther's concept of a eucharistic prayer. The splitting of the Narrative and the administration now became mandatory; and a solution to the accompanying devotions was provided. The consecration of the bread was followed by the German Sanctus or the popular Corpus Christi hymn "God be blest" or the Hus hymn "Jesus Christ our God and Savior," during which there was an elevation; while the consecration of the wine was followed by Agnus Dei or the remainder of the hymns.

Many of these changes did not prove to be popular: indeed the only one to gain wide acceptance was the placing of the Lord's Prayer and Exhortation before the Institution Narrative. What emerged were a series of Church Orders which fell into two main groups—the Brandenburg-Nürnberg family following the more conservative *Formula Missae* and the Bugenhagen family following *Deutsche Messe*. But Luther's share in the development of Lutheran rites cannot be judged simply by the forms he himself produced. Other rites for which he himself was not responsible emerged; and of some of these he was critical. Nevertheless, they owed their existence to the impetus he provided.

It should be noted that of the works referred to in the Bibliography, Brilioth's *Eucharistic Faith and Practice* in 1930 was a pioneer study, adopting a rather critical view of Luther's work as a liturgist. Other subsequent writers—Bouyer, Maxwell, and Reed—tended to repeat his views. More recently, however, Spinks has re-examined Luther's writing and has produced a rather different and much more positive estimate.

BIBLIOGRAPHY
Coena Domini I (1983), pp. 33–39.
Bouyer, pp. 384–391.
Y. Brilioth, *Eucharistic Faith and Practice Evangelical and Catholic* (1930), pp. 94–144.
Ulrich S. Leupold (ed.), *Luther's Works* (American edition), vol. 53 (1965), pp. 15–40, 51–90.
W. D. Maxwell, *An Outline of Christian Worship* (1945), pp. 73–80.
N. Micklem(ed.), *Christian Worship* (1936), pp. 119–136.
Luther D. Reed, *The Lutheran Liturgy* (1947, 1959) pp.69–87.
F. C. Senn, "Martin Luther's Revision of the Eucharistic Canon in the *Formula Missae* of 1523," *Concordia Theological Monthly*, vol.44 (1973), pp. 101–118.
B. D. Spinks, *Luther's Liturgical Criteria and his Reform of the Canon of the Mass*, (Grove Liturgical Study 30, 1981). This contains extensive reference to other works on Luther.
Bard Thompson, pp. 95–137.

a. Formula Missae et Communionis for the Church at Wittenberg 1523

. . . That utter abomination follows which forces all that precedes in the Mass into its service and is, therefore, called the offertory. From here on almost everything smacks and savors of sacrifice. And the words of life and salvation (the Words of Institution) are imbedded in the midst of it all, just as the ark of the Lord once stood in the idol's temple next to Dagon. And there was no Israelite who could approach or bring back the ark until it "smote his enemies in the hinder parts, putting them to a perpetual reproach," and forced them to return it—which is a parable of the present time. Let us, therefore, repudiate everything that smacks of sacrifice, together with the entire canon and retain only that which is pure and holy, and so order our mass.

I. After the Creed or after the sermon let bread and wine be made ready for blessing in the customary manner. I have not yet decided whether or not water should be mixed with the wine. I rather incline, however, to favor pure wine without water; for the passage, "Thy wine is mixed with water," in Isaiah 1:22 gives the mixture a bad connotation.

Pure wine beautifully portrays the purity of gospel teaching. Further, the blood of Christ, whom we here commemorate, has been poured out unmixed with ours. Nor can the fancies of those be upheld who say that this is a sign of our union with Christ; for that is not what we commemorate. In fact, we are not united with Christ until he sheds his blood; or else we would be celebrating the shedding of our own blood together with the blood of Christ shed for us. Nonetheless, I have no intention of cramping anyone's freedom or of introducing a law which might again lead to superstition. Christ will not care very much about these matters, nor are they worth arguing about. Enough foolish controversies have been fought on these and many other matters by the Roman and Greek churches. And though some direct attention to the water and blood which flowed from the side of Jesus, they prove nothing. For that water signified something entirely different from what they wish that mixed water to signify. Nor was it mixed with blood. The symbolism does not fit, and the reference is inapplicable. As a human invention, this mixing (of water and wine) cannot, therefore, be considered binding.

II. The bread and wine having been prepared, one may proceed as follows:
The Lord be with you.
Response: *And with thy spirit.*
Lift up your hearts.

Response: *Let us lift them to the Lord.*
Let us give thanks unto the Lord our God.
Response: *It is meet and right.*
It is truly meet and right, just and salutary for us to give thanks to Thee always and everywhere, Holy Lord, Father Almighty, Eternal God, through Christ our Lord . . .

III. Then: . . . *Who the day before he suffered, took bread, and when he had given thanks, brake it, and gave it to his disciples, saying, Take, eat; this is my body, which is given for you.*

After the same manner also the cup, when he had supped, saying, This cup is the New Testament in my blood, which is shed for you and for many, for the remission of sins; this do, as often as ye do it, in remembrance of me.

I wish these words of Christ—with a brief pause after the preface—to be recited in the same tone in which the Lord's Prayer is chanted elsewhere in the canon, so that those who are present may be able to hear them, although the evangelically minded should be free about all these things and may recite these words either silently or audibly.

IV. The blessing ended, let the choir sing the Sanctus. And while the Benedictus is being sung, let the bread and cup be elevated according to the customary rite for the benefit of the weak in faith who might be offended if such an obvious change in this rite of the Mass were suddenly made. This concession can be made especially where through sermons in the vernacular they have been taught what the elevation means.

V. After this, the Lord's Prayer shall be read. Thus, *Let us pray: Taught by thy saving precepts.* . . . The prayer which follows, *Deliver us, we beseech thee* . . . , is to be omitted together with all the signs they were accustomed to make over the host and with the host over the chalice. Nor shall the host be broken or mixed into the chalice. But immediately after the Lord's Prayer shall be said, *The peace of the Lord,* etc., which is, so to speak, a public absolution of the sins of the communicants, the true voice of the gospel announcing remission of sins, and therefore the one and most worthy preparation for the Lord's Table, if faith holds to these words as coming from the mouth of Christ himself. On this account I would like to have it pronounced facing the people, as the bishops are accustomed to do, which is the only custom of the ancient bishops that is left among our bishops.

VI. Then, while the Agnus Dei is sung, let him (the liturgist) communicate, first himself and then the people. But if he should wish to pray the prayer, *O Lord Jesus Christ, Son of the Living God, who according to the will of the Father*, etc., before the communion, he does not pray wrongly, provided he changes the singular *mine* and *me* to the plural *ours* and *us*. The same thing holds for the prayer, *The body of our Lord Jesus Christ preserve my (or thy) soul unto life eternal*, and *The blood of our Lord preserve thy soul unto life eternal*.

VII. If he desires to have the communion sung, let it be sung. But instead of the *complenda* or final collect, because it sounds almost like a sacrifice, let the following prayer be read in the same tone: *What we have taken with our lips, O Lord. . . .* The following one may also be read: *May thy body which we have received . . .* (changing to the plural number) *. . . who livest and reignest world without end. The Lord be with you*, etc. In place of the *Ite missa*, let the *Benedicamus domino* be said, adding Alleluia according to its own melodies where and when it is desired. Or the *Benedicamus* may be borrowed from Vespers.

VIII. The customary benediction may be given; or else the one from Numbers 6:24–27, which the Lord himself appointed:

The Lord bless us and keep us. The Lord make his face shine upon us and be gracious unto us. The Lord lift up his countenance upon us, and give us peace.

Or the one from Psalm 67:6–7:

God, even our own God shall bless us. God shall bless us; and all the ends of the earth shall fear him

I believe Christ used something like this when, ascending into heaven, he blessed his disciples (Luke 24:50–51)

The bishop should also be free to decide on the order in which he will receive and administer both species. He may choose to bless both bread and wine before he takes the bread. Or else he may, between the blessing of the bread and of the wine, give the bread both to himself and to as many as desire it, then bless the wine and administer it to all. This is the order Christ seems to have observed, as the words of the Gospel show, where he told them to eat the bread before he had blessed the cup (Mark 14:22–23). Then is said expressly, *Likewise also the cup after he supped* (Luke 22:20; 1 Corinthians 11:25). Thus you see that the cup was not blessed until after the bread had been eaten. But this order is (now) quite new and allows no room for those prayers which heretofore were said after the blessing, unless they would also be changed.

Thus we think about the Mass. But in all these matters we will want to beware lest we make binding what should be free, or make sinners of those who may do some things differently or omit others. All that matters is that the Words of Institution should be kept intact and that everything should be done by faith. For these rites are supposed to be for Christians, i.e. children of the "free woman" (Galatians 4:31), who observe them voluntarily and from the heart, but are free to change them how and when ever they wish. Therefore, it is not in these matters that anyone should either seek or establish as law some indispensable form by which he might ensnare or harass consciences. Nor do we find any evidence for such an established rite, either in the early Fathers or in the primitive church, but only in the Roman church. But even if they had decreed anything in this matter as a law, we would not have to observe it, because these things neither can nor should be bound by laws.

b. *The German Mass* 1526

HYMN or GERMAN PSALM
KYRIES
COLLECT
EPISTLE
GERMAN HYMN
GOSPEL
APOSTLES' CREED in German hymn form—*In one true God we all believe*

Martin Luther   195

SERMON

After the sermon shall follow a public paraphrase of the Lord's Prayer and admonition for those who want to partake of the sacrament, in this or a better fashion:

Friends in Christ: since we are here assembled in the name of the Lord to receive his Holy Testament, I admonish you first of all to lift up your hearts to God to pray with me the Lord's Prayer, as Christ our Lord has taught us and graciously promised to hear us.

That God, our Father in heaven, may look with mercy on us, his needy children on earth, and grant us grace so that his holy name be hallowed by us and all the world through the pure and true teaching of his Word and the fervent love of our lives; that he would graciously turn from us all false doctrine and evil living whereby his precious name is being blasphemed and profaned.

That his kingdom may come to us and expand; that all transgressors and they who are blinded and bound in the devil's kingdom be brought to know Jesus Christ his Son by faith, and that the number of Christians may be increased.

That we may be strengthened by his Spirit to do and to suffer his will, both in life and in death, in good and in evil things, and always to break, slay, and sacrifice our own wills.

That he would also give us our daily bread, preserve us from greed and selfish cares, and help us to trust that he will provide for all our needs.

That he would forgive our debts as we forgive our debtors, so that our hearts may rest and rejoice in a good conscience before him, and that no sin may ever fright or alarm us.

That he would not lead us into temptation but help us by his Spirit to subdue the flesh, to despise the world and its ways, and to overcome the devil with all his wiles.

And lastly, that he would deliver us from all evil, both of body and soul, now and forever.

All those who earnestly desire these things will say from their very hearts: Amen, trusting without any doubt that it is Yea and answered in heaven as Christ has promised: Whatever you ask in prayer, believe that you shall receive it, and you will (Mark 11:24). Amen.

Secondly, I admonish you in Christ that you discern the Testament of Christ in true faith and, above all, take to heart the words wherein Christ imparts to us his body and his blood for the remission of our sins. That you remember and give thanks for his boundless love which he proved to us when he redeemed us from God's wrath, sin, death, and hell by his own blood. And that in this faith you externally receive the bread and wine, i.e. his body and his blood, as the pledge and guarantee of this. In his name therefore, and according to the command that he gave, let us use and receive the Testament.

Whether such paraphrase and admonition should be read in the pulpit immediately after the sermon or at the altar, I would leave to everyone's judgement. It seems that the ancients did so in the pulpit, so that it is still the custom to read general prayers or to repeat the Lord's Prayer in the pulpit. But the admonition itself has since become a public confession. In this way, however, the Lord's Prayer together with a short exposition would be current among the people, and the Lord would be remembered, even as he commanded at the Supper.

I would, however, like to ask that this paraphrase or admonition followed a prescribed wording or be formulated in a definite manner for the sake of the common people. We cannot have one do it one way today, and another, another way tomorrow, and let everybody parade his talents and confuse the people so that they can neither learn nor retain anything. What chiefly matters is the teaching and guiding of the people. That is why we must limit our freedom and keep to one form of paraphrase or admonition, particularly in a given church or congregation—if for the sake of freedom it does not wish to use another.

Thereupon THE OFFICE *and* CONSECRATION. . . .

Our Lord Jesus Christ, in the night in which he was betrayed, took bread; and when he had given thanks, he brake it and gave it to his disciples, saying, Take, eat; this is my body, which is given for you; this do in remembrance of me. After the same manner also, he took the cup, when he had supped, and when he had given thanks, he gave it to them, saying, Drink ye all of it; this cup is the New Testament in my blood, which is shed for you, and for many, for the remission of sins; this do, as oft as ye drink it, in remembrance of me.

It seems to me that it would accord with (the institution of) the Lord's Supper to administer the sacrament immediately after the consecration of the bread, before the cup is blessed; for both Luke and Paul say: He took the cup after they had supped, etc.(Luke 22:20; 1 Corinthians 11:25). Meanwhile, the German Sanctus or the hymn *Let God be blest*, or the hymn of John Hus, *Jesus Christ, our God and Savior*, could be sung. Then shall the cup be blessed and administered, while the remainder of these hymns are sung, or the German Agnus Dei. Let there be a decent and orderly approach, not men and women together, but the women after the men, wherefore they should also stand apart from each other in separate places. What should be done about the private confession, I have written elsewhere, and my opinion can be found in the *Betbüchlein*.

We do not want to abolish the elevation, but retain it because it goes well with the German Sanctus and signifies that Christ has commanded us to remember him. For just as the sacrament is bodily elevated, and yet Christ's body and blood are not seen in it, so he is also remembered and elevated by the word of the sermon and is confessed and adored in the reception of the sacrament. In each case he is apprehended only by faith, for we cannot see how Christ gives his body and blood for us and even now daily shows and offers it before God to obtain grace for us.

THE GERMAN SANCTUS

Isaiah 'twas the prophet who did see
Seated above the Lord in majesty
High on a lofty throne in splendor bright;
The train of his robe filled the temple quite.
Standing beside him were two seraphim;
Six wings, six wings he saw on each of them.
With twain they hid in awe their faces clear;

Martin Luther

With twain they hid their feet in rev'rent fear.
And with the other twain they flew about:
One to the other loudly raised the shout:
Holy is God, the Lord of Sabaoth,
Holy is God, the Lord of Sabaoth,
Holy is God, the Lord of Sabaoth,
Behold his glory filleth all the earth.
The angels' cry made beams and lintels shake;
The house also was filled with clouds of smoke.

POST-COMMUNION COLLECT
AARONIC BLESSING

Martin Luther

27 Olavus Petri: *The Swedish Mass* 1531

Liturgical reform in Sweden provides an interesting parallel with
that in Germany, being Lutheran in character with little or no
Zwinglian or Calvinistic influence. It owed a great debt to Olavus
Petri, who had been a student at Wittenberg from 1516 to 1518.
His Swedish Mass, which appeared in Stockholm in 1531, was
one of the most complete early Lutheran liturgies in the
vernacular. While it could be generally regarded as a rite of Luther's *Formula Missae* type, it was also indebted to Döber's
Evangelische Messe, a rite used at Nuremberg in the hospital chapel
from 1524 onwards, which Petri discovered at Rostock on the Bal-
tic. Like Luther, Petri retained the order of the medieval Roman
rite but introduced some distinctive features. He replaced the old
Latin *confiteor* of the priest by a congregational confession in the
vernacular, one of the first Lutheran rites to do so. He also introduced after the Sursum corda quite a lengthy preface of penitential character, but including the incarnation, death, and resurrection of Jesus Christ. Brilioth believed it to have been based—at
least in general idea though not in wording—on the Roman Paschal Preface; while Bouyer, although in general agreement,
thought it might also have been the first instance of a Protestant
rite being influenced by the Eastern liturgies, which Petri knew,
or at least by the Greek Fathers. The Institution Narrative was
accompanied by an elevation and was followed, as in *Formula
Missae*, by Sanctus and Benedictus. The exhortation before Communion became optional, being used "if the priest think it necessary and the time permit": strongly penitential in character, it
closely resembled that of the Church Order of Nuremberg. The
Nuremberg practice of singing the Nunc Dimittis during the administration was also adopted.

This rite, like Luther's, was not intended to displace the Latin
high mass, but replaced the Latin low mass at which people communicated at a side altar. In fact the Swedish mass and the Latin
high mass existed side by side for some years, until the former
supplanted the latter, at the same time adding some of the latter's
liturgical and ceremonial features. These became evident in the

Olavus Petri

revisions of Olavus Petri's younger brother, Laurentius, Archbishop of Uppsala. Laurentius Petri revised the 1531 rite five times before producing his own Church Order of 1571, the culmination of thirty years' work, and to all intents and purposes a Swedish high mass. It embodied the positive results of the whole Swedish Reformation. While remaining distinctively Lutheran, it restored certain traditional features, principally the system of pericopes, the sermon, and the proper prefaces. These prefaces, together with the introit, the gradual, and the creed, could—if so desired—be sung in Latin to their traditional chants. Furthermore, if the proper prefaces were used, they concluded with the singing of the Sanctus, thereby restoring it to its traditional position.

For some years from 1576 onwards this Church Order of Laurentius Petri was eclipsed by the rite from the notorious Red Book produced by King John III, himself a zealous liturgist and patristic scholar. This rite, which restored the Offertory and included a Canon based on the latter part of the traditional Roman Canon, satisfied neither Catholics nor Protestants and was rejected after his death in 1592. Sweden then returned to the Petri Church Order of 1571, which remained practically intact until the present day.

BIBLIOGRAPHY
Coena Domini I (1983), pp.113–121.
Bouyer, pp. 396–407.
Y. Brilioth, *Eucharistic Faith and Practice Evangelical and Catholic* (1930), pp.231–253.
Luther D. Reed, *The Lutheran Liturgy* (1947, 1959), pp.111–127.
F. C. Senn, "Liturgia Svecanae Ecclesiae," in *Studia Liturgica*, vol.14 (1980), pp. 20–36.
E.E. Yelverton, *The Mass in Sweden* (Henry Bradshaw Society, vol.57,1920).

INVITATION AND CONFESSION
PRAYER OF FORGIVENESS AND GRACE
INTROIT
KYRIES
GLORIA IN EXCELSIS
SALUTATION

COLLECT
EPISTLE
GRADUAL HYMN
GOSPEL
APOSTLES' OR NICENE CREED

Then the priest commences the Preface, saying thus:

The Lord be with you.
R̞. And with your spirit.
Lift up your hearts to God.
R̞. We lift up our hearts.
Let us give thanks unto our Lord God.
R̞. It is right and meet.

Truly it is meet, right and blessed that we should in all places give
you thanks and praise, holy Lord, almighty Father, everlasting
God, for all your benefits; and especially for that benefit which
you gave us when by reason of sins we were all in so bad a case
that nothing but damnation and eternal death awaited us, and no
creature in heaven or earth could help us. Then you sent forth
your only-begotten son Jesus Christ, who was of the same divine
nature as yourself; you suffered him to become a man for our
sake; you laid our sins upon him; and you suffered him to un-
dergo death instead of our all dying eternally. And as he has overcome death and risen again and now is alive for evermore, so
likewise shall all those who put their trust in him overcome sin
and death and through him attain to everlasting life.

And for our admonition that we should bear in mind and never
forget such a benefit, in the night that he was betrayed, he celebrated a supper, in which he took the bread in his holy hands,
gave thanks to his heavenly Father, blessed it, broke it, and gave
it to his disciples, and said: Take and eat; this is my body which
will be given for you; do this in remembrance of me.

Then the priest lifts it up, lays it down again, and takes the cup, saying:

Likewise also he took the cup in his holy hands, gave thanks to
his heavenly Father, blessed it, and gave it to his disciples and
said: Take and drink all from this; this is the cup of the new testament in my blood, which will be shed for you and for many for

Olavus Petri

the remission of sins; as often as you do this, do it in remembrance of me.

Then he lifts it up and sets it down again.

Then is read or sung

Holy, holy, holy, Lord God of Sabaoth; heaven and earth are full of your glory. Hosanna in the highest. Blessed is he who comes in the name of the Lord. Hosanna in the highest.

Then the priest says:

Let us all now pray as our Lord Jesus Christ himself has taught us, saying,

Our Father . . .

Then the priest turns to the people and says:

The peace of the Lord be with you.
And also with your spirit.

AGNUS DEI
EXHORTATION (OPTIONAL)

Afterwards he administers the bread to the people and says:

The body of our Lord Jesus Christ preserve your soul unto everlasting life. Amen.

Afterwards the cup, saying:

The blood of our Lord Jesus Christ, etc.

HYMN OR NUNC DIMITTIS (in Swedish)
SALUTATION
POST-COMMUNION COLLECT (FIXED)
BENEDICAMUS
AARONIC BLESSING

Olavus Petri   203

28 Martin Bucer: *The Psalter, with complete Church Practice,* 1539

Martin Bucer was a Dominican monk who came into contact with Luther in 1518 and was excommunicated five years later when he began to preach Lutheranism actively. At approximately the same time he went to live in Strasbourg, where Diebold Schwarz, another former Dominican monk, celebrated the first Reformed mass in German on February 16, 1524. This was very conservative, being an almost literal translation of the Roman rite with certain omissions or modifications which had the effect of excluding all reference to the sacrifice of the Mass. From 1525 onwards Bucer became increasingly influential in church affairs in the city and was largely responsible for the thirteen revisions of Schwarz's rite which took place between 1526 and 1539, moving towards greater simplicity, a greater emphasis on preaching, and a greater element of congregational participation. In 1539 he published his service book *The Psalter with complete Church Practice*. In this the Mass had become the Lord's Supper; the priest had become the pastor or minister; he celebrated at the holy table facing the congregation; and vestments had been replaced by the cassock and black gown. Only the principal festivals of the year were observed, although the eucharist was celebrated every Sunday in the cathedral and monthly in the parish churches. The Word had also assumed a greater significance: the epistle had disappeared, but the Gospels were read through systematically Sunday by Sunday and the reading was then expounded in the sermon. Bucer firmly believed that the Holy Spirit worked through the preaching of the Gospel and that by this means the people received spiritual food.

Bucer's sacramental views represented a *via media* between those of Luther and Zwingli. Like Luther he asserted that the communicant did indeed receive the body and blood of Christ; but like Zwingli he denied that the body and blood were united to the sacramental signs of bread and wine. His own view stated in 1530 in his *Nine Propositions concerning the Holy Eucharist* was that the communicant only received bread and wine; but when doing so his faith uplifted him to a real participation of the body and blood of Christ in heaven. So the Exhortation appended to the sermon stated, "The Lord truly offers and gives his holy and sanctifying body and blood to us in the Holy Supper, with the visible things of bread and wine, through the ministry of the Church."

After the Sermon and Exhortation came the Apostles' Creed in a German metrical version—or a psalm or a hymn—and the elements were prepared without words or ceremony. Then followed a choice of three eucharistic prayers: the first was the original form, and the second and third were added about 1536: the third was the basis of Calvin's Great Prayer and that of the 1562 *Scottish Book of Common Order*. The minister was not limited to this choice, however; he was free to use his own form of words if he so desired. In the three prayers provided the Sursum corda, preface, Sanctus and Benedictus all disappeared, but there were nevertheless elements of a traditional eucharistic prayer—intercession, a memorial of Christ's saving work, a prayer of humble access and a prayer for a good communion with a specific reference in the first and third of lifting up the hearts to God. It could be said that what the prayers were concerned with was not a consecration of the bread and wine but of the communicants themselves. They all ended with the Lord's Prayer, after which the minister read the Institution Narrative, followed immediately—as in Luther—by communion. There was a single Word of Delivery, simply exhorting the communicants—as in Zwingli—to remember, believe, and proclaim that Christ had died for them. Communion was received standing or kneeling at the table, the bread being distributed at the north end and the cup at the south. The rite then ended briefly with a psalm or hymn, a choice of three thanksgivings, and the blessing and dismissal. This Strasbourg rite of Bucer had considerable influence on later reformed rites, particularly those of Calvin and Scotland. Hermann also used it in the preparation of his *Consultation*, and it therefore had some influence on Anglican rites.

BIBLIOGRAPHY
Coena Domini I (1983), pp.317–325.
W. D. Maxwell, *An Outline of Christian Worship* (1945), pp.87–111. *The Liturgical Portions of the Genevan Service Book* (1965),pp.24–32,188–198.

Bard Thompson, pp. 159–181.

G. J. Van de Poll, *Martin Bucer's Liturgical Ideas* (1954).

Order for the Lord's Supper

CONFESSION (3 forms)

ABSOLUTION or WORD OF COMFORT

PSALM or HYMN

KYRIE ELEISON (sometimes)

GLORIA IN EXCELSIS (sometimes)

PRAYER FOR ILLUMINATION

PSALM

GOSPEL

SERMON

EXHORTATION (or before INSTITUTION NARRATIVE)

APOSTLES' CREED (or PSALM or HYMN)

PREPARATION OF THE ELEMENTS

The Pastor stands behind the Table and speaks to the people:

The Lord be with you.

Let us pray.

Then he leads the prayer, with these or similar words:

Almighty God, merciful God and Father, you have promised us through your Son, that you will grant us whatever we ask of you in his name; and you have also commanded us through your Spirit to pray for those in authority and for all men. We heartily pray, through your beloved Son our Savior Jesus Christ, that you will enlighten with the knowledge of your Gospel the hearts of our lord emperor and king, all princes and nobles, and the magistrates and ruling body of this city, that they and all those in power may acknowledge you as their true and sovereign Lord, serve you with fear and trembling, and rule over us, who are your handiwork and the sheep of your pasture, according to your will and good pleasure.

Bring all men everywhere to the knowledge of the truth. In particular send upon this congregation, now assembled in your name, your Holy Spirit, the Master and Teacher, that he may write your law upon our hearts, take away our blindness, and lead us to acknowledge our sin, which otherwise is death, and whose baseness and shame is hidden from us. Make it clear to us, O Lord, and enlighten our eyes, that we may see the truth and recognize that there is indeed nothing in us except sin, death, hell and your deserved wrath. Grant that we may hunger and thirst after the rich springs of your goodness and grace, and gratefully receive of them what you have given to us through your only-begotten Son, who, having become man like us poor sinners, suffered, died, and rose from the dead, that he might save us from sin, death and hell, and bring us to the resurrection and our inheritance of the kingdom of God.

Grant us, Lord and Father, that we may celebrate with true faith this Supper of your dear Son, our Lord Jesus, as he has commanded, so that we truly receive and enjoy the true communion of his body and blood, of our Savior himself, the truly heavenly bread of salvation. In this holy sacrament, he wills to offer and give himself so that he may live in us, and we in him, as members of his body, serving you fruitfully in every way for the building up of your Church, set free from every passion of our evil and corrupt flesh, from all anger, vexation, envy, hatred, selfishness, lewdness, unchastity, and any other wicked works of the flesh. So that we may, as your obedient children, always and in every way lift our hearts and souls to you with real childlike trust, and call upon you, saying as our Lord Jesus Christ, our only Master and Savior, has taught us: Our Father . . .

Another prayer

Almighty, heavenly Father, you have promised through your Son, our Lord Jesus Christ, that you will give us whatever we ask in his name; and you have commanded us to pray for all men, and especially for those who are in authority. We therefore pray, dear and faithful Father, through your Son our Savior, for our lord emperor and king, for all princes and nobles, and for all the magistrates of this city. Give your Spirit and a godly fear to those whom you have set to rule over us in your stead, that they may administer their office in accordance with your will and for your glory, that your children everywhere may lead calm and peaceful lives, in all godliness and propriety.

We also pray for all who are called to be pastors of your Church and proclaim your holy word. Grant them your word and Spirit that they may so serve you that all your elect may be drawn to you, and those who already bear your name and are counted as Christians may be true to their calling, promote your glory, and build up your Church.

We pray also for those whom you chasten through sickness and other adversity. Enable them to recognize your gracious hand and accept your discipline for their health's sake, that in your grace you may grant them comfort and help.

And we pray for those who have not yet heard your holy word, but remain in error and depravity. Enlighten their eyes that they recognize you as their God and creator, and accept your will.

We also pray, heavenly Father, for ourselves here present, that we may be gathered in your name. Drive from our hearts and souls all that displeases you. Help us to understand that in you we live and have our being; and that our sins are so heavy and grievous that only by the death of your Son, our Lord Jesus Christ, could we be restored to your life and grace. Help us to grasp by true faith how great is your love for us, that you have given your dear Son to die for us, so that when we believe in him we shall not perish but have everlasting life. Merciful God and Father, draw our hearts and souls to your Son, that as he gives himself to us in his holy Gospel and sacraments, and bestows his body and blood that we, corrupt as we are, may live in him, so may we receive a love such as his with lively faith and eternal gratitude, and so day by day increasingly die to all evil, grow and increase in all goodness and lead our lives in all soberness, patience and love towards our neighbor. It is to this that our Lord calls us and invites us through his holy Gospel and the sacraments. Wherefore, heavenly Father, grant that we may now receive and enjoy the same in true faith for our salvation, always as true and living members of him who is our Lord and your dear Son; and through him may we be your true and obedient children, always calling upon you and praying to you in a right Spirit

Martin Bucer

and with truly faithful hearts: saying as he himself has taught us:
Our Father . . .

Another prayer

Almighty God and heavenly Father, you have promised through
your dear Son, our Lord Jesus Christ, that you will grant to us
whatever we ask in his Name. Your Son our Lord himself and his
beloved apostles taught us to come together in his name, and
promised to be there in the midst of us, and to obtain and procure
for us from you whatever we on earth agree to ask of you. Especially he has commanded us to pray for those whom you have set
over us as rulers and magistrates, and then for the needs both of
your people and of all men. And since we have all gathered together as in your sight, to your praise, and in the name of your
Son, our Lord Jesus: we heartily pray, merciful God and Father,
through our only Savior, your most beloved Son, that you will
graciously forgive us all our sins and offences, and so lift our
hearts and souls to you, that we may be able to ask and implore
you with all our heart, according to your will and pleasure which
alone are righteous.

Therefore, heavenly Father, we pray for our most gracious rulers,
your servants, our lord emperor and king, and all princes, and
nobles, and the magistrates of this city. Grant them always and
increasingly the gift of your holy and right sovereign Spirit, that
they may with a true faith acknowledge you as king of all kings,
and lord of all lords, and your Son, our Lord Jesus, as him to
whom you have given all power in heaven and on earth. May
they so rule over their subjects, the work of your hands and the
sheep of your pasture, in accordance with your good pleasure,
that we both here and everywhere may lead a quiet, peaceful life
in all godliness and sobriety, and by being delivered from the fear
of our enemies, may serve you in all holiness and righteousness.

Furthermore, faithful Father and Savior, we pray for all those you
have appointed as pastors and curates of souls of your faithful
people, and to whom you have entrusted the preaching of your
holy Gospel. Give them increasingly your Holy Sirit, that they
may be found faithful, always serving you in such a way that they

may always gather your poor wandering sheep into the fold of Christ, your Son, their chief shepherd and bishop, and daily be built up by him into all holiness and righteousness, to the eternal praise of your name.

Merciful God and gracious Father, we also pray for all mankind. As it is your will to be known as a Savior to the whole world, so draw to your Son, our Lord Jesus, those who are still estranged from him. And grant to those whom you have drawn to him and taught, that through him our only mediator, you will pardon sin and bestow every grace, that they may grow daily in such knowledge, and being filled with the fruit of all good works, may live without scandal, to your praise and the well-being of their neighbor, and await with confidence the advent and the day of your Son our Lord. And we pray especially for those whom you have disciplined, visiting and chastening them with poverty, misery, sickness, imprisonment and other adversities. Father of mercy and Lord of all consolation, may they recognize your gracious fatherly hand, that they may turn wholeheartedly to you, who alone chastens them, to receive from you as Father comfort and deliverance from all evil.

And may all of us, here gathered before you, in the name of your Son and at your table, O God and Father, truly and profoundly acknowledge the sin and depravity in which we were born, and into which we thrust ourselves more and more deeply by our sinful life. And since there is nothing good in our flesh, indeed since our flesh and blood cannot inherit your kingdom, grant that we may yield ourselves with all our hearts in true faith to your Son, our only Redeemer and Savior. And since, for our sake, he has not only offered his body and blood upon the cross to you for our sin, but also wishes to give them to us for food and drink unto eternal life, grant that we may accept his goodness and gift with complete longing and devotion, and faithfully partake of and enjoy his true Body and true Blood—even himself, our Savior, true God and true man, the only true bread from heaven; so that we may live no more in our sins and depravity, but that he may live in us and we in him—a holy, blessed and eternal life, verily partaking of the true and eternal testament, the covenant of grace, in sure confidence that you will be our gracious Father forever, never again reckoning our sins against us, and in all things providing for us in body and soul, as your heirs and dear children: so that we may at all times give thanks and praise, and glorify your holy name in all that we say and do. Wherefore, heavenly Father, grant that we may celebrate today the glorious and blessed memorial of your dear Son our Lord and proclaim his death, so that we shall continually grow and increase in faith to you and in all goodness. So, in sure confidence, we call upon you now and always, God and Father, and pray as our Lord taught us to pray, saying: Our Father . . .

At the conclusion of this prayer, the minister makes a short exhortation, if he has not done so at the end of the Sermon, to the effect that the Holy Supper is to be observed with true faith and meet devotion; and he explains this Mystery.

After doing this, he reads the account of the Supper from the evangelists and, particularly, Paul.

The Lord Jesus, in the night in which he was betrayed, took bread, and when he had given thanks, he broke it, and gave it to his disciples, and said: Take and eat, this is my body which is given for you; do this in remembrance of me. In the same manner also he took the cup, after they had eaten, and said: This is the cup of the new testament in my blood, which is shed for you and for many for the forgiveness of sins; take and drink from this, all of you. Do this in remembrance of me.

Then, after these words, the Pastor speaks thus:

Believe in the Lord, and give eternal praise and thanks to him.

Herewith he distributes the bread and cup of the Lord, first saying these words:

Remember, believe, and proclaim that Christ the Lord died for you, and gives himself to you for food and drink to eternal life.

Thereupon the church sings "Let God be blest" or another psalm appropriate to the occasion.

Martin Bucer

POST-COMMUNION PRAYER
PRAYER OF THANKSGIVING (3 forms)
AARONIC BLESSING
DISMISSAL

Martin Bucer

29 John Calvin: *The Form of Church Prayers* 1542

In 1536 Calvin was persuaded by Guillaume Farel to join him in establishing a Reformed Church at Geneva, but the opposition of the city authorities to their proposals led to their expulsion in 1538. Calvin then went to Strasbourg, where he came into close association with Bucer and became minister of the congregation of French exiles. Bucer's rite impressed him greatly, and he followed it closely in producing his own French service book in the following year. In 1542 he was recalled to Geneva, where his supporters had gained the ascendancy, and he replaced Farel's rite by a slightly modified form of his own Strasbourg liturgy, reducing the number of alternatives and slightly changing the structure. The full title of the service book gave a clear indication of his liturgical aims—*The Form of Prayers and Manner of Ministering the Sacraments according to the Usage of the Ancient Church.* Like Zwingli and Luther he was hostile to the medieval Roman mass, which involved what he called "magical mumblings." His purpose was to restore the eucharist to its primitive simplicity, with Word and Sacrament holding their rightful place and celebrated weekly as the central service of the Christian community. In creating the content and structure of the rite he was successful: but its establishment on a weekly basis was an ideal which he never succeeded in realizing. It had been a bone of contention during his first stay in Geneva; and now, rather than risk further trouble, he gave way to the magistrates' demands for only quarterly celebrations in the interests of peace. After a fruitless attempt to secure greater flexibility in the timing of eucharists, he finally agreed to the fixed times of Christmas, Easter, Pentecost, and Harvest. It was an arrangement which he never ceased to lament, regarding it as contrary to Scripture.

Like Bucer, he adopted a mediating position on the presence of Christ. The body of the risen and ascended Lord existed in heaven; and it could not be imprisoned and brought down into earthly matter. Nevertheless the sacrament was a divine act and a means of grace: God used the bread and the wine—outwardly nothing—to feed the faithful soul with spiritual food. The communicant therefore had to lift his heart and mind to heaven to receive the Lord. So Calvin's eucharistic prayer or exhortation stated, "Although we see only bread and wine, yet let us not doubt that he accomplishes spiritually in our souls all that he shows us outwardly by these visible signs; in other words, that he is heavenly food. . . . Let us raise our hearts and minds on high, where Jesus Christ is . . . in order to seek him there, as if he were enclosed in the bread or wine."

Calvin did not follow Bucer in including Intercession in his eucharistic prayer. Instead he made it a separate prayer, following the Sermon, although it continued to use a great deal of Bucer's material: it then ended with a lengthy paraphrase of the Lord's Prayer. After this the congregation professed their faith in the Apostles' Creed and the elements were prepared. The minister then proceeded to the Table, where he faced the congregation and read the Institution Narrative from 1 Corinthians 11. This led into the "Eucharistic Prayer," which was in fact not a prayer addressed to God but an exhortation addressed to the congregation. While undoubtedly containing elements reminiscent of both Bucer and Farel, it can legitimately be regarded as Calvin's own handiwork, expressing what he had said originally in his *Institutes* in 1536. It began with a fencing of the table—sinners were excommunicated and the faithful were called upon to examine themselves: then came a declaration of our Lord's promises to feed the faithful with his own body and blood "that he may live in us and we in him," with a very brief reference to his death and Passion: it concluded with the Farel type of Reformed Sursum corda, urging the faithful to raise their hearts and minds on high to receive the body and blood of Christ. In response they came forward to receive communion as in Bucer's rite: while the 1542 edition of the rite made no reference to Words of Delivery, these were provided in later editions and explicitly referred to the real presence—communicants were exhorted to eat and drink the body and blood of Christ. The rite then ended with the customary thanksgiving and blessing.

This rite, which became the basis of many Reformed rites (e.g. that of John Knox), was simple, subdued and austere. It had weaknesses—notably the replacement of the eucharistic prayer by an exhortation containing little of the elements of praise and thanksgiving or commemoration of our Lord's saving work: there was also perhaps an undue stress on worthy participation and holiness of life. Nevertheless it focussed attention on union with the risen and ascended Lord and clearly expressed the fact that the eucharist was the corporate instrument of God's chosen people, wherein they received spiritual sustenance through his Word and sacrament and by means of which they were enabled to show forth his glory.

BIBLIOGRAPHY
Coena Domini I (1983), pp.355–362.
A. Barclay, The Protestant Doctrine of the Lord's Supper (1927).
Y. Brilioth, Eucharistic Faith and Practice Evangelical and Catholic (1930), pp. 164–179.
W. D. Maxwell, An Outline of Christian Worship (1945), pp.112–119. The Liturgical Portions of the Genevan Service Book (1965), pp.17–36.
N. Micklem (ed.), Christian Worship (1936), pp. 154–171.
Bard Thompson, pp. 185–210.

The Manner of celebrating the Supper

SCRIPTURE SENTENCE—PSALM 124:8
CONFESSION
PRAYER FOR PARDON
METRICAL PSALM
PRAYER FOR ILLUMINATION
LESSON
SERMON
INTERCESSIONS
PARAPHRASE OF THE LORD'S PRAYER
APOSTLES' CREED
PLACING OF BREAD AND WINE ON THE TABLE

After the Prayers and the Confession of Faith, to testify in the name of the people that all wish to die in the doctrine and religion of Christ, he (the minister) says aloud:

Let us listen to the institution of the Holy Supper by Jesus Christ, as narrated by St. Paul in the eleventh chapter of the first epistle to the Corinthians:

John Calvin   215

For I have received, he says, from the Lord what I also delivered to you, that the Lord Jesus, on the night when he was betrayed, took bread, and when he had given thanks, he broke it, and said, This is my body, which is broken for you. Do this in remembrance of me. In the same way also he took the cup, after supper, saying, This cup is the new covenant in my blood. Do this, as oft as you drink it, in remembrance of me. For as often as you eat this bread and drink this cup, you will proclaim the Lord's death until he comes. Whoever, therefore, eats the bread or drinks the cup of the Lord in an unworthy manner will be guilty of the body and blood of the Lord. Let a man examine himself, and so eat of this bread and drink of this cup. For anyone who eats and drinks unworthily incurs condemnation, not discerning the Lord's body.

We have heard, brethren, how our Lord celebrated his Supper with his disciples, thereby indicating that strangers, and those who are not of the company of the faithful, ought not to be admitted. Therefore, in accordance with this rule, in the name and by the authority of our Lord Jesus Christ, I excommunicate all idolaters, blasphemers, despisers of God, heretics, and all who form private sects to break the unity of the Church, all perjurers, all who rebel against parents or their superiors, all who are seditious, mutinous, quarrelsome or brutal, all adulterers, fornicators, thieves, ravishers, misers, drunkards, gluttons, and all who lead a scandalous and dissolute life. I declare that they must abstain from this holy table, for fear of defiling and contaminating the holy food which our Lord Jesus Christ gives only to his household and believers.

Therefore, in accordance with the exhortation of St. Paul, let each man prove and examine his conscience, to see whether he has truly repented of his faults, and is dissatisfied with his sins, desiring to live henceforth a holy life and according to God. Above all, let each man see whether he puts his trust in the mercy of God, and seeks his salvation entirely in Jesus Christ; and whether, renouncing all hatred and rancor, he truly intends and resolves to live in peace and brotherly love with his neighbors.

If we have this testimony in our hearts before God, let us have no doubt at all that he claims us for his children, and that the Lord

John Calvin

Jesus addresses his words to us, to invite us to his table, and to present to us this holy sacrament which he communicated to his disciples.

And although we may feel within ourselves much frailty and misery from not having perfect faith, but being inclined to unbelief and distrust; from not being devoted to the service of God so entirely and with such zeal as we ought, but having to war daily against the lusts of our flesh; nevertheless, since our Lord has graciously permitted us to have his gospel imprinted on our hearts, in order to withstand all unbelief, and has given us the desire and longing to renounce our own desires, in order to follow righteousness and his holy commandments, let us all be assured that the sins and imperfections which remain in us will not prevent him from receiving us, and making us worthy to partake of this spiritual table: for we do not come to declare that we are perfect or righteous in ourselves; but, on the contrary, by seeking our life in Christ, we confess that we are in death. Let us therefore understand that this sacrament is a medicine for the spiritually poor and sick, and that the only worthiness which our Savior requires in us is to know ourselves, so as to be dissatisfied with our vices, and have all our pleasure, joy and contentment in him alone.

First, then, let us believe in those promises which Jesus Christ, who is the unfailing truth, has pronounced with his own lips, namely, that he is indeed willing to make us partakers of his own body and blood, in order that we may possess him entirely and in such a manner that he may live in us, and we in him. And although we see only bread and wine, yet let us not doubt that he accomplishes spiritually in our souls all that he shows us outwardly by these visible signs; in other words, that he is heavenly bread, to feed and nourish us unto eternal life.

Next, let us not be unmindful of the infinite goodness of our Savior, who displays all his riches and blessings at this table, in order to give them to us; for, in giving himself to us, he bears testimony to us that all which he has is ours. Moreover, let us receive this sacrament as a pledge that the virtue of his death and Passion is imputed to us for righteousness, just as if we had suffered it in our own persons. Let us never be so perverse as to hold back when Jesus Christ invites us so gently by his word. But, reflecting on the dignity of the precious gift which he gives us, let us present ourselves to him with ardent zeal, in order that he may make us capable of receiving him.

With this in mind, let us raise our hearts and minds on high, where Jesus Christ is, in the glory of his Father, and from whence we look for him at our redemption. Let us not be bemused by these earthly and corruptible elements which we see with the eye, and touch with the hand, in order to seek him there, as if he were enclosed in the bread or wine. Our souls will only then be disposed to be nourished and vivified by his substance, when they are thus raised above all earthly things, and carried as high as heaven, to enter the kingdom of God where he dwells. Let us therefore be content to have the bread and the wine as signs and evidences, spiritually seeking the reality where the word of God promises that we shall find it.

This done, the ministers distribute the bread and cup to the people, having warned them to come forward with reverence and in order. Meanwhile, some psalms are sung, or some passage of Scripture read, suitable to what is signified by the sacrament.

PRAYER OF THANKSGIVING
HYMN OF PRAISE (NUNC DIMITTIS from 1549)
AARONIC BLESSING

John Calvin

30 Hermann von Wied: *A Simple and Religious Consultation* 1545

Hermann von Wied, Archbishop-Elector of Cologne (1477–1552), was noted for the efficient manner in which he administered his archdiocese: discipline was improved and a number of canons removing abuses in the liturgy were passed, although it is doubtful whether they were ever fully observed. Initially hostile to the Reformers, he gradually became sympathetic; and in 1542 he invited Bucer and Melancthon to assist him in drawing up a Church Order. This Order, in which Bucer played a major part, was—at the Archbishop's request—based on the Brandenburg-Nürnberg Order of 1535, compiled by Johannes Brenz and Andreas Osiander, whose niece married Thomas Cranmer. But Bucer also used material from the Albertine Saxony Order (1539–40)—largely the work of Justus Jonas; the Swäbisch-Hall Order (1543) by Johannes Brenz; and from his own work in the Cassel Order (1539) and in his Strasbourg rite of the same year. There were also some original elements. The use of this varied material indicated a confluence of two main streams in the Reformation liturgies—those of Luther and Bucer: this fact made it particularly congenial to Cranmer.

The result was printed in 1543 for private distribution and in the following year for public distribution in German under the title *Einfältiges Bedenken*. This was revised, translated into Latin and republished in 1545 as *Simplex ac Pia Deliberatio*, and an English translation first appeared in 1547 as *A Simple and Religious Consultation*. Hermann's reforming zeal met with hostility both from the Emperor Charles V and Pope Paul III, who excommunicated and deposed him in 1546. He died a Lutheran in 1552. His Reformation at Cologne came to nothing: his Order was never used in the city, and only temporarily in Hesse. But Cranmer made extensive use of it in *The Order of the Communion 1548* and in the 1549 Prayer Book.

The Communion Service, called by Hermann "the Supper of the Lord," although unmistakably Lutheran, was in many ways very traditional. The first part of the rite as far as the Sermon followed the old Roman rite with only two variations. At the beginning, instead of the old *Confiteor* said privately by the priest, there was now a confession in German said by the priest "in the name of the whole Church" together with Comfortable Words and absolution, all borrowed extensively from the Strasbourg rite. Secondly the sermon was followed by intercessions "for all States of Men and Necessities of the Congregation" in longer or shorter form, taken from the Cassel Order and bearing some general resemblance to the 1662 Prayer for the Church. It should be remembered, however, that many congregations would be familiar with intercessions in the vernacular at this point as an element in the Prone.

At the Offertory the communicants made their offerings and then went to their appointed places near the altar for the eucharistic action, the men on one side and the women on the other. The eucharistic prayer then began with Sursum corda and a fixed preface of early Eastern type with thanksgiving for Creation and Redemption, followed by the Sanctus and Benedictus. The Sanctus was sung alternately by the clerks in Latin and by the people in German, while "Lord God of Sabaoth" and Benedictus were sung by everyone in German. This was followed immediately by the Institution Narrative sung by the priest in German "with great reverence and plainly, that they may be well understanded of all men": but, unlike Luther's rites, there was no mention of an elevation. Then came the Lord's Prayer and Peace before communion in both kinds, during which Agnus Dei was sung, again alternately in Latin and German by the clerks and congregation together with the two German hymns as in Luther's *Deutsche Messe*. The rite ended with the two alternative prayers of thanksgiving and the four alternative blessings from the Brandenburg-Nürnberg Order. The final rubrics made it clear that where there were no clerks, as for example in village congregations, everything was in German.

BIBLIOGRAPHY
Coena Domini I (1983), pp. 336–337.
F. E. Brightman, *The English Rite*, 2 vols. (1915), passim.

G. J. Cuming, *A History of Anglican Liturgy* (1982), pp. 24–27,41–43,286–304. *The Godly Order* (Alcuin Club Collections no.65, 1983), pp. 68–90.
J. Dowden, *Further Studies in the Prayer Book* (1908), pp. 44–71.
H. A. Wilson, *The Order of the Communion 1548* (Henry Bradshaw Society vol.34, 1908).

Of the Preparation to the Supper of the Lord
(to be used the night before the celebration)

PSALM

ANTIPHON AND HYMN

MAGNIFICAT

COLLECT

PSALM

NEW TESTAMENT LESSON

SERMON

EXHORTATION

PRAYERS

PRIVATE CONFESSION

How the Lord's Supper must be Celebrated

CONFESSION

COMFORTABLE WORDS

ABSOLUTION

INTROIT

KYRIES

GLORIA IN EXCELSIS

COLLECT

EPISTLE

ALLELUIA (or GRAIL or SEQUENCE)

GOSPEL

SERMON

PRAYER "FOR ALL STATES OF MEN AND NECESSITIES OF THE CONGREGATION"

ALTERNATIVE SHORTER FORM OF PRAYER

CREED

OFFERTORY

Hermann von Wied   221

WARNING AGAINST UNWORTHY RECEPTION AND NON-COMMUNICATING ATTENDANCE

But howsoever the rest be handled in the congregation at this time, they nevertheless that shall be admitted to the communion, as soon as they have made their oblation, must go together to that place that shall be appointed unto them, nigh to the altar. For in every temple there must some place be appointed nigh the altar for them which shall communicate at the Lord's table, according to the opportunity and fitness of every temple. They, then, which shall be admitted to the communion of the Lord's board shall stand in that place, the men in their proper place and the women in their place, and there they shall give thanks and pray religiously with the pastor. The giving of thanks shall be handled after the accustomed manner, but in Douch,[1] that the people universally may give thanks to the Lord, as both the example and the commandment of the Lord requireth, and also the old Church observed.

The priest: The Lord be with you.
The people: And with thy spirit.
The priest: Lift up your hearts.
The people: We have unto the Lord.
The priest: Let us give thanks unto the Lord our God.
The people: It is meet and right.

The priest:
It is verily a thing worthy, right, meet, and wholesome, that we give thanks unto thee always and everywhere, that we praise and magnify thee, Lord, holy Father, Almighty, everlasting God, through Jesus Christ our Lord, by whom thou madest us of nothing unto thine image, and hast appointed all other creatures to our uses; and whereas we, through the sin of Adam sliding from thee, were made thine enemies, and therefore subject to death and eternal damnation, thou of thy infinite mercy and unspeakable love, didst send the same thy Son, the eternal Word, into this world; who through the cross and death delivered us from sins and the power of the devil, and brought us again into thy favor by his holy Spirit whom he sent unto us from thee; and gave his body and blood to be the food of a new and eternal life, that,

1. i.e. in German.

being more confirmed through the trust of thy mercy and love, we should ever go forward to all that that is thy pleasure by renewing and sanctifying of ourselves; and that we should glorify and exalt thee here and evermore in all our words and deeds, and sing unto thee without end with all thy holy angels and beloved children.

After these things, Sanctus *shall be sung; where clerks be, in Latin, but of the people in Douch, one side answering the other, thrice of both parts. As for that that is wont to be added,* "The Lord God of Hosts" *and* Benedictus, *it shall be sung communally of the whole congregation, and therefore in Douch.*

Straightway after this, let the priest sing the words of the Lord's Supper in Douch, "Our Lord, the night in which he was delivered," *etc. But these words must be sung of the priest with great reverence and plainly, that they may be well understanded of all men. And the people shall say to these words, Amen, which all the old churches observed, and the Greeks do yet observe the same. For the whole substance of this sacrament is contained in these words. And it consisteth altogether in the true understanding and faith of these words that the sacrament be wholesomely administered and received.*

After[2] the people then have answered their Amen, the priest shall add:

Let us pray.

Our Father, which art in heaven, etc.

To which prayer of the Lord the people shall say again their Amen.

The priest: The Lord's peace be ever with you.
The people: And with thy spirit.

After this, they which be admitted to the communion and do look for the same in their place shall come to the Lord's board religiously in order, first men and then women; and the whole sacrament shall be given to them all, that they may be partakers of the body and blood of the Lord, receiving not only bread but also the cup, even as he instituted it.

At the exhibition of the body let the pastor say:

2. Latin: *Postquam;* 1547 and 1548: *when.*

Take and eat to thy health the body of the Lord, which was delivered for thee.[3]

At the exhibition of the cup:

Take and drink to thy health the blood of the Lord, which was shed for thy sins.

After the communion, let Agnus Dei *be sung both in Douch and Latin, one side answering the other, where clerks be. And then let this Douch song be sung, "Gott sei gelobet," item, "Jesus Christus unser Heiland," if the communion of the sacraments shall give so much time and leisure.*

When the communion is ended, let the priest sing, turning to the people:
The Lord be with you.
The people: And with thy spirit.

The priest: Let us pray.

Almighty, everlasting God, we give thanks to thy exceeding goodness, because thou hast fed us with the body of thy only-begotten Son our Lord and given us his blood to drink. We humbly beseech thee, work in us with thy Spirit, that, as we have received this divine sacrament with our mouths, so we may also receive and ever hold fast with true faith thy grace, remission of sins, and communion with Christ thy Son. All which things thou hast exhibited unto us in these sacraments through our Lord Jesus Christ thy Son, which liveth and reigneth with thee in unity of the Holy Ghost, very God and very man, forever. Amen.

Another thanksgiving:

We give thee thanks, Father, Almighty God, which hast refreshed us with the singular gift of thy body and blood; we beseech thy goodness that the same may help to confirm our faith in thee, and to kindle mutual love among us, by the same our Lord Jesus Christ, etc

Last of all, let the pastor bless the people with these words:

3. Latin: *pro te;* 1547 and 1548: *for thy sins.*

Hermann von Wied

The Lord bless thee and keep thee; the Lord lighten his countenance upon thee and have mercy on thee; the Lord lift up his face on thee and settle thee in peace. Amen.

Or thus:

God have mercy upon us and bless us, lighten his countenance upon us, and give us his peace. Amen.

Or thus:

God, the Father, the Son, and the Holy Ghost, bless and keep us.

Amen.

Or thus:

The blessing of God, the Father, the Son, and the Holy Ghost, be with us and remain with us for ever. Amen.

FINAL RUBRICS

31 *The Order of the Communion* 1548

The first steps in revising the medieval Latin Mass in England took place in 1547, first with the reading of the Epistle and Gospel in the vernacular, and a little later with the administration of communion in both kinds to the laity. To make proper provision for the latter, an *Order of the Communion* was produced by a commission of bishops and scholars in March 1548. This was not a complete eucharistic rite, but primarily a set of penitential devotions in the vernacular to be inserted into the Latin Mass immediately after the priest's communion. It was closely modelled on the relevant sections in Hermann's rite and may have been inspired by what Cranmer had experienced in Germany.

A preliminary rubric ensured that sufficient bread and wine were provided, and in particular the priest was reminded not to drink all the wine himself, as he would normally have done hitherto, but to take only "one sup or draught." Then came two exhortations—the first to be read on the previous Sunday and the second immediately before communion. Both owed something to Hermann's forms, the first of which came from the Cassel Order and the second from the Brandenburg-Nürnberg Order: Cranmer used Hermann's introductory phrases verbatim but then employed his own wording, although relying on Hermann for inspiration. Both exhortations urged the duty of self-examination; but whereas the first spoke of private confession when necessary and desirable, the second was more general and was followed by an invitation to a general confession. The Confession, however, was said in the communicants' name either by the priest or by another minister or by one of the communicants: to most people it would not be known by heart, and few, if any, would have books. The Absolution was composite, the first half coming from Hermann and the second half from Sarum. The Comfortable Words differed both in choice and position from those in Hermann: he provided five sentences of Scripture, from which only one was said before the Absolution; Cranmer, however, provided four Words—three from Hermann and one from Zwingli (Matthew 11:28)—all of which were said after the Absolution—a less satisfactory arrangement.

The Prayer of Humble Access immediately before Communion was a pastiche of phrases found in a wide variety of sources—Scripture, the early liturgies, Missals, German Church Orders and theological treatises: but few could be reliably identified as the original source. It corresponded to the priest's prayer before communion in the Roman rite and did in fact begin with a phrase from a priest's prayer found in two missals printed before 1548: but whereas the Roman prayer was private to the priest, here he said it in the name of the communicants. The Words of Administration were from the Roman Order for the Communion of the Sick with the Lutheran additions "given for thee" and "shed for thee." They also expressed the idea found in the Prayer of Humble Access, that the bread preserved the body and the blood preserved the soul. This was a matter of concern to some people, involving the old debates on concomitance, and it was modified in the first Prayer Book in 1549. The Blessing was compiled by Cranmer from a conflation of Philippians 4:7 and 2 Peter 1:2. A final rubric highlighted the fact that more frequent communion in both kinds was a practice unknown to the parish priest. The wafers of bread could be divided into two or more pieces, and the assurance was given that the whole body of Jesus Christ was given in each piece of wafer. Provision was also made for the consecration of further wine by the recitation of the relevant portion of the Institution Narrative over a fresh supply.

When the Order appeared, the Bishops were ordered to direct their clergy to use "such good, gentle, and charitable instruction of their simple and unlearned parishioners, that there might be one uniform manner quietly used in all parts of the realm." However, some bishops were apparently tardy or less than enthusiastic in complying; and some of the clergy opposed it. Nevertheless, it was incorporated into the eucharistic rite of the first Prayer Book within a year.

BIBLIOGRAPHY
Coena Domini I (1983), pp.388–394.

The Order of the Communion *1548*   227

F. E. Brightman, *The English Rite*, 2 vols. (1915).
C. O. Buchanan, *Eucharistic Liturgies of Edward VI* (Grove Liturgical Studies no.34, 1983).
G. J. Cuming, *A History of Anglican Liturgy* (1982), pp.40–44.
J. Dowden, *The Workmanship of the Prayer Book* (1908), pp.317–343.
H. A. Wilson, *The Order of the Communion 1548* (Henry Bradshaw Society, vol. 34, 1908).

First the Parson, Vicar, or Curate, the next Sunday or holy day, or at the least, one day before he shall minister the Communion, shall give warning to his parishioners, or those which be present, that they prepare themselves thereto, saying to them openly and plainly as hereafter followeth or such like.

Dear Friends, and you especially . . . of God's word for the same.

The time of the Communion shall be immediately after that the priest himself hath received the sacrament, without the varying of any other rite or ceremony in the Mass, until other order shall be provided; but as heretofore usually the priest hath done with the sacrament of the Body, to prepare, bless, and consecrate so much as will serve the people, so it shall continue still after the same manner and form, save that he shall bless and consecrate the biggest chalice, and some fair and convenient cup or cups, full of wine with some water put into it, and that day not drink it up all himself, but, taking only one sup or draught, leave the rest upon the altar covered, and turn to them that are disposed to be partakers of the Communion, and shall thus exhort them as followeth.

Dearly beloved in the Lord . . . all the days of our life. Amen.

Then shall the priest say to them which be ready to take the sacrament.

If any man here be an open blasphemer, an adulterer, in malice, or envy, or any other notable crime, and be not truly sorry therefore, and earnestly minded to leave the same vices, or that doth not trust himself to be reconciled to almighty God, and in charity with all the world, let him yet a while bewail his sins and not come to this holy table, lest after the taking of this most blessed bread, the devil enter into him, as he did into Judas, to fulfill in him all iniquity, and to bring him to destruction, both of body and soul.

Here the priest shall pause a while to see if any man will withdraw himself: and if he perceive any so to do, then let him commune with him privily at convenient leisure, and see whether he can with good exhortation bring him to grace: and after a little pause, the priest shall say:
You that do truly and earnestly repent you of your sins and offences committed to almighty God, and be in love and charity with your neighbours, and intend to lead a new life and heartily to follow the commandments of God, and to walk from henceforth in his holy ways, draw near, and take this holy sacrament to your comfort, make your humble confession to almighty God, and to his holy Church, here gathered together in his name, meekly kneeling upon your knees.

Then shall a general confession be made in the name of all those that are minded to receive the holy Communion, either by one of them, or else by one of the ministers, or by the priest himself, all kneeling humbly upon their knees.

Almighty God, Father of our Lord Jesus Christ, Maker of all things, Judge of all men, we acknowledge and bewail our manifold sins and wickedness, which we from time to time most grievously have committed by thought, word, and deed against thy divine Majesty, provoking most justly thy wrath and indignation against us: we do earnestly repent, and be heartily sorry for these our misdoings; the remembrance of them is grievous unto us; the burden of them is intolerable; have mercy upon us, have mercy upon us, most merciful Father, for thy son our Lord Jesus Christ's sake. Forgive us all that is past, and grant that we may ever hereafter serve and please thee in newness of life, to the honour and glory of thy name, through Jesus Christ our Lord.

Then shall the priest stand up, and turning him to the people, say thus:

Our blessed Lord, who hath left power to his Church to absolve penitent sinners from their sins, and to restore to the grace of the heavenly Father such as truly believe in Christ, have mercy upon you, pardon and deliver you from all sins, confirm and strengthen you in all goodness, and bring you to everlasting life.

Then shall the priest stand up, and turning him toward the people, say thus:

The Order of the Communion 1548   229

Hear what comfortable words our Savior Christ saith to all that truly turn to him.

Come unto me, all that travail and be heavy laden, and I shall refresh you. God so loved the world that he gave his only begotten Son, to the end that all that believe in him should not perish, but have life everlasting.

Hear also what S. Paul saith.

This is a true saying, and worthy of all men to be embraced and received, that Jesus Christ came into this world to save sinners.

Hear also what S. John saith.

If any man sin, we have an advocate with the Father, Jesus Christ the righteous, he it is that obtained grace for our sins.

Then shall the priest kneel down and say in the name of all them that shall receive the Communion this prayer following.

We do not presume to come to this thy table, O merciful Lord, trusting in our own righteousness, but in thy manifold and great mercies; we be not worthy so much as to gather up the crumbs under thy table. But thou art the same Lord, whose property is always to have mercy: Grant us therefore, gracious Lord, so to eat the flesh of thy dear Son Jesus Christ, and to drink his blood in these holy mysteries, that we may continually dwell in him and he in us, that our sinful bodies may be made clean by his body, and our souls washed through his most precious blood. Amen.

Then shall the priest rise, the people still reverently kneeling; and the priest shall deliver the Communion, first to the ministers, if any be there present, that they may be ready to help the priest, and after to the others. And when he doth deliver the Sacrament of the body of Christ, he shall say to every one these words following.

The body of our Lord Jesus Christ, which was given for thee, preserve thy body unto everlasting life.

And the priest delivering the Sacrament of the blood, and giving every one to drink once and no more, shall say:

The blood of our Lord Jesus Christ, which was shed for thee, preserve thy soul unto everlasting life.

If there be a deacon or other priest, then shall he follow with the chalice, and as the priest ministereth the bread, so shall he for more expedition minister the wine, in form before written.

Then shall the priest, turning him to the people, let the people depart with this blessing:

The peace of God which passeth all understanding, keep your hearts and minds in the knowledge and love of God, and of his Son Jesus Christ, our Lord.

To the which the people shall answer Amen.

Note, that the bread that shall be consecrated shall be such as heretofore hath been accustomed. And every of the said consecrated breads shall be broken in two pieces at the least, or more, by the discretion of the minister, and so distributed. And men must not think less to be received in part than in the whole, but in each of them the whole body of our Savior Jesus Christ.

Note, that if it doth so chance, that the wine hallowed and consecrated doth not suffice or be enough for them that do take the Communion, the priest after the first cup or chalice be emptied, may go again to the altar, and reverently and devoutly prepare and consecrate another, and so the third, or more likewise, beginning at these words. Simili modo, postquam cenatum est, *and ending at these words* qui pro uobis et pro multis effundetur in remissionem peccatorum, *and without any elevation or lifting up.*

Although Henry VIII had broken with Rome in 1532, no serious reformation of the liturgy took place until the accession of Edward VI in 1547. *The Order of the Communion* appeared in March of the following year, and the Windsor Commission, composed of "certain of the most learned and discreet bishops and other learned men of this realm" under Archbishop Cranmer completed work on the first Book of Common Prayer in September. It was approved by Parliament in January 1549 and was ordered to come into use not later than the Feast of Pentecost (June 9). It was intended as a congregational book, written in the vernacular and grounded in Scripture. Compared with material produced on the Continent it was conservative, retaining in considerable measure not only the structure but the wording of the medieval rites.

In the case of the eucharist the layman would have noticed little serious departure from the Roman rite beyond the use of the vernacular. The first sign of change came after the Gospel, which was no longer followed by the sermon but by the creed. The sermon was now in the Lutheran position after the creed, followed by the optional use of the two exhortations from *The Order of the Communion*. Then came a radical change with the offertory, which, although retaining the title, was concerned solely with alms. The practice of Hermann was adopted: the communicants came up to place their money in "the poor men's box" near the altar and remained there for communion, men on one side and women on the other. Bread and wine mixed with water were then placed on the altar with no accompanying words or ceremony.

For a Reformed rite the eucharistic prayer was remarkably conservative. After the Sursum corda Cranmer used the first part of the Roman preface; and although including five proper prefaces for the major festivals, he omitted the ferial preface before continuing with the Sanctus and Benedictus. The result was a short and impoverished introduction to the actual prayer, with no reference to the mighty divine acts for which praise and thanksgiving were traditionally offered. This was followed by the intercessions, different in structure and position from those in the Roman canon, but remarkable in retaining a prayer for the departed: they were introduced by a bidding similar to Hermann's and retained his order; but the wording was Cranmer's own, coming from a variety of sources. In the central section of the prayer there was a petition which, while related to the *Quam oblationem* clause of the Roman canon, nevertheless requested that the bread and wine might be blessed and sanctified by the divine word and the Holy Spirit. While at first sight this might appear to have affinities with an Eastern epiclesis, it was in fact in line with a longstanding tradition dating from Paschasius Radbertus (c.785–860). This led into the Institution Narrative which, as in other Reformed rites, was shorn of non-Scriptural elements and was a conflation of the various New Testament accounts. The prayer concluded with an anamnesis-oblation, but so worded as to exclude any suggestion of the medieval sacrificial doctrine of the Mass: as in Bucer and other Reformers, the offering was of oneself and of praise and thanksgiving. Nor was the priest allowed any ceremonies at the Institution Narrative beyond taking the bread and wine into his hands, and there was no elevation suggestive of adoration of the consecrated elements. The Lord's Prayer and the Peace were then followed by the penitential material from *The Order of the Communion*, the only small change being in the absolution, where Cranmer substituted a new preamble for that of Hermann. The words of administration were also modified from those in *The Order* so that they both referred to the preservation of the body and soul of the communicants.

Unlike the Continental Reformers, Cranmer retained other traditional features. Vestments were used, singing was envisaged, unleavened wafer bread was required, and communion was received kneeling, with the bread directly into the communicant's mouth. On the other hand, there was no mention of reservation or further consecration, and private masses were forbidden. Probably Cranmer did not intend the rite to express exclusively any one doctrinal position but regarded it as an interim step edging towards a more Reformed point of view. As a compromise it satisfied neither reformers nor traditionalists: indeed a further revision was on the way even as the book came into use. But it did have a

The Book of Common Prayer *1549*

long-term influence; and Anglican worship in subsequent centuries might well have been impoverished had Cranmer never produced it but adopted a more extreme line from the outset.

BIBLIOGRAPHY
Coena Domini I (1983), pp.395–406.
Bouyer, pp. 407–417.
F. E. Brightman, *The English Rite*, 2 vols. (1915).
C. O. Buchanan, *What did Cranmer think he was doing?* (Grove Liturgical Studies no.7 (1976). *Eucharistic Liturgies of Edward VI* (Grove Liturgical Studies no.34, 1983). *Background Documents on Liturgical Revision 1547–9* (Grove Liturgical Studies no.35, 1983).
G. J. Cuming, *A History of Anglican Liturgy*(2nd ed. 1982), pp.30–69. *The Godly Order* (Alcuin Club Collections no.65, (1983), pp.91–121.
D. Horton Davies, *Worship and Theology in England*, vol.I (1970),pp.3–39,76–123,165–201.
P. Hall, *Fragmenta Liturgica*, vol.I (1848), pp.101–148.
D. E. W. Harrison, *The First and Second Prayer Books of King Edward the Sixth* (1972).
C. Hopf, *Martin Bucer and the English Reformation* (1946).
E. C. Ratcliff, *The Booke of Common Prayer: its Making and Revisions 1549–1661* (Alcuin Club Collections no.37, 1949). "The Liturgical Work of Archbishop Cranmer", in *Journal of Ecclesiastical History* vol. 7 (1956),pp.189–203. "The English Usage of Eucharistic Consecration 1548–1662," in *Theology* vol.60 (1957), pp.229–236, 273–280. These last two essays have been reprinted in *Liturgical Studies* (eds. A. H. Couratin and D. H. Tripp, 1976), pp. 184–221.
Jasper Ridley, *Thomas Cranmer* (1962), pp.272–289.
C. H. Smyth, *Cranmer and the Reformation under Edward VI* (1972).

The literature on the 1549 Prayer Book is extensive and the volumes cited here are only a selection. For further study, consult the bibliographies in Buchanan, Cuming, and Horton Davies.

The Supper of the Lord, and the Holy Communion, commonly called the Mass

INTRODUCTORY RUBRICS
INTROIT PSALM (CLERKS)
LORD'S PRAYER (PRIEST)
COLLECT FOR PURITY (PRIEST)

INTROIT PSALM (PRIEST)

KYRIES (NINEFOLD)

GLORIA IN EXCELSIS

SALUTATION AND COLLECT OF THE DAY

COLLECT FOR THE KING

EPISTLE

GOSPEL

NICENE CREED

SERMON OR HOMILY

EXHORTATIONS (OPTIONAL)

OFFERTORY WITH SENTENCES

While the Clerks do sing the offertory, so many as are disposed shall offer to the poor men's box, every one according to his ability and charitable mind. And at the offering days appointed, every man and woman shall pay to the Curate the due and accustomed offerings.

Then so many as shall be partakers of the holy communion shall tarry still in the quire, or in some convenient place nigh the quire, the men on the one side, and the women on the other side. All other, that mind not to receive the said holy communion, shall depart out of the quire, except the Ministers and Clerks.

Then shall the Minister take so much bread and wine as shall suffice for the persons appointed to receive the holy communion, laying the bread upon the corporal, or else in the paten, or in some other comely thing prepared for that purpose: and putting the wine into the chalice, or else in some fair or convenient cup prepared for that use, if the chalice will not serve, putting thereto a little pure and clean water, and setting both the bread and wine upon the altar. Then the Priest shall say,

       The Lord be with you.

Answer: And with thy spirit.

Priest: Lift up your hearts.

Answer: We lift them up unto the Lord.

Priest: Let us give thanks to our Lord God.

Answer: It is meet and right so to do.

The Priest: It is very meet, right, and our bounden duty that we should at all times and in all places give thanks to thee, O Lord, holy Father, almighty, everlasting God.

The Book of Common Prayer *1549*   235

Here shall follow the proper Preface, according to the time, if there be any specially appointed, or else immediately shall follow,

Therefore with angels, etc.

PROPER PREFACES

Upon Christmas Day

Because thou didst give Jesus Christ thine only Son to be born as this day for us; who, by the operation of the Holy Ghost, was made very man of the substance of the Virgin Mary his mother; and that without spot of sin, to make us clean from all sin. Therefore, etc.

Upon Easter Day

But chiefly are we bound to praise thee for the glorious resurrection of thy Son Jesus Christ our Lord: for he is the very paschal Lamb, which was offered for us, and hath taken away the sin of the world; who by his death hath destroyed death, and by his rising to life again hath restored to us everlasting life. Therefore, etc.

Upon the Ascension Day

Through thy most dear beloved Son Jesus Christ our Lord; who, after his most glorious resurrection, manifestly appeared to all his disciples, and in their sight ascended up into heaven to prepare a place for us; that where he is, thither might we also ascend, and reign with him in glory. Therefore, etc.

Upon Whit Sunday

Through Jesus Christ our Lord; according to whose most true promise the Holy Ghost came down this day from heaven with a sudden great sound, as it had been a mighty wind, in the likeness of fiery tongues, lighting upon the apostles, to teach them, and to lead them to all truth, giving them both the gift of divers languages, and also boldness with fervent zeal constantly to preach the gospel unto all nations; whereby we are brought out of darkness and error into the clear light and true knowledge of thee, and of thy Son Jesus Christ. Therefore, etc.

Upon the feast of the Trinity

It is very meet, right, and our bounden duty, that we should at all times and in all places give thanks to thee, O Lord, Almighty, everlasting God, which art one God, one Lord; not one only Person, but three Persons in one substance. For that which we believe of the glory of the Father, the same we believe of the Son, and of the Holy Ghost, without any difference or inequality. Whom the angels, etc.

After which Preface shall follow immediately,

Therefore with angels and archangels, and with all the holy company of heaven, we laud and magnify thy glorious name; evermore praising thee, and saying,
Holy, holy, holy, Lord God of hosts: heaven and earth are full of thy glory. Hosanna in the highest. Blessed is he that cometh in the name of the Lord. Glory to thee, O Lord, in the highest.

This the Clerks shall also sing.

When the Clerks have done singing, then shall the Priest or Deacon turn him to the people, and say,

Let us pray for the whole state of Christ's Church.

Then the priest, turning him to the altar, shall say or sing, plainly and distinctly, this prayer following.

Almighty and everliving God, which by thy holy apostle hast taught us to make prayers, and supplications, and to give thanks for all men; We humbly beseech thee most mercifully to receive these our prayers, which we offer unto thy divine Majesty; beseeching thee to inspire continually the universal church with the spirit of truth, unity, and concord: and grant, that all they that do confess thy holy name may agree in the truth of thy holy word, and live in unity and godly love. Specially we beseech thee to save and defend thy servant Edward our king; that under him we may be godly and quietly governed; and grant unto his whole council, and to all that be put in authority under him, that they may truly and indifferently minister justice, to the punishment of wickedness and vice, and to the maintenance of God's true religion and virtue. Give grace, O heavenly Father, to all bishops, pastors and curates that they may both by their life and doctrine set forth thy true and lively word, and rightly and duly administer thy holy sacraments. And to all thy people give thy heavenly grace; that with meek heart and due reverence, they may hear and receive thy holy word; truly serving thee in holiness and righteousness all the days of their life. And we most humbly beseech thee of thy goodness, O Lord, to comfort and succour all them, which in this transitory life be in trouble, sorrow, need, sickness, or any other adversity. And especially we commend unto thy merciful goodness this congregation, which is here assembled in thy name, to celebrate the commemoration of the most glorious death of thy son. And here we do give unto thee most high praise, and hearty thanks, for the wonderful grace and virtue declared in thy saints, from the beginning of the world; and chiefly in the glorious and most blessed Virgin Mary, mother of thy Son Jesu Christ our Lord and God; and in the holy patriarchs, prophets, apostles and martyrs, whose examples, O Lord, and stedfastness in thy faith, and keeping thy holy commandments, grant us to follow. We commend unto thy mercy, O Lord, all other thy servants, which are departed hence from us with the sign of faith, and now do rest in the sleep of peace: grant unto them, we beseech thee, thy mercy, and everlasting peace; and that, at the day of the general resurrection, we and all they which be of the mystical body of thy Son, may altogether be set on his right hand, and hear that his most joyful voice, Come unto me, O ye that be blessed of my Father, and possess the kingdom, which is prepared for you from the beginning of the world. Grant this, O Father, for Jesus Christ's sake, our only Mediator and Advocate.

O God, heavenly Father, which of thy tender mercy didst give thine only Son Jesu Christ to suffer death upon the cross for our redemption; who made there, by his one oblation once offered, a full, perfect, and sufficient sacrifice, oblation, and satisfaction, for the sins of the whole world; and did institute, and in his holy gospel command us to celebrate a perpetual memory of that his precious death, until his coming again: hear us, O merciful Father, we beseech thee; and with thy Holy Spirit and word vouchsafe to ble✠ss and sanc✠tify these thy gifts and creatures of bread and wine, that they may be unto us the body and blood of thy most dearly beloved Son Jesus Christ, who in the same night that he was betrayed, took bread,[1] and when he had blessed, and given thanks, he brake it, and gave it to his disciples, saying, Take, eat; this is my body which is given for you; do this in remembrance of me.

Likewise after supper he took the cup,[2] and when he had given thanks, he gave it to them, saying, Drink ye all of this; for this is my blood of the new Testament, which is shed for you and for many for remission of sins. Do this, as oft as you shall drink it, in remembrance of me.

These words before rehearsed are to be said, turning still to the altar, without any elevation or shewing the sacrament to the people.

Wherefore, O Lord and heavenly Father, according to the institution of thy dearly beloved Son our Saviour Jesu Christ, we thy humble servants do celebrate and make here before thy divine Majesty, with these thy holy gifts, the memorial which thy Son hath willed us to make; having in remembrance his blessed passion, mighty resurrection, and glorious ascension; rendering unto thee most hearty thanks for the innumerable benefits procured unto us by the same; entirely desiring thy fatherly goodness mercifully to accept this our sacrifice of praise and thanksgiving; most humbly beseeching thee to grant, that by the merits and death of thy Son Jesus Christ and through faith in his blood, we and all thy whole church may obtain remission of our sins, and all other benefits of his passion. And here we offer and present unto thee, O Lord, our self, our souls and bodies, to be a reasonable, holy, and lively sacrifice unto thee; humbly beseeching thee, that whosoever shall be partakers of this holy communion may worthily receive the most precious body and blood of thy Son Jesus Christ, and be fulfilled with thy grace and heavenly benediction, and made one body with thy Son Jesu Christ, that he may dwell in them, and they in him. And although we be unworthy, through

1. Here the priest must take the bread into his hands.
2. Here the priest shall take the cup into his hands.

our manifold sins, to offer unto thee any sacrifice, yet we beseech thee to accept this our bounden duty and service, and command these our prayers and supplications, by the ministry of thy holy angels, to be brought up into thy holy tabernacle, before the sight of thy divine Majesty; not weighing our merits, but pardoning our offences, through Christ our Lord; by whom, and with whom, in the unity of the Holy Ghost, all honour and glory be unto thee, O Father almighty, world without end. Amen.

Let us pray.

As our Saviour Christ hath commanded and taught us, we are bold to say, Our Father, which art in heaven, hallowed be thy name. Thy kingdom come. Thy will be done in earth, as it is in heaven. Give us this day our daily bread. And forgive us our trespasses, as we forgive them that trespass against us. And lead us not into temptation.
The answer. But deliver us from evil.

Then shall the Priest say,

The peace of the Lord be always with you.
The Clerks: And with thy spirit.
The Priest: Christ our Paschal Lamb is offered up for us, once for all, when he bare our sins on his body upon the cross; for he is the very Lamb of God that taketh away the sins of the world: therefore let us keep a joyful and holy feast with the Lord.

Here the Priest shall turn him toward those that come to the holy Communion, and shall say,

You that do truly and earnestly repent you of your sins to almighty God, and be in love and charity with your neighbours, and intend to lead a new life, following the commandments of God, and walking from henceforth in his holy ways; Draw near, and take this holy sacrament to your comfort; make your humble confession to Almighty God, and to his holy Church here gathered together in his name, meekly kneeling upon your knees.

Then shall this general confession be made, in the name of all those that are minded to receive the holy communion, either by one of them, or else

The Book of Common Prayer *1549*

by one of the Ministers, or by the Priest himself, all kneeling humbly upon their knees.

Almighty God, Father of our Lord Jesus Christ, Maker of all things, Judge of all men; we acknowledge and bewail our manifold sins and wickedness, which we, from time to time, most grievously have committed, by thought, word, and deed, against thy divine Majesty, provoking most justly thy wrath and indignation against us. We do earnestly repent, and be heartily sorry for these our misdoings; the remembrance of them is grievous unto us; the burden of them is intolerable. Have mercy upon us, have mercy upon us, most merciful Father; for thy Son our Lord Jesus Christ's sake, forgive us all that is past; and grant that we may ever hereafter serve and please thee in newness of life, to the honour and glory of thy name; through Jesus Christ our Lord.

Then shall the Priest stand up, and turning himself to the people, say thus:

Almighty God, our heavenly Father, who of his great mercy hath promised forgiveness of sins to all them which with hearty repentance and true faith turn unto him; Have mercy upon you; pardon and deliver you from all your sins; confirm and strengthen you in all goodness; and bring you to everlasting life; through Jesus Christ our Lord. Amen.

Then shall the Priest say.

Hear what comfortable words our Saviour Christ saith to all that truly turn to him.

Come unto me all that travail, and be heavy laden, and I shall refresh you. So God loved the world, that he gave his only-begotten Son, to the end that all that believe in him should not perish, but have life everlasting.

Hear also what Saint Paul saith.

This is a true saying, and worthy of all men to be received, that Jesus Christ came into this world to save sinners.

Hear also what Saint John saith.

If any man sin, we have an Advocate with the Father, Jesus Christ the righteous; and he is the propitiation for our sins.

The Book of Common Prayer *1549* 241

Then shall the Priest, turning him to God's board, kneel down, and say in the name of all them that receive the communion, this prayer following:

We do not presume to come to this thy table, O merciful Lord, trusting in our own righteousness, but in thy manifold and great mercies. We be not worthy so much as to gather up the crumbs under thy table; but thou art the same Lord whose property is always to have mercy: Grant us therefore, gracious Lord, so to eat the flesh of thy dear Son Jesus Christ, and to drink his blood, in these holy mysteries, that we may continually dwell in him, and he in us, that our sinful bodies may be made clean by his body, and our souls washed through his most precious blood. Amen.

Then shall the Priest first receive the communion in both kinds himself, and next deliver it to other Ministers, if any be there present, that they may be ready to help the chief Minister, and after to the people. And when he delivereth the sacrament of the body of Christ, he shall say to every one these words:

The body of our Lord Jesus Christ, which was given for thee, preserve thy body and soul unto everlasting life.

And the Minister delivering the sacrament of the blood, and giving every one to drink once, and no more, shall say,

The blood of our Lord Jesus Christ, which was shed for thee, preserve thy body and soul unto everlasting life.

If there be a Deacon or other Priest, then shall he follow with the chalice; and as the Priest ministereth the sacrament of the body, so shall he, for more expedition, minister the sacrament of the blood, in the form before written.

In the communion time the Clerks shall sing,

ii. O Lamb of God, that takest away the sins of the world; have mercy upon us.

O Lamb of God, that takest away the sins of the world; grant us thy peace.

Beginning so soon as the Priest doth receive holy communion, and when the communion is ended, then shall the Clerks sing the post-communion.

POST-COMMUNION SENTENCES
PRAYER OF THANKSGIVING
BLESSING
FINAL RUBRICS AND COLLECTS

The Book of Common Prayer 1549   243

The 1549 Prayer Book was not well received: but a successor was apparently already envisaged when it was being produced. Certainly by January 1551 the bishops had agreed to a number of changes, and in the same year Martin Bucer submitted a thorough-going criticism of the 1549 Book in his *Censura*. The fact that a number of bishops and divines claimed that it was still possible to interpret the 1549 rite in accordance with traditional eucharistic theology undoubtedly encouraged its demise. A second, more Protestant Book duly appeared in 1552, to come into use on All Saints' Day, with none of the ambiguity of doctrine and conservatism of practice of its predecessor. In the eucharist there was a clear expression of a theology which regarded it as essentially an eating of bread and a drinking of wine in thankful remembrance of Christ's death. The title "the Mass" disappeared; vestments were replaced by the surplice; the stone altar became a wooden table standing in the chancel or body of the church running east to west, with the priest on the north side of it; all singing ceased; and the whole rite became more penitential in tone.

The offertory underwent further modification. The term itself disappeared; there were no directions for setting the bread and wine on the table; and the communicants no longer approached to give their alms—instead the churchwardens came round and collected them. The eucharistic prayer was also dismembered. The Intercessions became a self-contained entity, said immediately after the almsgiving and shorn of all reference to the saints and the departed, so avoiding any idea of a propitiatory sacrifice for the living and the dead. This was followed by the Exhortations and the penitential material, now removed from its former position between the eucharistic prayer and communion—with the exception of the Prayer of Humble Access. This found a new home after the Sursum corda, Preface and Sanctus (but no Benedictus): it also lost the phrase "in these holy mysteries," and this together with its new position ensured that there would be no adoration of consecrated elements. The eucharistic prayer, in addition to losing its first section, also lost its last section. The anamnesis disappeared altogether, and the Prayer of Oblation was placed after communion. The abbreviated eucharistic prayer therefore ended abruptly with the Institution Narrative and was followed immediately by communion—the practice of Zwingli, Bucer, and other Reformers. It also underwent a significant change of wording. The epiclesis disappeared and the prayer no longer contained the petition for God to "bless and sanctify" the bread and wine; instead it prayed that "we, receiving these thy creatures of bread and wine . . . may be partakers of his most blessed body and blood." It had merely become a prayer for the fruitful reception of bread and wine—a fact further emphasized by two other changes. First, there were new words of distribution, strongly reminiscent of those put out by the Reformer John à Lasco and avoiding identification of the elements with the body and blood of Christ: his form had been, "Take, eat (drink), and remember the body (blood) of our Lord Jesus Christ who died for us on the cross for the remission of all our sins." Secondly, there was the rubric enjoining the use of ordinary bread and permitting the curate to have any remaining elements "to his own use." The prayer also lacked an Amen. This, together with the placing of the Prayer of Oblation and the Lord's Prayer immediately after communion, suggested that Cranmer envisaged the eating and drinking as occurring within the prayer itself. The communicants, having sealed their union with Christ in communion, were now in a position to ask God to accept their "sacrifice of praise and thanksgiving" and to offer themselves as a reasonable, holy, and living sacrifice to him. It was all very logical and consistent, but marred by the permission to use the Prayer of Thanksgiving as an alternative to the Prayer of Oblation.

These changes in 1552 brought Cranmer much closer to Zwingli's position: but he was still less radical. He still envisaged communion as a weekly and not a quarterly practice: and he could still regard the sacraments as "effectual signs of grace." The view of most scholars is that his eucharistic theology was in general agreement with that of Bucer. Apart from its temporary eclipse during the reign of Queen Mary, the 1552 rite remained substantially unchanged until 1662.

BIBLIOGRAPHY

Coena Domini I (1983),pp.406–408.

F. E. Brightman, *The English Rite*, 2 vols. (1915).

C. O. Buchanan,*What did Cranmer think he was doing?* (Grove Liturgical Study no.7,1976). *Eucharistic Liturgies of Edward VI* (Grove Liturgical Study no.34,1983).

G. J. Cuming, *A History of Anglican Liturgy* (1982), pp.70–81.

D. Horton Davies, *Worship and Theology in England*, vol.1 (1970), pp.3–39,76–123,194–210.

C. W.Dugmore, "The First Ten Years 1549–1559," in *The English Prayer Book 1549–1662* (essays published for the Alcuin Club, 1963), pp.6–30.

D. E. W.Harrison, *The First and Second Prayer Books of King Edward the Sixth* (1972).

C. Hopf, *Martin Bucer and the English Reformation* (1946).

E. C. Ratcliff, *The Booke of Common Prayer: its Making and Revisions 1549–1661,* (Alcuin Club Collections no.37,1949). "The Liturgical Work of Archbishop Cranmer." *Journal of Ecclesiastical History*, vol. 7 (1956), pp.189–203. This essay also appears in *Liturgical Studies*(eds.A. H.Couratin and D. H.Tripp,1976),pp.184–221.

Jasper Ridley, *Thomas Cranmer* (1962),pp.290–342.

C. H.Smyth, *Cranmer and the Reformation under Edward VI* (1972).

E. C.Whitaker, *Martin Bucer and the Book of Common Prayer* (Alcuin Club Collections no.55,1974).

As with the 1549 Prayer Book, consult the bibliographies of Buchanan, Cuming, and Horton Davies.

The Order for the Administration of the Lord's Supper or Holy Communion

INTRODUCTORY RUBRICS

LORD'S PRAYER (Priest)

COLLECT FOR PURITY (Priest)

TEN COMMANDMENTS

COLLECT OF THE DAY

COLLECT FOR THE KING

EPISTLE

GOSPEL

NICENE CREED

SERMON OR HOMILY

ALMSGIVING WITH SENTENCES

PRAYER FOR THE CHURCH MILITANT "Almighty and everliving God . . ."

EXHORTATIONS

INVITATION "Ye that do truly . . ."

CONFESSION "Almighty God, Father of our Lord . . ."

ABSOLUTION "Almighty God, our heavenly Father . . ."

COMFORTABLE WORDS

After which the Priest shall proceed, saying,

Lift up your hearts.

Answer: We lift them up unto the Lord.

Priest: Let us give thanks unto our Lord God.

Answer: It is meet and right so to do.

Priest: It is very meet, right, and our bounden duty, that we should at all times, and in all places, give thanks unto thee, O Lord, holy Father, almighty, everlasting God.

Here shall follow the proper Preface, according to the time, (if there be any especially appointed), or else immediately shall follow,

Therefore with angels, etc.

PROPER PREFACES

Upon Christmas Day, and seven days after
  Because thou didst give Jesus Christ . . .
Upon Easter Day, and seven days after
  But chiefly are we bound to praise thee . . .
Upon the Ascension Day, and seven days after
  Through thy most dearly beloved Son, Jesus Christ . . .
Upon Whit Sunday, and six days after
  Through Jesus Christ our Lord, according . . .
Upon the feast of Trinity only
  Who art one God, one Lord . . .

After which Preface shall follow immediately
  Therefore with angels and archangels, and with all the company of heaven, we laud and magnify thy glorious name, evermore praising thee, and saying,

The Book of Common Prayer 1552   247

Holy, holy, holy, Lord God of hosts, heaven and earth are full of thy glory. Glory be to thee, O Lord most high.

"We do not presume . . . and he in us. Amen."

Then the Priest, standing up, shall say as followeth:

Almighty God, our heavenly Father, which of thy tender mercy didst give thine only Son Jesus Christ to suffer death upon the cross for our redemption; who made there, by his one oblation of himself once offered, a full, perfect, and sufficient sacrifice, oblation, and satisfaction for the sins of the whole world; and did institute, and in his holy gospel command us to continue, a perpetual memory of that his precious death until his coming again; Hear us, O merciful Father, we beseech thee; and grant that we, receiving these thy creatures of bread and wine, according to thy Son our Savior Jesus Christ's holy institution, in remembrance of his death and passion, may be partakers of his most blessed body and blood; who, in the same night that he was betrayed, took bread; and when he had given thanks, he brake it, and gave it to his disciples, saying, Take, eat; this is my body which is given for you. Do this in remembrance of me. Likewise after supper he took the cup; and when he had given thanks, he gave it to them, saying, Drink ye all of this; for this is my blood of the New Testament, which is shed for you and for many for remission of sins: do this, as oft as ye shall drink it in remembrance of me.

Then shall the Minister first receive the communion in both kinds himself, and next deliver it to other Ministers, if any be there present, that they may help the chief Minister, and after to the people in their hands kneeling. And when he delivereth the bread he shall say,

Take and eat this, in remembrance that Christ died for thee, and feed on him in thy heart by faith with thanksgiving.

And the Minister that delivereth the cup, shall say,

Drink this in remembrance that Christ's blood was shed for thee, and be thankful.

Then shall the Priest say the Lord's Prayer, the people repeating after him every petition.

After shall be said as followeth:

O Lord and heavenly Father, we thy humble servants entirely desire thy fatherly goodness mercifully to accept this our sacrifice of praise and thanksgiving; most humbly beseeching thee to grant, that by the merits and death of thy Son Jesus Christ, and through faith in his blood, we and all thy whole church may obtain remission of our sins, and all other benefits of his passion. And here we offer and present unto thee, O Lord, our selves, our souls and bodies, to be a reasonable, holy, and lively sacrifice unto thee; humbly beseeching thee, that all we which be partakers of this holy communion, may be fulfilled with thy grace and heavenly benediction. And although we be unworthy, through our manifold sins to offer unto thee any sacrifice, yet we beseech thee to accept this our bounden duty and service; not weighing our merits, but pardoning our offences, through Jesus Christ our Lord; by whom, and with whom in the unity of the Holy Ghost, all honour and glory be unto thee, O Father Almighty, world without end. Amen.

or PRAYER OF THANKSGIVING
GLORIA IN EXCELSIS
BLESSING
FINAL RUBRICS AND COLLECTS

34 John Knox: *The Form of Prayers and Ministration of the Sacraments* 1556

The group of English refugees from the Marian persecution gathered at Frankfurt-on-Main were divided on matters of worship. Some preferred to follow the 1552 Prayer book, others—among whom was John Knox—preferred the Genevan rites of John Calvin. In January 1555, in an attempt to resolve these differences, a committee—including Knox—produced an independent liturgy in the hope that it would be acceptable to all parties. This was the original version of *The Form of Prayers*. Their hopes were not fulfilled, however, and the liturgy was never used. The quarrelling continued, and eventually Knox was forced to leave. He settled in Geneva, where in due course he became minister of a group of like-minded English exiles. *The Form of Prayers* was revived and additions were made, including Calvin's Catechism and some metrical psalms, much of the work being done by William Whittingham (later Dean of Durham). It was published in February 1556, the first Reformed liturgy in English, subsequently passing through several editions. It owed a great deal to Calvin's service book *La Forme des Prières* and to a lesser degree the 1552 Prayer Book. On the accession of Elizabeth in 1559 the English congregation in Geneva was dissolved and the exiles returned home. Knox went to Scotland, taking his enthusiasm for Calvin with him. In 1560 the first General Assembly of the Church of Scotland directed that the sacraments were to be administered according to the Genevan rite, and this was confirmed in 1562. In 1564 *The Form of Prayers* was accepted as the standard of worship in the Church of Scotland, and a Scottish edition was published. It gradually became known as *The Book of Common Order* and continued in use until superseded by *The Westminster Directory* in 1645.

In structure and doctrine *The Form of Prayers* belonged primarily to the liturgical traditions of Strasbourg and Geneva. It was not a fixed rite, however, like the *Book of Common Prayer*. It provided a standard of worship, leaving a great deal to the minister's discretion, although in the case of the sacraments he was expected to "honour the liturgy." The first rubric of the Communion Service indicated a monthly celebration in Geneva, but a quarterly celebration became the norm in Scotland. Nevertheless, when communion was not celebrated, as much as possible of the rite was retained, only the portions specifically pertaining to consecration and communion being omitted. The major part of the service was conducted from the pulpit, the minister wearing a black preaching gown. The Scottish edition of 1564 followed Calvin's *La Forme* even more closely than the Geneva edition. For example, the confession of sin, with which the service began and which was a new composition in the Genevan edition, was provided with Calvin's shorter form as an alternative in the Scottish edition. The same thing happened with the Intercessions—the original prayer of Geneva was given Calvin's form as an alternative in Scotland.

As in Calvin, the Intercessions were followed by the Lord's Prayer and Apostles' Creed, after which the bread and wine were brought forward to the Table: but since the minister was still in the pulpit, this was done by his assistants. He then read the Institution Narrative, which was based on that in 1 Corinthians 11: it was not from any known version of the Bible, but followed Huycke's English translation of the text in Calvin. Clearly it was in no sense consecratory but was the warrant in Scripture for what was about to take place. The Table was then fenced and unworthy communicants warned off in an Exhortation, the first half of which was Cranmer's from 1552 and the second half of which was Calvin's. It ended with a passage which was strongly suggestive of the Sursum corda, and which could be traced to Farel's *La Manière et Fasson*. It was at this stage that the minister left the pulpit and came to sit at the Table with the communicants. This practice of sitting together at what was known as the Long Table was quite unique, but having been established in Geneva it was also brought to Scotland. It not only expressed the idea of fellowship but was a precise following of Scripture. As with the Confession and Intercessions, the Eucharistic Prayer in the Genevan edition was an original composition although akin to Calvin's; but in the Scottish edition Calvin's prayer was included as an alternative. The prayer did not refer to the consecration of the bread and wine, but it contained many of the constituent elements of the canon—praise and thanksgiving for Creation and redemption, an anamnesis, and, in conclusion, a doxology. After the prayer, the bread was broken. Although there was no reference in the Genevan edition, there is evidence that the Institution Narrative was repeated again at this point in Scotland, and it certainly appeared here in *The Westminster Directory*. Similarly there was no reference to Words of Delivery at the communion, but it seems most likely that they were used: both Calvin and Pullain used them, and they appeared in the Scottish edition. Calvin was also followed in the Prayer of Thanksgiving after communion.

BIBLIOGRAPHY
Coena Domini 1 (1983),pp.472–479.
J. M. Barkley, *The Worship of the Reformed Church* (1966), pp.22–26.
G. B. Burnet, *The Holy Communion in the Reformed Church of Scotland* (1960),pp.1–25.
G. J. Cuming, "John Knox and the Book of Common Prayer," in *Liturgical Review*, vol.II (1981), pp.80–81.
D. Horton Davies, *The Worship of the English Puritans* (1948), pp. 116–122.
D. Forrester and D. Murray (eds.), *Studies in the History of Worship in Scotland* (1984), pp.33–42.
R. A. Leaver, *The Liturgy of the Frankfurt Exiles 1555* (Grove Liturgical Study no.38, 1984).
W. D. Maxwell, *An Outline of Christian Worship* (1945), pp.120–125. *The Liturgical Portions of the Genevan Service Book* (1965).
Bard Thompson, pp.287–307.

The Manner of the Lord's Supper

CONFESSION OF SIN (1 form in 1556, 2 forms in 1562)
PRAYER FOR PARDON
PSALM
PRAYER FOR ILLUMINATION
LESSON
SERMON
INTERCESSIONS (1 form in 1556, 2 forms in 1562)
LORD'S PRAYER
APOSTLES' CREED

PSALM during which THE ELEMENTS ARE PREPARED
The day when the Lord's Supper is ministered, which commonly is used once a month, or so oft as the Congregation shall think expedient, the minister useth to say as followeth:

Let us mark, dear brethren, and consider how Jesus Christ did ordain unto us his holy supper, according as St. Paul maketh rehearsal in the eleventh chapter of the first Epistle to the Corinthians, I have (saith he) received of the Lord that which I have delivered unto you, to wit, that the Lord Jesus, the same night he was betrayed, took bread; and when he had given thanks, he brake it, saying, "Take ye, eat ye; this is my body, which is broken for you: do ye this in remembrance of me." Likewise after supper, he took the cup, saying, "This cup is the new testament, or covenant, in my blood; do ye this, so oft as ye shall drink thereof, in remembrance of me. For so oft as ye shall eat this bread, and drink of this cup, ye shall declare the Lord's death until his coming." Therefore, whosoever shall eat this bread, and drink the cup of the Lord unworthily, he shall be guilty of the body and blood of the Lord. Then see that every man prove and try himself, and so let him eat of this bread and drink of this cup; for whosoever eateth or drinketh unworthily, he eateth and drinketh his own damnation, for not having due regard and consideration of the Lord's body.

This done, the minister proceeded to the Exhortation.

Dearly beloved in the Lord, forasmuch as we be now assembled to celebrate the holy communion of the body and blood of our Savior Christ, let us consider these words of St. Paul, how he exhorteth all persons diligently to try and examine themselves, before they presume to eat of that bread, and drink of that cup. For as the benefit is great, if, with a truly penitent heart and lively faith, we receive that holy sacrament (for then we spiritually eat the flesh of Christ and drink his blood, then we dwell in Christ, and Christ in us, we be one with Christ, and Christ with us), so is the danger great if we receive the same unworthily, for then we be guilty of the body and blood of Christ our savior, we eat and drink our own damnation, not considering the Lord's body; we

John Knox   253

kindle God's wrath against us, and provoke him to plague us with divers diseases and sundry kinds of death.

Therefore, if any of you be a blasphemer of God, an hinderer or slanderer of his word, an adulterer, or be in malice or envy, or in any other grievous crime, bewail your sins, and come not to this holy table; lest after the taking of this holy sacrament, the devil enter into you as he entered into Judas, and fill you full of all iniquities, and bring you to destruction, both of body and soul. Judge therefore yourselves brethren, that ye be not judged of the Lord: repent you truly for your past sins, and have a lively and steadfast faith in Christ our savior, seeking only your salvation in the merits of his death and passion, from henceforth refusing and forgetting all malice and debate, with full purpose to live in brotherly amity and godly conversation all the days of your life.

And albeit we feel in ourselves much frailty and wretchedness, as that we have not our faith so perfect and constant as we ought, being many times ready to distrust God's goodness through our corrupt nature; and also that we are not so thoroughly given to serve God, neither have so fervent a zeal to set forth his glory, as our duty requireth, feeling still such rebellion in ourselves, that we have need daily to fight against the lusts of our flesh; yet nevertheless, seeing that our Lord hath dealt thus mercifully with us, and hath printed his gospel in our hearts, so that we are preserved from falling into desperation and misbelief: and seeing also that he hath endued us with a will and desire to renounce and withstand our own affections, with a longing for his righteousness and the keeping of his commandments, we may be now right well assured, that those defaults and manifold imperfections in us, shall be no hindrance at all against us, to cause him not to accept and impute us worthy to come to his spiritual table.

For the end of our coming thither is not to make protestation that we are upright or just in our lives; but contrariwise we come to seek our life and perfection in Jesus Christ, acknowledging in the meantime that we of ourselves be the children of wrath and damnation.

Let us consider, then, that this sacrament is a singular medicine for all poor sick creatures, a comfortable help to weak souls, and that our Lord requireth no other worthiness on our part, but that we unfeignedly acknowledge our naughtiness and imperfection. Then, to the end that we may be worthy partakers of his merits and most comfortable benefits, which is the true eating of his flesh and drinking of his blood, let us not suffer our minds to wander about the consideration of these earthly and corruptible things, which we see present to our eyes and feel with our hands, to seek Christ bodily present in them, as if he were enclosed in the bread and wine, or as if these elements were turned and changed into the substance of his flesh and blood.

For the only way to dispose our souls to receive nourishment, relief and quickening of his substance, is to lift up our minds by faith above all things worldy and sensible, and thereby to enter into heaven, that we may find and receive Christ, where he dwelleth undoubtedly very God and very Man, in the incomprehensible glory of his Father, to whom be all praise, honour and glory, now and ever. Amen.

The exhortation ended, the minister cometh down from the pulpit, and sitteth at the Table, every man and woman in like wise taking their places as occasion best serveth, then he taketh bread and giveth thanks, either in these words following, or like in effect:

O Father of mercy and God of all consolation, seeing all creatures do acknowledge and confess thee, as governor and lord, it becometh us the workmanship of thine own hands, at all times to reverence and magnify thy godly majesty, first that thou hast created us to thine own image and similitude: but chiefly that thou hast delivered us, from that everlasting death and damnation into the which Satan drew mankind by the means of sin: from the bondage whereof neither man nor angel was able to make us free, but thou, O Lord, rich in mercy and infinite in goodness, hast provided our redemption to stand in thy only and well-beloved son: whom of very love thou didst give to be made man, like unto us in all things, sin except, that in his body he might receive the punishments of our transgression, by his death to make satisfaction to thy justice, and by his resurrection to destroy him that was the author of death, and so to reduce and bring again life to the world, from which the whole offspring of Adam most justly was exiled.

O Lord, we acknowledge that no creature is able to comprehend the length and breadth, the deepness and height, of that thy most excellent love which moved thee to show mercy, where none was deserved; to promise and give life, where death had gotten victory; but to receive us into thy grace, when we would do nothing but rebel against thy justice.

O Lord, the blind dullness of our corrupt nature will not suffer us sufficiently to weigh these thy most ample benefits: yet nevertheless at the commandment of Jesus Christ our Lord, we present our selves to this his table, which he hath left to be used in remembrance of his death until his coming again, to declare and witness before the world, that by him alone we have received liberty and life: that by him alone, thou dost acknowledge us thy children and heirs: that by him alone, we have entrance to the throne of thy grace: that by him alone, we are possessed in our spiritual kingdom, to eat and drink at his table: with whom we have our conversation presently in heaven, and by whom our bodies shall be raised up again from the dust, and shall be placed with him in that endless joy, which thou, O father of mercy, hast prepared for thine elect, before the foundation of the world was laid.

And these most inestimable benefits, we acknowledge and confess to have received of thy free mercy and grace, by thy only beloved Son Jesus Christ, for the which therefore we thy congregation moved by thy Holy Spirit render thee all thanks, praise, and glory for ever and ever.

This done, the Minister breaketh the bread and delivereth it to the people, who distribute and divide the same amongst themselves, according to our savior Christ's commandment, and in like wise giveth the cup. During the which time, some place of the scriptures is read, which doth lively set forth the death of Christ, to the intent that our eyes and senses may not only be occupied in these outward signs of bread and wine, which are called the visible word: but that our hearts and minds also may be fully fixed in the contemplation of the Lord's death which is by this holy Sacra-

John Knox

ment represented. And after the action is done, he giveth thanks, saying . . .

PRAYER OF THANKSGIVING
PSALM 103 OR SOME OTHER PSALM OF THANKSGIVING
BLESSING

35 The Scottish *Book of Common Prayer* 1637

From 1616 onwards King James, who was king of both England and Scotland, had been urging the Scottish bishops to produce a new service book in place of *The Book of Common Order*. Little progress was made, but his successor Charles I revived the idea in 1629. He and Archbishop Laud were keen to promote the use of the Prayer Book of 1604, which was essentially that of 1559; but the Scottish bishops preferred a new liturgy of their own. In 1634 they were instructed to "draw up a liturgy as near that of England as might be" and drafts—mainly the work of John Maxwell, Bishop of Ross—were approved by Archbishop Laud and the king in April 1635. Within months, however, a new situation emerged. In February 1636 James Wedderburn, an able liturgical scholar, became Bishop of Dunblane. He was dissatisfied with the proposed eucharistic rite, desiring a more radical form closer to that of 1549, yet at the same time retaining a number of distinctive Scottish features. His own proposals, with strong support from Maxwell, were finally agreed by Laud and the king and authorized in April 1636.

The eucharistic rite was undoubtedly a fine piece of work, despite the fact that some of the rubrics were likely to cause misgivings. For example, the altar was to be placed at the "uppermost part of the Chancel or Church," and during the eucharistic prayer the presbyter—a title more acceptable to the Scots than priest—was required to stand "at such a part of the holy Table, where he may with more ease and decency use both his hands." This could be interpreted by the more suspicious as an encouragement to re-introduce the elevation and the adoration of the consecrated elements. Nor would the permission to consecrate further supplies of bread and wine when necessary simply by the use of the Words of Institution meet with universal approval. Nevertheless the rite was a skillful blending of 1549 and 1552 material, which at a number of points was in line with Scottish custom. The word "offertory" was restored, and six of Lancelot Andrewes' "peculiar sentences for the offertory" were included, thereby broadening the concept of offering to include the fruits of the earth and the labors of mankind as well as a collection of money: the presbyter was also required to "offer up" and place the bread and wine upon the Table in readiness for the consecration. The intercessions remained in the 1552 position immediately after the offertory but contained a petition for the communicants and a commemoration of the departed—both of which were in line with 1549 and Scottish custom. The penitential material also remained in its 1552 position, except for the Prayer of Humble Access, which came immediately before communion as in 1549. This arrangement permitted the Sursum corda and the Preface-Sanctus to be linked directly with the eucharistic prayer. The first part of this prayer was that of 1549 including the epiclesis, but with the addition of the essentials of the receptionist language of 1552 used at this point. The manual acts were introduced at the Institution Narrative, although with no reference to a fraction either here or later before communion; and significantly the 1549 rubric forbidding any elevation or showing of the sacrament to the people at this point was omitted. Here again both the manual acts and the epiclesis were elements in accordance with Scottish custom. After the Narrative the 1549 prayer of oblation was added almost verbatim with its anamnesis, but omitting the reference to the angels and the holy tabernacle: this again would be acceptable to the Scots, particularly with its references to the communicants being made one body with Christ, that "he may dwell in them and they in him." The eucharistic prayer was followed by the Lord's Prayer, the Prayer of Humble Access and communion, at which the words of administration were those of 1549 without the commemorative language of 1552—another feature acceptable to the Scots. Unlike 1552, the remains of the consecrated elements were not allowed to be taken by the presbyter for his own use but had to be veiled and then consumed at the end of the service.

Despite containing so many elements which one would have thought to be acceptable to Scottish feelings, the introduction of the new book in the spring of 1637 was bitterly opposed; rioting broke out, and it was quickly dropped. This hostility was probably due to the fact that the book was essentially an episcopal book; and the Scots were no lovers of episcopacy. Significantly in the following year the General Assembly not only repudiated the

The Scottish Book of Common Prayer *1637*   259

book; it also abolished episcopacy and ratified the National Covenant. Nevertheless, despite its fate, the rite—which was the first official attempt to depart from the 1552–1559 pattern—was influential in later Anglican revisions. It undoubtedly had some influence on 1662: its merits were recognized by the Nonjurors: and it was used in the compilation of the Scottish rite of 1764 and the first American rite of 1790.

BIBLIOGRAPHY

Coena Domini I (1983), pp.409–413.
G. J. Cuming, *The Godly Order* (Alcuin Club Collections no.65, 1983),pp.110–123.
G. Donaldson, *The Making of the Scottish Prayer Book of 1637* (1954).
W. J. Grisbrooke, *Anglican Liturgies of the Seventeenth and Eighteenth Centuries* (Alcuin Club Collections no.40,1958),pp.1–18,163–182.
P. Hall, *Reliquiae Liturgicae* vol.2 (1847), pp. 122–158. *Fragmenta Liturgica* vol.5 (1848), pp. 81–119.
G. W. Sprott, *Scottish Liturgies of the Reign of James VI* (1901).

The Order of the Administration of the Lord's Supper or Holy Communion

INTRODUCTORY RUBRIC
LORD'S PRAYER (Presbyter)
COLLECT FOR PURITY
TEN COMMANDMENTS
COLLECT FOR THE KING
COLLECT OF THE DAY
EPISTLE
GOSPEL
NICENE CREED
SERMON (or HOMILY or EXHORTATION)
OFFERTORY WITH SENTENCES
PRAYER FOR THE CHURCH MILITANT
EXHORTATIONS (3)
INVITATION "Ye that do truly . . ."
CONFESSION "Almighty God, Father of our Lord . . ."
ABSOLUTION "Almighty God, our heavenly Father . . ."
COMFORTABLE WORDS

After which the Presbyter shall proceed, saying:

Lift up your hearts.
Answer: We lift them up unto the Lord.
Presbyter: Let us give thanks unto our Lord God.
Answer: It is meet and right so to do.
Presbyter: It is very meet, right, and our bounden duty, that we should at all times, and in all places, give thanks unto thee, O Lord, holy Father, almighty, everlasting God.

Here shall follow the proper Preface, according to the time, if there be any especially appointed; or else immediately shall follow,

Therefore with Angels and Archangels, etc.

PROPER PREFACES

Upon Christmas Day, and seven days after
  Because thou didst give Jesus Christ . . .

Upon Easter Day, and seven days after
  But chiefly are we bound to praise thee . . .

Upon Ascension Day, and seven days after
  Through thy most dearly beloved Son Jesus Christ . . .

Upon Whitsunday, and six days after
  Through Jesus Christ our Lord; according . . .

Upon the Feast of Trinity only.
  Who art one God, one Lord . . .

After which Prefaces shall follow immediately this Doxology:

Therefore with Angels and Archangels, and with all the company of heaven, we laud and magnify thy glorious Name, evermore praising thee, and saying, Holy, holy, holy, Lord God of hosts. Heaven and earth are full of thy glory. Glory be to thee, O Lord most high.

Then the Presbyter, standing up, shall say the Prayer of Consecration, as followeth. But then, during the time of Consecration, he shall stand at such a part of the holy Table, where he may with the more ease and decency use both his hands.

The Scottish Book of Common Prayer *1637*   **261**

Almighty God, our heavenly Father, which of thy tender mercy didst give thy only Son Jesus Christ to suffer death upon the cross for our redemption; who made there (by his one oblation of himself once offered) a full, perfect, and sufficient sacrifice, oblation, and satisfaction for the sins of the whole world, and did institute, and in his holy gospel command us to continue, a perpetual memory of that his precious death and sacrifice, until his coming again: Hear us, O merciful Father, we most humbly beseech thee, and of thy Almighty goodness vouchsafe so to bless and sanctify with thy word and Holy Spirit these thy gifts and creatures of bread and wine, that they may be unto us the body and blood of thy most dearly beloved Son; so that we, receiving them according to thy Son our Saviour Jesus Christ's holy institution, in remembrance of his death and passion, may be partakers of the same his most precious body and blood: Who, in the night that he was betrayed, *took bread,*[1] and when he had given thanks, he brake it, and gave it to his disciples, saying, Take, eat, this is my body, which is given for you: do this in remembrance of me. Likewise after supper he *took the cup,*[2] and when he had given thanks, he gave it to them, saying, Drink ye all of this, for this is my blood of the new testament which is shed for you, and for many, for the remission of sins; do this, as oft as ye shall drink it, in remembrance of me.

Immediately after shall be said this Memorial or Prayer of Oblation, as followeth.

Wherefore, O Lord and heavenly Father, according to the institution of thy dearly-beloved Son, our Savior Jesus Christ, we thy humble servants do celebrate and make here before thy Divine Majesty with these thy holy gifts, the memorial which thy Son hath willed us to make; having in remembrance his blessed passion, mighty resurrection, and glorious ascension; rendering unto thee most hearty thanks for the innumerable benefits procured unto us by the same. And we entirely desire thy Fatherly goodness mercifully to accept this our sacrifice of praise and thanksgiv-

1. *At these words* took bread *the Presbyter that officiates is to take the paten in his hand.*
2. *At these words* took the cup *he is to take the chalice in his hand, and lay his hand upon so much, be it in chalice or flagons, as he intends to consecrate.*

ing, most humbly beseeching thee to grant, that by the merits and death of thy Son Jesus Christ, and through faith in his blood, we and all thy whole Church may obtain remission of our sins and all other benefits of his passion. And here we offer and present unto thee, O Lord, ourselves, our souls and bodies, to be a reasonable, holy, and lively sacrifice unto thee; humbly beseeching thee, that whosoever shall be partakers of this holy Communion, may worthily receive the most precious body and blood of thy Son Jesus Christ, and be fulfilled with thy grace and heavenly benediction, and made one body with him, that he may dwell in them, and they in him. And although we be unworthy, through our manifold sins, to offer unto thee any sacrifice: yet we beseech thee to accept this our bounden duty and service, not weighing our merits, but pardoning our offences, through Jesus Christ our Lord: by whom, and with whom, in the unity of the Holy Ghost, all honour and glory be unto thee, O Father Almighty, world without end. Amen.

Then shall the Presbyter say

As our Savior Christ hath commanded and taught us, we are bold to say,

Our Father, which art in heaven . . . Amen.

Then shall the Presbyter, kneeling down at God's board, say in the name of all them that shall communicate, this Collect of humble access to the holy Communion, as followeth.

We do not presume . . . and he in us. Amen.

Then shall the Bishop, if he be present, or else the Presbyter that celebrateth first receive the Communion in both kinds himself, and next deliver it to the other Bishops, Presbyters and Deacons (if any be there present), that they may help him that celebrateth; and after to the people in due order, all humbly kneeling. And when he receiveth himself, or delivereth the bread to others, he shall say this benediction:

The body of our Lord Jesus Christ, which was given for thee, preserve thy body and soul unto everlasting life.

Here the party receiving shall say, Amen.

And the Presbyter or Minister that receiveth the cup himself, or delivereth it to others, shall say this benediction.

The blood of our Lord Jesus Christ, which was shed for thee, preserve thy body and soul unto everlasting life.

Here the party receiving shall say, Amen.

COLLECT OF THANKSGIVING
GLORIA IN EXCELSIS
BLESSING
ABLUTIONS AND FINAL RUBRICS
COLLECTS

36 A Directory for the Public Worship of God throughout the Three Kingdoms of England, Scotland, and Ireland 1645

One of the aims of the Solemn League and Covenant, established both in England and in Scotland in 1643–44 was the reformation in worship "according to the Word of God and the example of the best reformed Churches." This meant a Scottish-Genevan type of reformation, the English or Lutheran type being regarded as defective and incomplete. A Commission was therefore established at Westminster, composed of about 150 Englishmen, mostly Presbyterian with a smaller number of Independents, and eight Scottish "commissioners," who although not permitted to vote, nevertheless exerted considerable influence. All were agreed on a rejection of the Prayer Book, but differed on what should replace it: the Presbyterians wanted a Genevan type service with fixed elements and set prayers, but the Independents preferred greater freedom relying on ministerial inspiration. Inevitably the outcome was a compromise: and *The Directory for the Public Worship of God* took the form of a set of directions and suggestions, some of which could be converted into set prayers should the minister so choose, and allowing for considerable variation. The only set texts were the formulae for baptism, the marriage vows, and the words of delivery at communion, while the Lord's Prayer was recommended as "a pattern prayer" and "a most comprehensive prayer," but was to be said by the minister and not by the congregation. *The Directory* was authorized by the Long Parliament in England as the sole manual for public worship in January 1645, and by the Scottish Parliament and General Assembly in the following month.

Communion was to be celebrated "frequently"—a direction widely ignored—and was to take place after the Morning Sermon. This meant that it was preceded by prayer, the reading of the Old and New Testaments, metrical psalmody and preaching. Differences of opinion were apparent in the setting of the rite. English

Puritans preferred to sit "about" the Table; i.e., to remain in their pews and receive communion there from the ministers: but the Scots preferred to sit "at" the Long Table and hand the elements of communion to one another. Both arrangements were therefore provided for. After a brief exhortation, the Institution Narrative was read as the scriptural warrant and was followed by the eucharistic prayer. The directions, which could easily be used as a set prayer and contained an explicit petition for the bread and wine to be blessed and sanctified by Word and Prayer, was evidently introduced under Scottish pressure. It omitted any reference to the Sursum corda but stressed all the positive features of Calvin's liturgy. The ideas of humble access, thanksgiving for all God's benefits and especially for redemption (possibly the starting point for the 1662 General Thanksgiving), an anamnesis of the Passion of Christ, and the working of the Holy Spirit were all included: and the emphasis was on the reception of Christ's body and blood, that "he may be one with us, and we with Him." The bread and the wine were consecrated together—an arrangement favored by the Scots—and they were then distributed to the communicants "at" or "about" the Table with collective words of delivery. The rite ended with a brief exhortation to lead a worthy life, a thanksgiving, a metrical psalm, and a blessing.

This rite was bare, lacked seasonal variation, and lost any sense of order with its permitted variations. Too much was left to the whim of the minister, who—if he had little liturgical sense or ability to extemporize—could easily produce a form of service that failed to commend itself either to Anglicans or to Presbyterians. On the other hand the Independents still found it too limiting and precise for their liking. *The Directory* in fact did nothing to enhance or even maintain the standards of public worship. In England many Anglicans tended to use the Prayer Book privately, while by 1660 Presbyterians were more than ready to support both the restoration of the King and a Church settlement with a set liturgy. In Scotland the Rescissory Act at the Restoration deprived *The Directory* of all civil and ecclesiastical authority, and ministers tended to turn to the old *Book of Common Order* if needing a guide to worship.

BIBLIOGRAPHY

Coena Domini I (1983), pp. 486–489.

Ian Breward, *The Westminster Directory of Public Worship* (Grove Liturgical Study no.21, 1980).

G. B.Burnet, *The Holy Communion in the Reformed Chruch of Scotland* (1960), pp. 105–111.

D. Horton Davies, *The Worship of the English Puritans* (1948),pp.127–142. *Worship and Theology in England* vol.2 (1975), pp.405–426.

D. Forrester and D. Murray(eds.), *Studies in the History of Worship in Scotland* (1984), pp. 52–64.

P. Hall, *Reliquiae Liturgicae*, vol.3 (1847), pp.52–58.

T. Leishman, *The Westminster Directory* (1901).

E. C. Ratcliff, "Puritan Alternatives to the Prayer Book: The Directory and Richard Baxter's Reformed Liturgy," in *The English Prayer Book 1549–1662* (essays published for the Alcuin Club, 1963), pp.56–81. This essay can also be found in *Liturgical Studies* (eds. A. Couratin and D. H. Tripp,1976), pp.222–243.

Bard Thompson, pp.354–371.

CALL TO WORSHIP

PRAYER OF APPROACH

LESSON—OLD TESTAMENT

LESSON—NEW TESTAMENT

METRICAL PSALMS (before and/or between lessons)

PRAYER OF CONFESSION AND INTERCESSION

SERMON

EXHORTATION

After this exhortation, warning, and invitation, the Table being before decently covered, and so conveniently placed, that the communicants may orderly sit about it, or at it, the minister is to begin the action with sanctifying and blessing the elements of bread and wine set before him (the bread in comely and convenient vessels, so prepared that, being broken by him, and given, it may be distributed among the communicants; the wine also in large cups), having first, in a few words, showed that those elements, otherwise common, are now set apart and sanctified to this holy use, by the Word of Institution and prayer.

Let the Words of Institution be read out of the Evangelists, or out of the first Epistle of the Apostle Paul to the Corinthians, chapter 11:23. I have received of the Lord, etc., *to the 27th verse, which the minister may, when he seeth requisite, explain and apply.*

Let the prayer, thanksgiving, or blessing of the bread and wine, be to this effect:

With humble and hearty acknowledgement of the greatness of our misery, from which neither man nor angel was able to deliver us, and of our great unworthiness of the least of all God's mercies: to give thanks to God for all his benefits, and especially for that benefit of our redemption, the love of God the Father, the sufferings and merits of the Lord Jesus Christ the Son of God, by which we are delivered; and for all the means of grace, the Word and sacraments; and for this sacrament in particular, by which Christ, and all his benefits, are applied and sealed up unto us, which, notwithstanding the denial of them unto others, are in great mercy continued unto us, after so much and long abuse of them all.

To profess that there is no other name under heaven by which we can be saved, but the name of Jesus Christ, by whom alone we receive liberty and life, have access to the throne of grace, are admitted to eat and drink at his own table, and are sealed by his Spirit to an assurance of happiness and everlasting life.

Earnestly to pray to God, the Father of all mercies, and God of all consolation, to vouchsafe his gracious presence, and the effectual working of his Spirit in us; and so to sanctify these elements, both of bread and wine, and to bless his own ordinance, that we may receive by faith the body and blood of Jesus Christ, crucified for us, and so to feed upon him, that he may be one with us, and we with him; that he may live in us, and we in him, and to him who hath loved us, and given himself for us.

All which he is to endeavor to perform with suitable affections, answerable to such an holy action, and to stir up the like in the people.
The elements being now sanctified by the Word and prayer, the minister, being at the table, is to take the bread in his hand and say, in these expressions (or other the like, used by Christ or his apostle upon this occasion):

According to the holy institution, command, and example of our blessed Savior Jesus Christ, I take this bread, and having given thanks, I break it, and give it unto you.

There the minister, who is also himself to communicate, is to break the bread, and give it to the communicants.

Take ye, eat ye; this is the body of Christ, which is broken for you: do this in remembrance of him.

In like manner the minister is to take the cup, and say, in these expressions (or other the like, used by Christ or the apostle upon the same occasion):

According to the institution, command, and example of our Lord Jesus Christ, I take this cup, and give it unto you.

Here he giveth it to the communicants.

This cup is the New Testament in the blood of Christ, which is shed for the remission of the sins of many: drink ye all of it.

EXHORTATION TO A WORTHY LIFE
PRAYER OF THANKSGIVING
PSALM
BLESSING

(The Lord's Prayer was not directed to be said at any specific point, as a concession to the Independents: but its use was "recommended" in the Prayers of the Church after the sermon as "a most comprehensive prayer.")

37 Richard Baxter: *The Reformation of the Liturgy* 1661

When Charles II returned to England in 1660 at the invitation of a parliament which was largely Presbyterian, his Declaration concerning Ecclesiastical Affairs held promise of a broadly-based Church comprehending moderate Anglicans, Presbyterians, and even some Independents. He went on to say that while he considered the Prayer Book liturgy to be "the best we have seen," because exception had been taken to certain things in it, he would appoint a commission of both persuasions to review it and propose such additions and alterations as were thought necessary; and in March 1661, 12 bishops and 12 Presbyterian divines met at the Master's lodgings in the Savoy. At the request of the bishops the Presbyterians submitted their criticisms and proposals in two documents—*The Exceptions*, containing their criticisms of the Prayer Book, and *The Reformation of the Liturgy*, which was in fact a new service book combining both Anglican and Genevan elements. This was the work of Richard Baxter, the most able liturgist on the Presbyterian side and one of those who had supported the return of the king. Although compiled in a fortnight, it was the fruit of long study and his experience of *The Directory* while pastor at Kidderminster. He had no thought of rejecting the Prayer Book, for though he considered it defective and disorderly, it was nevertheless permissible when no better was available. Consequently his aim was to provide alternative rites expressed "in scripture words" and he believed that if such alternatives were placed side by side with the Prayer Book rites, the former would be seen to be preferable.

His eucharistic rite was intended to be used at the conclusion of the normal Sunday service, which had its full quota of psalmody, Old and New Testament readings, prayers, and sermon. It began with an exhortation on the nature, use and benefits of the sacrament followed by a prayer of penitence and confession echoing the confession and Prayer of Humble Access in the Prayer Book rite. The bread and wine were then brought to the minister and set upon the Table, after which came a series of elements which together might be described as Baxter's "Canon" and including three prayers each addressed to a different person of the Trinity. First there was a brief prayer to the Father containing a commemoration of creation and redemption together with a specific petition for God to sanctify the bread and wine. Then came the Institution Narrative from 1 Corinthians 11, followed by a declaration that the elements were no longer common bread and wine, but sacramentally the body and blood of Christ. Thirdly there was a prayer addressed to the Son which might be regarded as the anamnesis and containing the petition that "by thine intercession with the Father, through the sacrifice of thy body and blood" the communicants might be given pardon of their sins and Christ's quickening Spirit. At this point there was not only a fraction but a libation, representing in symbol the sacrificial death of Christ and accompanied by words echoing the Agnus Dei. Finally there was a third prayer, addressed to the Holy Spirit and praying for a good communion—"sanctify and quicken us, that we may relish the spiritual food and feed on it to our nourishment and growth in grace." The consecrated elements were then delivered to the communicants with the Scriptural formulae from *The Directory*. There was, however, provision for considerable flexibility in this rite. The bread and wine could be consecrated and distributed separately, in which case the same prayers were repeated over each element. On the other hand the bread and the wine could be consecrated and distributed together, in which case Baxter provided a single prayer addressed to the Father which was a combination of the other three. The use of the Institution Narrative was also flexible: it could be used either before the first prayer or after it. Communion could also be distributed in various ways: communicants could sit, stand or kneel; they could come to the Table or remain in their places. The rite concluded with a thanksgiving, an optional exhortation, a hymn or psalm of praise, and a blessing.

It was an admirable and dignified liturgy, attempting to harmonize Genevan liturgical traditions with those of the Prayer Book in an imaginative way. E.C.Ratcliff regarded Baxter's conception of the eucharist as "nearer to the historic Western tradition than the conception which Cranmer embodied in the Communion Service of the Prayer Book of 1552" (*From Uniformity to Unity*, p.123). Unfortunately it had little or no impact on the Savoy Conference or on the subsequent revision of the Prayer Book. This may have been due in large measure to Baxter himself. He was not a good negotiator and was intolerant of those who disagreed with him: he was an awkward ally as well as a difficult opponent. His own Presbyterian colleagues had misgivings about his liturgy and in fact its consideration only came at a late stage in the Conference. The Anglicans then judged it to be unhelpful. Indeed both sides would find in it little over which to enthuse. Possibly it was too much ahead of its time.

BIBLIOGRAPHY
Coena Domini I (1983),pp.490–493.
R. S. Bosher, *The Making of the Restoration Settlement* (1951), pp. 226–230.
G. J. Cuming, *The Godly Order* (Alcuin Club Collections no.65,1983), pp.142–152. *The Durham Book*, (1961).
D. Horton Davies, *Worship and Theology in England*, vol.2 (1975), pp.426–434. *The Worship of the English Puritans* (1948), pp.155–161.
P. Hall, *Reliquiae Liturgicae*, vol.4 (1847), pp.9–33,55–79.
W. Orme, *The Practical Works of the Revd. Richard Baxter*, vol.15 (1830),pp.450–527.
E. C. Ratcliff, "The Savoy Conference and the Revision of the Book of Common Prayer," in *From Uniformity to Unity 1662–1962* (eds. G. F. Nuttall and O. Chadwick,1962), pp.89–148. "Puritan Alternatives to the Prayer Book: *The Directory* and Richard Baxter's *Reformed Liturgy*," in *The English Prayer Book 1549–1662* (essays published for the Alcuin Club 1963), pp.56–81. This essay can also be found in *Liturgical Studies* (eds. A. Couratin and D. Tripp,1976),pp.222–243.

The Ordinary Public Worship on the Lord's Day

(This preceded the celebration of the Sacrament of the Body and Blood of Christ)

OPENING PRAYER FOR GOD'S ASSISTANCE (long and short
   forms)
APOSTLES' OR NICENE CREED, "AND SOMETIMES
   ATHANASIUS' CREED"
TEN COMMANDMENTS

SCRIPTURE SENTENCES MOVING THE PEOPLE TO PENITENCE
AND CONFESSION (optional)
CONFESSION OF SIN AND PRAYER FOR PARDON AND SANCTI-
FICATION (long and short forms) ENDING WITH THE LORD'S
PRAYER
SCRIPTURE SENTENCES "FOR THE STRENGTHENING OF
FAITH" (optional)
PSALM 95 OR 100 OR 84
PSALMS IN ORDER FOR THE DAY
OLD TESTAMENT LESSON
PSALM OR TE DEUM
NEW TESTAMENT LESSON
PRAYER FOR THE KING AND MAGISTRATES
PSALM 67 OR 98 OR SOME OTHER, OR BENEDICTUS, OR
MAGNIFICAT
PRAYER FOR THE CHURCH (extempore)
SERMON
PRAYERS FOR A BLESSING ON THE WORD OF INSTRUCTION
AND INTERCESSIONS
BENEDICTION (omitted when the sacrament followed)

The Order for Celebrating the Sacrament of the Body and Blood of Christ

EXHORTATION ON THE NATURE, USE AND BENEFITS OF THE
SACRAMENT (optional)
EXHORTATION TO PENITENCE
PRAYER OF PENITENCE AND CONFESSION (by the minister)

Here let the Bread be brought to the Minister, and received by him, and set upon the Table; and then let the Wine in like manner: or if they be set there before, however let him bless them, praying in these or like words.

Almighty God, thou art the Creator and the Lord of all things. Thou art the Sovereign Majesty whom we have offended. Thou art our most loving and merciful Father, who hast given thy Son to reconcile us to thyself: who hath ratified the new testament and covenant of grace with his most precious blood; and hath instituted this holy Sacrament to be celebrated in remembrance of him

Richard Baxter   273

till his coming. Sanctify these thy creatures of bread and wine, which, according to thy institution and command, we set apart to this holy use, that they may be sacramentally the body and blood of thy Son Jesus Christ. Amen.

Then (or immediately before this Prayer) let the Minister read the words of the institution, saying:

Hear what the apostle Paul saith: For I have received of the Lord that which also I deliver unto you; that the Lord Jesus the same night in which he was betrayed, took bread, and when he had given thanks, he brake it, and said, Take, eat, this is my body which is broken for you: this do in remembrance of me. After the same manner also he took the cup, when he had supped, saying, This cup is the new testament in my blood; this do ye, as oft as ye drink it in remembrance of me: for as often as ye eat this bread, and drink this cup, ye do shew the Lord's death till he come.

Then let the Minister say:

This bread and wine, being set apart, and consecrated to this holy use by God's appointment, are now no common bread and wine, but sacramentally the body and blood of Christ.

Then let him thus pray:

Most merciful Savior, as thou hast loved us to the death, and suffered for our sins, the just for the unjust, and hast instituted this holy Sacrament to be used in remembrance of thee till thy coming; we beseech thee, by thine intercession with the Father, through the sacrifice of thy body and blood, give us the pardon of our sins, and thy quickening Spirit, without which the flesh will profit us nothing. Reconcile us to the Father: nourish us as thy members to everlasting life. *Amen.*

Then let the Minister take the Bread, and break it in the sight of the people, saying:

The body of Christ was broken for us, and offered once for all to sanctify us: behold the sacrificed Lamb of God that taketh away the sins of the world.

In like manner let him take the Cup, and pour out the Wine in the sight of the congregation, saying:

Richard Baxter

We were redeemed with the precious blood of Christ, as of a Lamb without blemish and without spot.

Then let him thus pray:

Most holy Spirit, proceeding from the Father and the Son: by whom Christ was conceived; by whom the prophets and apostles were inspired, and the ministers of Christ are qualified and called: that dwellest and workest in all the members of Christ, whom thou sanctifiest to the image and for the service of their Head, and comfortest them that they may shew forth his praise: illuminate us, that by faith we may see him that is here represented to us. Soften our hearts, and humble us for our sins. Sanctify and quicken us, that we may relish the spiritual food, and feed on it to our nourishment and growth in grace. Shed abroad the love of God upon our hearts, and draw them out in love to him. Fill us with thankfulness and holy joy, and with love to one another. Comfort us by witnessing that we are the children of God. Confirm us for new obedience. Be the earnest of our inheritance, and seal us up to everlasting life. *Amen.*

Then let the Minister deliver the Bread, thus consecrated and broken to the Communicants, first taking and eating it himself as one of them, when he hath said:

Take ye, eat ye; this is the body of Christ, which is broken for you. Do this, in remembrance of him.

In like manner he shall deliver them the Cup, first drinking of it himself, when he hath said:

This cup is the New Testament in Christ's blood (*or*, Christ's blood of the New Testament), which is shed for you for the remission of sins. Drink ye all of it, in remembrance of him.

Let it be left to the Minister's choice, whether he will consecrate the bread and wine together, and break the bread, and pour out the wine immediately; or whether he will consecrate and pour out the wine, when the communicants have eaten the bread. If he do the latter, he must use the foregoing prayers and expressions twice accordingly. And let it be left to his discretion, whether he will use any words at the breaking of the bread and pouring out the wine, or not.

Richard Baxter

And if the Minister choose to pray but once at the consecration, commemoration, and delivery, let him pray as followeth, or to this sense.

Almighty God, thou art the Creator and the Lord of all. Thou art the Sovereign Majesty whom we have offended. Thou art our merciful Father, who hast given us thy Son to reconcile us to thyself; who hath ratified the New Testament and covenant of grace with his most precious blood, and hath instituted this holy Sacrament to be celebrated in memorial of him till his coming. Sanctify these thy creatures of bread and wine, which, according to thy will, we set apart to this holy use, that they may be sacramentally the body and blood of thy Son Jesus Christ. And, through his sacrifice and intercession, give us the pardon of all our sins, and be reconciled to us, and nourish us by the body and blood of Christ to everlasting life. And to that end, give us thy quickening Spirit to shew Christ to our believing souls, that is here represented to our senses. Let him soften our hearts, and humble us for our sins, and cause us to feed on Christ by faith. Let him shed abroad thy love upon our hearts, and draw them on in love to thee, and fill us with holy joy and thankfulness, and fervent love to one another. Let him comfort us by witnessing that we are thy children, and confirm us for new obedience, and be the earnest of our inheritance, and seal us up to life everlasting, through Jesus Christ, our Lord and Savior. Amen.

Let it be left to the Minister's discretion, whether to deliver the bread and wine to the people, at the table, only in general, each one taking it and applying it to themselves: or to deliver it in general to so many as are in each particular form; or to put it into every person's hand: as also at what season to take the contribution for the poor. And let none of the people be forced to sit, stand, or kneel, in the act of receiving, whose judgment is against it.

THANKSGIVING
EXHORTATION (optional)
HYMN OR PSALM OF PRAISE
BLESSING

Richard Baxter

In March 1661 the Savoy Conference (see p.270) was called to consider the revision of the Book of Common Prayer. Despite the wealth of proposals the Conference ended inconclusively on July 25, for the majority of the bishops were unwilling to accept anything but the most insignificant changes. Meanwhile a Bill of Uniformity, imposing the 1604 Book on the Church had already passed its third reading in the House of Commons. Before it could be considered by the House of Lords, however, Convocation met; and as the Church's constitutional body responsible for the Prayer Book, it decided to undertake its revision. A committee of eight bishops was appointed to produce proposals between full sessions. It had before it the *Durham Book,* containing the suggestions of Bishop Matthew Wren of Ely and Bishop John Cosin of Durham, and successfully completed its task in the record time of 22 days. Consideration by both Upper and Lower Houses was equally rapid. The entire revision was endorsed by the Convocations on December 21 and duly annexed to the Uniformity Bill, which received the royal assent on May 19, 1662. The new Prayer Book officially came into use on St. Bartholomew's Day (August 24).

Numerically there was a large number of changes—some six hundred: but most were of a very minor nature, and only few concessions were made either to the Laudians as represented by Cosin and Wren or to the Presbyterians. In the eucharistic rite, however, the changes—though small—were none the less significant, having the effect not only of making it more acceptable to the Laudians but also of meeting some of the Presbyterian *Exceptions.* The title "Offertory" reappeared, and both alms and bread and wine were directed to be placed upon the Table, although the rubric did not go so far as the Scottish rite of 1637 in enjoining the bread and wine to be "offered up." The eucharistic prayer was called "The Prayer of Consecration," and rubrics made it clear that manual acts were to be used and a fraction was to take place at the Institution Narrative. This, of course, pleased not only the Laudians but also the Presbyterians, who had commented in the

Exceptions that in the 1604 Prayer Book "the manner of the consecrating of the elements is not here explicit and distinct enough, and the minister's breaking of the bread is not so much as mentioned." The consecration of the elements during the prayer was further emphasized, first by the insertion of *Amen* at the end of the prayer, but also by the inclusion of the Scottish 1637 provision for the consecration of additional supplies of bread and wine if required, by the recital of the appropriate parts of the Institution Narrative over them. The Scottish rite was also followed in making proper provision for the consecrated remains after communion: they were to be veiled until the end of the service and then consumed: and on no account were they to be taken out of church, nor—as in the previous Prayer Book—could the priest have them for his own use. Finally the Declaration on Kneeling was restored, but with a significant alteration as a concession to the Presbyterians: the words "corporal presence" replaced the earlier "real and essential presence," thus turning it into a denial of one particular mode of Christ's presence in the bread and wine and not of his presence altogether.

The 1662 rite was therefore a compromise not really reflecting fully any one theological position. The words of the rite were substantially unchanged: what changed was the manner of celebrating the rite in small but significant ways. Nevertheless, it was a compromise which has successfully withstood change in England for over three hundred years. Today it still remains one of the official rites of the Church of England, while many parts of the Anglican communion throughout the world and many generations of Methodists have found its use acceptable.

BIBLIOGRAPHY
Coena Domini I (1983), pp.414–426.
F. E. Brightman, *The English Rite*, 2 vols. (1915).
G. J. Cuming, *The Durham Book* (1961). *A History of Anglican Liturgy* (1982), pp.112–127. *The Godly Order* (Alcuin Club Collections no.65, 1983), pp.110–122. "The Making of the Prayer Book of 1662," in *The English Prayer Book 1549–1662* (essays published for the Alcuin Club, 1963), pp.82–110.
D. Horton Davies, *Worship and Theology in England*, vol.2 (1975), pp.378–389.

W. J. Grisbrooke, *Anglican Liturgies of the Seventeenth and Eighteenth Centuries* (Alcuin Club Collections no.40, 1958), pp.349–374.
E. C. Ratcliff, *The Booke of Common Prayer: its Making and Revisions 1549–1661* (Alcuin Club Collections no.37, 1949).

The Order for the Administration of the Lord's Supper or Holy Communion

INTRODUCTORY RUBRICS
LORD'S PRAYER (Priest)
COLLECT FOR PURITY (Priest)
TEN COMMANDMENTS
COLLECT FOR THE KING
COLLECT OF THE DAY
EPISTLE
GOSPEL
NICENE CREED
NOTICES
SERMON or HOMILY
OFFERTORY WITH SENTENCES
PRAYER FOR THE CHURCH MILITANT
EXHORTATIONS (3)
INVITATION "Ye that do truly . . ."
CONFESSION "Almighty God, Father of our Lord . . ."
ABSOLUTION "Almighty God, our heavenly Father . . ."
COMFORTABLE WORDS

After which the Priest shall proceed, saying:
      Lift up your hearts.
Answer: We lift them up unto the Lord.
Priest: Let us give thanks unto our Lord God.
Answer: It is meet and right so to do.

Then shall the Priest turn to the Lord's Table, and say:

It is very meet, right, and our bounden duty, that we should at all times, and in all places, give thanks unto thee, O Lord, holy Father,* almighty, everlasting God.

*These words holy Father *must be omitted on Trinity Sunday.*

The Book of Common Prayer 1662   279

Here shall follow the proper Preface, according to the time, if there be any specially appointed: or else immediately shall follow:

Therefore with angels and archangels, and with all the company of heaven, we laud and magnify thy glorious Name, evermore praising thee, and saying, Holy, holy, holy, Lord God of hosts, heaven and earth are full of thy glory: Glory be to thee, O Lord most High. Amen.

PROPER PREFACES

Upon Christmas Day, and seven days after.
   Because thou didst give Jesus Christ . . .
Upon Easter Day, and seven days after.
   But chiefly are we bound to praise thee . . .
Upon Ascension Day, and seven days after.
   Through thy most dearly beloved Son Jesus Christ our
   Lord . . .
Upon Whitsunday, and six days after.
   Through Jesus Christ our Lord; according . . .
Upon the Feast of Trinity only.
   Who art one God, one Lord . . .
After each of which Prefaces shall immediately be sung or said:
   Therefore with Angels and Archangels . . .

Then shall the Priest, kneeling down at the Lord's Table, say in the name of all them that shall receive the Communion this prayer following.

We do not presume . . . and he in us. Amen.

When the Priest, standing before the Table, hath so ordered the Bread and Wine, that he may with the more readiness and decency break the Bread before the people, and take the Cup into his hands, he shall say the Prayer of Consecration, as followeth:

Almighty God, our heavenly Father, who of thy tender mercy didst give thine only Son Jesus Christ to suffer death upon the Cross for our redemption; who made there (by his one oblation of himself once offered) a full, perfect, and sufficient sacrifice, oblation, and satisfaction, for the sins of the whole world; and did institute, and in his holy Gospel command us to continue, a perpetual memory of that his precious death, until his coming again;

Hear us, O merciful Father, we most humbly beseech thee; and grant that we receiving these thy creatures of bread and wine, according to thy Son our Savior Jesus Christ's holy institution, in remembrance of his death and passion, may be partakers of his most blessed Body and Blood: who in the same night that he was betrayed, took Bread;[1] and, when he had given thanks, he brake it,[2] and gave it to his disciples, saying, Take, eat; this is my Body[3] which is given for you: Do this in remembrance of me. Likewise after supper he took the Cup;[4] and, when he had given thanks, he gave it to them, saying, Drink ye all of this; for this[5] is my Blood of the New Testament, which is shed for you and for many for the remission of sins: Do this, as oft as ye shall drink it, in remembrance of me. *Amen.*

Then shall the Minister first receive the Communion in both kinds himself, and then proceed to deliver the same to the Bishops, Priests, and Deacons, in like manner (if any be present), and after that to the people also in order, into their hands, all meekly kneeling. And, when he delivereth the Bread to any one, he shall say,

The Body of our Lord Jesus Christ, which was given for thee, preserve thy body and soul unto everlasting life: Take and eat this in remembrance that Christ died for thee, and feed on him in thy heart by faith with thanksgiving.

And the Minister that delivereth the Cup to any one shall say,

The Blood of our Lord Jesus Christ, which was shed for thee, preserve thy body and soul unto everlasting life: Drink this in remembrance that Christ's blood was shed for thee, and be thankful.

If the consecrated Bread or Wine be all spent before all have communicated, the Priest is to consecrate more, according to the Form before prescribed: beginning at (Our Savior Christ in the same night, etc.) *for*

---

1. *Here the Priest is to take the paten into his hands:*
2. *And here to break the Bread:*
3. *And here to lay his hand upon all the Bread.*
4. *Here he is to take the Cup into his hands:*
5. *And here to lay his hand upon every vessel (be it Chalice or Flagon) in which there is any Wine to be consecrated.*

the blessing of the Bread; and at (Likewise after supper, etc.) *for the blessing of the Cup.*

When all have communicated, the Minister shall return to the Lord's Table, and reverently place upon it what remaineth of the consecrated Elements, covering the same with a fair linen cloth.

LORD'S PRAYER
PRAYER OF OBLATION "O Lord and heavenly Father . . ."
or

PRAYER OF THANKSGIVING
·GLORIA IN EXCELSIS
BLESSING
F INAL RUBRICS AND COLLECTS

39 J.F. Osterwald: *The Liturgy of Neuchâtel and Vallangin* 1713

Jean Frédéric Osterwald was born in 1663, studied at Saumur in France, was ordained in 1683 at Neuchâtel, and served there until his death in 1747. Although he did not travel widely and never visited England, he was a great Anglophile—a friend of Archbishop Wake and Bishop Burnet—and a pioneer of ecumenism. He believed that a liturgy, founded on Scripture and the best in both early and modern rites, was the most effective means of revitalizing the Church and achieving unity. At Neuchâtel he found the church using a modified form of Farel's *Manner and Fashion*, a rite in the Zwinglian mould: but neither this nor Calvin's liturgy satisfied him. He began work on a new rite in 1701; by 1707 it was in use: and it was finally published in 1713 for the churches of Neuchâtel and Vallangin. Subsequently it came to be recognized as a landmark in the liturgical history of the Reformed Churches.

For a man reared in the Calvinist tradition, Osterwald's liturgical views were unusual. His understanding of the eucharist was moralist: there was no question of communion with Christ himself, but an engagement of love and a participation in the fruits of his Passion and death. His position was therefore nearer to that of Zwingli: and while he believed in the corporate aspect of worship, he regarded fellowship as symbolized by the rite of communion rather than effected by its means. He was also influenced by the Anglican Prayer Book, breaking new ground in the Reformed Churches by having a prayer of consecration. Nevertheless his liturgical ideas and his theology were not in full agreement: and while he was critical of Calvin, he does not appear to have understood the real thrust of Calvin's teaching and he lacked awareness of Calvin's insistence on the unity of word and sacrament. His communion service, for example, seems to have been an entity in itself without any relation to a Ministry of the Word, and with no visible connection with or reference to the Sunday Service.

It came from a variety of sources—Calvin, Zwingli, the Anglican Prayer Book, the Roman rite—and some elements were his own.

After a Trinitarian invocation and an opening prayer, the Scriptural Warrant from 1 Corinthians 11 was read, leading into an exhortation. This was borrowed extensively from Calvin, and the ending was particularly interesting. It had the Reformed type of Sursum corda, as in Calvin, but continued with a Preface and Sanctus on Anglican lines. There were in fact proper Prefaces for Christmas, Easter, Pentecost, and September; the prefaces for Christmas and Easter being basically those of the Anglican Prayer Book, Pentecost having a choice of two—one from the Roman rite and one from the Prayer Book, and September being by Osterwald. The intercessions and confession also relied heavily on Anglican forms, the former on the Prayer for the Church and the latter on the Prayer of Humble Access. After the absolution, the minister left the pulpit and went to the table, where the consecration prayer was said, although there were no directions for the preparation of the elements. This prayer was also heavily reliant on the Prayer Book form, although much briefer: the Institution Narrative was repeated, this time with manual acts; but the sacrificial phraseology and the invocation were omitted, and there was no Amen at the end. Since communion followed immediately, the pattern of linking it with the Narrative was therefore identical with that of 1552 and with that of Luther and Zwingli. Nor did the 1552 similarity end there: the faithful came forward for communion and the minister used brief words of delivery, telling them simply to remember what Christ had done and be thankful. The post-communion devotions were a remarkable combination: the Nunc Dimittis and the prayer of thanksgiving both came from Calvin: the Gloria in excelsis came from the Prayer Book: the final exhortation appeared to have links with exhortations from Zwingli and Farel: and the Aaronic blessing was in line with Lutheran and Reformed practice.

However mixed his theology may have been, Osterwald certainly succeeded in producing a much richer liturgical form than his Reformed predecessors. His rite remained in use in Neuchâtel with minor modifications until the present century, and elsewhere had considerable influence. In the nineteenth century it became the rite of the Huguenot congregation in Charleston, South Carolina, an English edition being published in 1853: and from there it found its way to Scotland, where it was used in 1867 in the compilation of the Church Service Society's famous *Euchologion*, the precursor of the Church of Scotland's modern *Book of Common Order*.

BIBLIOGRAPHY

P. Le Brun, *Explication de la Messe*, (1787),vol.7, pp.252–276.
B. Bürki, *Cène de Seigneur—Eucharistie de l'Église*, 2 vols. (1985); vol.1, pp. 11–24; vol.2, pp.21–36, 57–94.
J.J. von Allmen, *L'Église et ses Fonctions d'après J. F. Osterwald* (1947).
Y. Brilioth, *Eucharistic Faith and Practice, Evangelical and Catholic* (1930), pp.179–180.
E. Doumergue, *Essai sur l'Histoire du Culte Reformé* (1890).
H. G. Hageman, *Pulpit and Table* (1962), pp. 60–66.
Verbum Caro, vol. 60, no.34 (1953), pp. 69–81.
The Liturgy, or Forms of Divine Service of the French Protestant Church, Charleston, South Carolina (1853).

TRINITARIAN INVOCATION
PRAYER FOR GRACE
INSTITUTION NARRATIVE—1 Corinthians 11: 23–29.

You have heard how Jesus Christ instituted the holy Supper, and how it should be celebrated with faith and reverence in the Church by all the faithful until the end of the world. From which we see that only those who are truly Christians should be admitted to it. So, following the precept which we have in Scripture and by the authority of our Lord Jesus Christ, I excommunicate all those who are not numbered among the faithful: blasphemers, unbelievers, the profane, those who curse, those who rebel against their superiors, the quarrelsome, those who hate others; the impure, the sensual and the lustful; drunkards, the unjust, liars, the greedy, the proud, slanderers; all those dominated by worldly desires; and in particular all who have been excluded from participation in the sacrament, either in this church or in another. As long as they do not amend, I publicly warn them that the wrath of God will remain with them, and they must abstain from this holy table, lest they defile this holy sacrament, which Jesus Christ gives only to his servants and to true believers.

You Christians, who intend to come to this holy communion, should well consider the importance of what you are about to do,

J.F. Osterwald   285

and the great danger involved in eating this bread and drinking this cup unworthily. Judge yourselves therefore, and you will not be judged by the Lord. Examine your lives in the light of God's commandments; and in whatever you realize that you have offended—either by deed, word, will, or thought—be sorry, everyone of you, for your sin and make confession of it to Almighty God with a humble trust in his mercy and a true desire to live henceforth a godly and righteous life. Furthermore, be charitable towards your neighbor: if you have done wrong to anyone, or if you have come into possession of something unfairly, make restitution of it: reconcile yourselves one with another, and forgive those who have offended you, as you desire God's forgiveness for your offences. If these are your dispositions, and if you can acknowlege them with a good conscience before God, who knows what is in your hearts, then you can come to this sacred Table, and you need have no doubt that the Lord Jesus will enable you to participate in all the fruits of his death and Passion.

But above all it is necessary for you to offer to almighty God humble and thankful hearts for his redemption of the world by our Lord Jesus Christ, who humbled himself to die upon the Cross for us poor sinners, in order to make us children of God and to raise us to eternal life. And that we might have continual remembrance of the tremendous love of our blessed Savior, who thus died for us, and of those infinite good things which he has provided for us, he instituted this holy sacrament to be for us a pledge of his love and a perpetual memorial of his death to our great and everlasting comfort. Let us then offer today and at all times to our loving Redeemer, as well as to the Father and to the Holy Spirit, our praises and thanksgivings, which is our bounden duty.

To do so, let us lift up our hearts on high and render thanks to our Lord God.

It is just and fitting, and a duty for our salvation that we should at all times and in all places give thanks to you, Lord God, Holy Father, God Eternal.

At Christmas.

J.F. Osterwald

Through Jesus Christ your Son our Lord, who was born at this time for us, and who by the operation of the Holy Spirit was made very man of the substance of the Blessed Virgin his mother; and that without spot of sin, to make us clean from all sin. Therefore, with angels, etc.

At Easter.

Through Jesus Christ our Lord, who died for our sins and was raised for our justification (We praise you for the glorious resurrection of our savior*), for he is the true Lamb, who has been sacrificed and who takes away the sins of the world. By his death he has destroyed death and by his resurrection has given us everlasting life. Therefore with angels, etc.

At Pentecost.

Through Jesus Christ our Lord, who after his resurrection ascended above all heavens to the throne of your glory, and sitting at your right hand poured out the Holy Spirit on the Apostles and on your adopted children. Wherefore the whole earth rejoices, and we pay you our homage, saying with angels, etc.

or this

Through Jesus Christ our Lord, who according to his promise sent down from heaven at this time (on this day) the Holy Spirit on the Apostles, to lead them into all truth and to give them the gift of speaking divers languages, that they might be able to preach the Gospel to all nations. By the same Spirit we have been brought out of darkness into light, and from error to the truth and to knowledge of you, our God, and of Jesus Christ, whom you sent. Therefore with angels, etc.

In September.

Through Jesus Christ our Lord, because you delivered him to death to redeem us from our sins, and he must return from heaven on the day of his glorious appearing. He has also instituted the Holy Supper and commanded us to eat this bread and drink this cup to proclaim his death until he comes.

*To be said on Easter Day.

J.F. Osterwald   287

Therefore with angels and archangels and with all the company of heaven, we magnify your glorious name and we sing a hymn to your glory, saying, Holy, holy, holy, Lord God of hosts. Heaven and earth are full of your glory, Lord most High.

INTERCESSIONS
CONFESSION
ABSOLUTION

The consecration is done at the Table.
Almighty God and heavenly Father, who of your tender mercy gave your Son to suffer death upon the cross for our redemption, who offered himself as a sacrifice for the sins of the whole world and ordained that a perpetual commemoration of his death be made in his Church until he comes on the last day: receive our prayers and praises, merciful God, which we offer you through Jesus Christ, who in the night that he was betrayed took bread,[1] and having given thanks, eternal Father, broke it and said, Take, eat, this is my body which is broken for you; do this in remembrance of me.[2] Likewise after supper, he took the cup,[3] and when he had given thanks, gave it, saying, Drink of this all of you, for this is my blood, the blood of the new covenant, which is shed for many for the remission of sins. Do this as often as you drink of it in remembrance of me.[4]

The people come to the Communion, and while this is taking place psalms are sung and select passages of Scripture are read.

In giving the bread the minister says,

Remember that Jesus Christ your Savior died for you and give him thanks.

In giving the cup.

Remember that Jesus Christ your Savior shed his blood for you and give him thanks.

1. *Here the minister takes the bread into his hands.*
2. *Here the minister communicates and then gives the bread to the ministers who are at the Table with him.*
3. *Here he takes the cup.*
4. *Here he communicates from the cup and gives it to the other ministers.*

J.F. Osterwald

NUNC DIMITTIS
PRAYER OF THANKSGIVING
GLORIA IN EXCELSIS
FINAL EXHORTATION
AARONIC BLESSING

J.F. Osterwald

The Nonjurors were those who refused to take the oath of alle-
giance to King William and Queen Mary in 1689 and in conse-
quence were deprived of their livings or offices in the Church of
England. Nevertheless, many of them still regarded themselves as
loyal adherents to Anglican orthodoxy. They therefore still continued to use the 1662 Prayer Book, simply changing the royal
names in the prayers. Others, however, were not so minded, regarding the Anglican liturgy as defective at certain crucial points.
For example, George Hickes, the titular Bishop of Thetford, in his
treatise *Of the Christian Priesthood* (1707) objected to three changes
which later revisions of the Prayer Book had made to the 1549
rite—the omission of the word "altar," the omission of the offertory rubric requiring the priest to set the bread and wine upon the
altar, and the transference of the prayer of oblation to a position
after communion. In 1716 a number of Nonjuring priests and laymen petitioned their bishops, not only for a greater degree of uniformity in their forms of worship, but also for the inclusion of
four elements in the eucharist—the mixed chalice, prayer for the
departed, and a prayer of oblation and an epiclesis in the eucharistic prayer. Unfortunately a meeting to discuss these questions
broke up in disarray and resulted in schism. On one side were the
Non-usagers, insisting on no change from established custom: on
the other were the Usagers, who decided to draw up a new Communion rite "agreeable to the primitive liturgies, taking in as
much of the present established office as might be conveniently
done," and as an interim measure to introduce certain changes
into the existing liturgy—the substitution of the Summary of the
Law for the Decalogue, the provision of a ceremonial commixture,
the omission of the phrase "militant here in earth" and the inclusion of prayer for the departed in the prayer for the Church, and
the inclusion of an anamnesis, an epiclesis, and the 1662 prayer of
oblation after the Institution Narrative in the eucharistic prayer.

The new rite, largely the work of Thomas Brett, Jeremy Collier,
and Thomas Deacon, was published in 1718 together with offices

for Confirmation and the Visitation of the Sick. Brett in his *A Collection of the Principal Liturgies* (1720) outlined the principles on which it was compiled. First the existing 1662 Prayer Book rite was retained where it was considered acceptable; secondly the 1549 rite was followed, both in order and text, where it was considered preferable; and thirdly, where both 1662 and 1549 were considered defective, the ancient liturgies—and in particular the Clementine liturgy in Book 8 of *The Apostolic Constitutions*—were employed. Thus the general order from the offertory onwards was that of 1549, including a commixture at the offertory and "Christ our Paschal Lamb" after the peace. In matters of detail, however, there were differences: an offertory prayer, based on a form in the rite of St. Basil, was included; the rite of St. James was followed in the use of "holy/holiness" as the tie-words between the Sanctus and the thanksgivings for Creation and redemption; the text of the anamnesis-oblation-epiclesis was taken almost verbatim from the Clementine liturgy; the intercessions followed the Clementine pattern in coming at the end of the eucharistic prayer, but the text was a combination of material from 1549 and the Scottish rite of 1637; the words of administration were those of 1549; and the Gloria was in its 1662 position before the blessing.

Of all the rites produced in England in the post-1662 period, this was the most practical and satisfactory. Restrained and largely familiar in language, reasonable in length and primitive in structure, it is not surprising that it was a model to which others— notably Scotland and America—were glad to turn in the creation of a new family of Anglican liturgies which took 1549 rather than 1662 as their parent. It was certainly more widely followed than the later Nonjuring rite of 1734, which was longer and more complicated and produced when the movement was past its zenith.

BIBLIOGRAPHY
H. Broxap, *The Later Nonjurors* (1924).
G. J. Cuming, *A History of Anglican Liturgy* (1982), pp. 141–143.
J. Dowden, *The Scottish Communion Office of 1764* (1922), pp. 210–222.
W. Jardine Grisbrooke, *Anglican Liturgies in the Seventeenth and Eighteenth Centuries* (Alcuin Club Collections no. 40, 1958), pp. 71–112, 273–296.
P. Hall, *Fragmenta Liturgica*, vol. 5. (1848), pp. 9–52.

The Order for the Administration of the Lord's Supper or Holy Communion.

INTRODUCTORY RUBRICS

INTROITS FOR SUNDAYS AND HOLY DAYS

SALUTATION AND LESSER LITANY

LORD'S PRAYER (Priest)

COLLECT FOR PURITY

SUMMARY OF THE LAW

COLLECT FOR THE KING

COLLECT OF THE DAY

EPISTLE

GOSPEL

NICENE CREED

NOTICES

SERMON or HOMILY

EXHORTATIONS (3)

OFFERTORY (Alms, Bread, Wine) with SENTENCES

OFFERTORY COLLECT

Then shall the Priest turn to the People, and say,

	The Lord be with you.
Answer.	And with thy Spirit.
Priest.	Lift up your hearts.
Answer.	We lift them up unto the Lord.
Priest.	Let us give thanks unto our Lord God.
Answer.	It is meet and right so to do.

Then shall the Priest turn to the Altar, and say,

It is very meet, right, and our bounden duty, that we should at all times, and in all places, give thanks unto thee, O Lord, holy Father,* almighty everlasting God.

Here shall follow the proper preface according to the time, if there be any specially appointed: or else immediately shall follow,

These words (holy Father) must be omitted on Trinity Sunday.

Therefore with angels and archangels, and with all the company of heaven, we laud and magnify thy glorious Name, evermore praising thee, and saying,

Here the People shall join with the Priest, and say,

Holy, holy, holy, Lord God of Hosts: heaven and earth are full of thy glory: Hosanna in the highest: Blessed is he that cometh in the Name of the Lord: glory be to thee, O Lord most high. Amen.

Proper Prefaces.

Upon Christmas-day, and seven days after.

Because thou didst give Jesus Christ thine only Son. . . .

Upon Easter-day, and seven days after.

But chiefly are we bound to praise thee. . . .

Upon Ascension-day, and seven days after.

Through thy most dearly beloved Son Jesus Christ. . . .

Upon Whitsunday, and six days after.

Through Jesus Christ our Lord; according to whose most true promise. . . .

Upon the Feast of Trinity only.

Who art one God, one Lord. . . .

After each of which Prefaces shall follow immediately.

Therefore with angels and archangels, and with all the company of heaven, we laud and magnify thy glorious Name, evermore praising thee, and saying,

Here the People shall join with the Priest and say,

Holy, holy, holy, Lord God of Hosts: heaven and earth are full of thy glory: Hosanna in the highest: Blessed is he that cometh in the Name of the Lord: glory be to thee, O Lord most high. Amen.

Immediately after, the Priest shall say,

Holiness is thy nature, and thy gift, O Eternal King; Holy is thine only begotten Son our Lord Jesus Christ, by whom thou hast made the worlds; Holy is thine Ever-blessed Spirit, who searcheth all things, even the depths of thine infinite perfection. Holy art thou, almighty and merciful God; thou createdst Man in thine own image, broughtest him into Paradise, and didst place him in a state of dignity and pleasure: And when he had lost his happiness by transgressing thy command, thou of thy goodness didst not abandon and despise him. Thy Providence was still continued, thy law was given to revive the sense of his duty, thy Prophets were commissioned to reclaim and instruct him. And when the fullness of time was come, thou didst send thine only begotten Son to satisfy thy Justice, to strengthen our Nature, and renew thine Image within us: For these glorious ends thine Eternal Word came down from heaven, was incarnate by the Holy Ghost, born of the Blessed Virgin, conversed with mankind, and directed his life and miracles to our salvation: And when his hour was come to offer the Propitiatory Sacrifice upon the Cross; when he, who had no sin himself, mercifully undertook to suffer death for our sins, in the same night that he was betrayed (a) took bread; and when he had given thanks, (b) he brake it, and gave it to his disciples, saying, Take, eat, (c) THIS IS MY BODY, which is given for you, Do this in remembrance of me.

Here the People shall answer. Amen.

Then shall the Priest say,

Likewise after Supper, (d) he took the Cup; and when he had given thanks, he gave it to them, saying, Drink ye all of this, for (e) THIS IS MY BLOOD of the New Testament, which is shed for you and for many for the remission of sins; Do this, as oft as ye shall drink it, in remembrance of me.

Here the People shall answer, Amen.

(a) *Here the Priest is to take the Paten into his hands:*
(b) *And here to break the Bread;*
(c) *And here to lay his hands upon all the Bread.*
(d) *Here he is to take the Cup into his hands:*
(e) *And here to lay his hand upon every vessel (be it Chalice or Flagon) in which there is any Wine and Water to be consecrated.*

The Nonjurors' Liturgy *1718*

Then shall the Priest say,

Wherefore, having in remembrance his Passion, Death, and Resurrection from the dead; his Ascension into heaven, and second coming with glory and great power to judge the quick and the dead, and to render to every man according to his works; we Offer to Thee, our King and our God, according to his holy Institution, this Bread and this Cup; giving thanks to thee through him, that thou hast vouchsafed us the honour to stand before thee, and to Sacrifice unto thee. And we beseech thee to look favourably on these thy Gifts, which are here set before thee, O thou self-sufficient God: And do thou accept them to the honour of thy Christ; and send down thine Holy Spirit, the witness of the Passion of our Lord Jesus, upon this Sacrifice, that he may make this (f) Bread the Body of thy Christ, and (g) this Cup the Blood of thy Christ; that they who are partakers thereof, may be confirmed in godliness, may obtain remission of their sins, may be delivered from the Devil and his snares, may be replenished with the Holy Ghost, may be made worthy of thy Christ, and may obtain everlasting life, Thou, O Lord Almighty, being reconciled unto thee through the merits and mediation of thy Son our Savior Jesus Christ; who, with thee and the Holy Ghost, liveth and reigneth ever one God, world without end. Amen.

Almighty and everliving God, who by thy holy Apostle hast taught us to make prayers and supplications, to give thanks for all men; We humbly beseech thee most mercifully to accept these our oblations, and to receive these our prayers, which we offer unto thy Divine Majesty, beseeching thee to inspire continually the Universal Church with the Spirit of truth, unity, and concord; and grant, that all they that do confess thy holy Name, may agree in the truth of thy holy Word, and live in unity and godly love. Give grace, O heavenly Father, to all Bishops and Curates, that they may both by their life and doctrine set forth thy true and lively Word, and rightly and duly administer thy holy Sacraments. We beseech thee also to save and defend all Christian kings, princes, and governours; and especially thy servant our King, that under

(f) *Here the Priest shall lay his hand upon the Bread.*
(g) *And here upon every vessel (be it Chalice or Flagon) in which there is any Wine and Water.*

him we may be godly and quietly governed: and grant unto his whole Council and to all that are put in authority under him, that they may truly and indifferently minister justice, to the punishment of wickedness and vice, and to the maintenance of thy true religion and virtue. And to all thy people given thy heavenly grace, that with meek heart and due reverence they may hear and receive thy holy Word, truly serving thee in holiness and righteousness all the days of their life. And we commend especially unto thy merciful goodness this Congregation, which is here assembled in thy Name to celebrate the commemoration of the most glorious death of thy Son. And we most humbly beseech thee of thy goodness, O Lord, to comfort and succour all them, who in this transitory life are in trouble, sorrow, need, sickness, or any other adversity; (*especially those for whom our prayers are desired.**) And here we do give unto thee most high praise and hearty thanks, for the wonderful grace and virtue declared in all thy Saints, from the beginning of the world; and particularly in the glorious and ever-blessed Virgin Mary, mother of thy Son Jesus Christ our Lord and God; and in the holy Patriarchs, Prophets, Apostles, Martyrs, and Confessors; whose examples, O Lord, and stedfastness in thy faith and keeping thy holy commandments, grant us to follow. We commend unto thy mercy, O Lord, all thy Servants, who are departed from us with the sign of faith, and now do rest in the sleep of peace: Grant unto them, we beseech thee, thy mercy and everlasting peace; and that at the day of the general resurrection, we and all they who are of the mystical Body of thy Son, may altogether be set on his right hand, and hear that his most joyful voice: Come, ye blessed of my Father, inherit the Kingdom prepared for you from the foundation of the world. Grant this, O Father, for Jesus Christ's sake, our only Mediator and Advocate. *Amen.*

Then the Priest shall say the Lord's Prayer, the People repeating after him every Petition.

Our Father, which . . . for ever and ever. Amen.

Then shall the Priest turn to the People, and say,

*This is to be said when any desire the Prayers of the Congregation.

The peace of the Lord be always with you.

Answer.   And with thy spirit.
Priest.   Christ, our Paschal Lamb, is offered up for us, once
for all, when he bare our sins in his body upon the Cross; for he is
the very Lamb of God, that taketh away the sins of the world:
Wherefore let us keep a joyful and holy feast unto the Lord.

Then the Priest shall say to all those that come to receive the Holy Com-
munion:

INVITATION "Ye that do truly . . ."
CONFESSION "Almighty God, Father of our Lord . . ."
ABSOLUTION "Almighty God, our heavenly Father . . ."
COMFORTABLE WORDS
PRAYER OF HUMBLE ACCESS "We do not presume . . ."

Then shall the Bishop if he be present, or else the Priest that officiateth,
kneel down and receive the Communion in both kinds himself, and then
proceed to deliver the same to other Bishops, Priests, and Deacons in like
manner, if any be there present; and after that to the People also in order
into their hands, all meekly kneeling.

And when he delivereth the Sacrament of the Body of Christ to any one,
he shall say,

The Body of our Lord Jesus Christ, which was given for thee,
preserve thy Body and Soul unto everlasting life.

Here the Person receiving shall say, Amen.

And the Priest or Deacon that delivereth the Sacrament of the Blood of
Christ to any one, shall say,

The Blood of our Lord Jesus Christ, which was shed for thee,
preserve thy Body and Soul unto everlasting life.

Here the Person receiving shall say, Amen.

COMMUNION
PRAYER OF THANKSGIVING
GLORIA IN EXCELSIS
BLESSING
FINAL COLLECTS AND RUBRICS

The Nonjurors' Liturgy 1718   297

41 Henry Muhlenberg: *The Church Agenda* 1748

The earliest Lutherans came to America from Holland and Sweden in the seventeenth century, and they were greatly increased in the early years of the eighteenth by the German immigration, which settled mainly in Pennsylvania. They founded local congregations, making use of the liturgical resources of their native churches: but there was no general organization or oversight until the congregations of Philadelphia, New Hanover and Trappe sent a delegation to the Lutheran authorities in London and Halle, asking for a leader to be sent to take charge of the scattered communities. In response Henry Melchior Muhlenberg, a thirty-one year old German pastor from Halle, near Leipzig, was sent in 1742. He proved to be a great and respected leader and has deservedly been regarded as the Patriarch of the Lutheran Church in America. One of his achievements was the creation of a common liturgy which was adopted by the first Lutheran Synod in Philadelphia in August 1748.

According to Muhlenberg's journal for April 28, 1748, he was assisted by Pastors Brunholtz and Handschuh, and they took the liturgy of the Lutheran Savoy Church in London as the basis of their work. This may have been the only printed text available to them; and if so, they clearly made substantial changes. Subsequent careful research by Dr. Beale Schmucker has revealed that in fact they owed remarkably little to the London Savoy liturgy, but that they actually produced from memory a great deal from the Church Orders of Northern Germany with which they had been familiar—those of Lüneburg, used at Muhlenberg's home in Einbeck; Calenberg, used at Göttingen during his student days; Brandenburg-Magdeburg, used at Halle while he resided there; and Saxony, which he used when pastor at Grosshennersdorf. These four Orders are remarkably similar; and a detailed comparison indicated that Muhlenberg's liturgy substantially agreed with them. The result was a fine Lutheran rite of considerable independence. This liturgy was never printed. Each minister was responsible for making his own manuscript copy; and two of these—one by Jacob Van Buskerk in 1763 and one by Peter Muhlenberg in

1769—eventually came into the hands of Dr. J. W. Richards, a descendant of Henry Muhlenberg. It is from these two copies that the text below is taken. Printed copies of the liturgy were not made until 1786, when it underwent minor revision, and was published in Philadelphia under the title *Kirchen-agenda der Evangelisch-Lutherischen Vereinigten Gemeinen in Nord-America.*

Its eclectic character is very evident. The propers were all taken from the Marburg Hymnal, which was widely used in America. The pattern of the abbreviated Sursum corda and Sanctus followed Luther's *Formula Missae*, but the paraphrase of the Lord's Prayer and the Exhortation followed the *Deutsche Messe*. The Invitation to Communion was the only distinctive element borrowed from the London Savoy liturgy. The Institution Narrative and Administration were no longer split, while the addition of the Trinitarian Invocation to the Aaronic Blessing came from the Swedish Liturgy. Dr. Schmucker commented: "It is the Service of widest acceptance in the Lutheran Church of middle and north Germany, Denmark, Norway and Sweden. . . . It is very fortunate for the Lutheran Church in America that the Fathers gave them at the beginning so pure and beautiful an Order of Service" (*The Lutheran Church Review*, 1882, p. 172).

BIBLIOGRAPHY

Luther D. Reed, *The Lutheran Liturgy* (1959), pp. 161–169.
H. E. Jacobs, *A History of the Evangelical Lutheran Church in the United States* (1893), pp. 266–275.
Beale M. Schmucker, "The First Pennsylvania Liturgy," in *The Lutheran Church Review*, 1882, pp. 16–27, 161–172.

An English translation of the German text was made by Dr. C.W. Schaeffer and appeared in the volume by H. E. Jacobs above pp. 269ff.

The Order for the Administration of the Lord's Supper

HYMN—Invocation of the Holy Spirit
EXHORTATION, CONFESSION, KYRIE (Confession from the Calenberg Order 1569)
GLORIA IN EXCELSIS (metrical form)

COLLECT (from the Marburg Hymnal—widely used in the
  U.S.A.)
EPISTLE (Marburg Hymnal)
HYMN (Marburg Hymnal)
GOSPEL (Marburg Hymnal)
NICENE CREED (Luther's metrical version)
HYMN
SERMON
GENERAL PRAYER WITH INTERCESSIONS or LITANY
LORD'S PRAYER
VOTUM ("The Peace of God, which passeth . . .")
HYMN
SALUTATION and COLLECT
AARONIC BLESSING and TRINITARIAN INVOCATION

The minister goes before the altar, places the bread and wine in order, then turns to the congregation and says:

Minister.   The Lord be with you,
Congregation. And with thy spirit.
Minister.   Let us lift up our hearts,
Congregation. We lift them up unto the Lord.
Minister.   Holy, holy, holy is the Lord of Sabaoth.
Congregation. The whole world is full of his glory.

Before the communion the pastor addresses the communicants in the exhortation here following. Beloved in the Lord!

Here follows Luther's Paraphrase of the Lord's Prayer, and his Exhortation to the Sacrament, exactly as it occurs in his Deutsche Messe 1526.

The pastor turns his face to the bread and wine, and repeats the Lord's Prayer and the Words of Institution.

Let us pray: Our Father, ...

Our Lord Jesus Christ in the night. . . . in remembrance of me.

Then the pastor turns to the congregation and says:

Now let all those who are found to be prepared, by the experience of sincere repentance and faith, approach, in the name of the Lord, and receive the Holy Supper.

In giving the bread the pastor shall say these words:

Take and eat: This is the true body of your Lord Jesus Christ,
given unto death for you; may this strengthen you in the true
faith unto everlasting life. Amen.

In giving the cup:

Take and drink: This is the true blood of your Lord Jesus Christ,
of the New Testament, shed for you for the forgiveness of your
sins, unto everlasting life. Amen.

The communion being finished, the pastor shall say:

O give thanks unto the Lord, for he is good: Hallelujah.

The congregation responds:

And his mercy endureth forever: Hallelujah.

FINAL COLLECT
AARONIC BLESSING and TRINITARIAN INVOCATION

Henry Muhlenberg

After the restoration of Charles II in 1660 the Scottish bishops made little effort to introduce either the Scottish Prayer Book of 1637 or the revised English Prayer Book of 1662. For nearly half a century there was little essential difference between Episcopalian and Presbyterian public worship. In the early years of the eighteenth century, however, Episcopalian patterns began to change. The use of the 1662 Book began to spread, aided by the Toleration Act of 1712 and by grants of books from England, while the 1637 Book also had its adherents. Some people in the diocese of Edinburgh, for example, tended to combine the eucharistic liturgies of the two books, interjecting an epiclesis into the 1662 consecration prayer and adding the prayer of oblation immediately after the Institution Narrative. In 1722–24 the "Wee Bookies" were published—reprints of the 1637 eucharistic rite beginning at the offertory and omitting the first two exhortations and the collects and rubrics after the blessing. Then in 1731 the entire Scottish episcopate signed a concordat undertaking to use only the 1637 or 1662 rites in public worship. In this way the use of the prayer of oblation and the epiclesis in the eucharistic prayer received specific sanction.

In this period one of the most learned figures in the Episcopal Church was Thomas Rattray, Laird of Craighall and successively Bishop of Brechin (1727), Dunkeld (1731), and Primus (1739). In 1743 he was elected to the see of Edinburgh but died before he could take office. His liturgical learning was immense; and he devoted himself to a study of the Liturgy of St. James, comparing it with other known texts of the early Church. This was published the year after his death under the title *The Ancient Liturgy of the Church of Jerusalem*, together with an appendix containing a proposed rite for current use. This proposed rite, which indicated his preference for the content and structure of the Nonjurors' rite of 1718 rather than those of 1637 or 1662, was never used publicly, but proved to be influential. In 1755 the Primus, Bishop Falconar of Edinburgh, issued a revision of the communion office which clearly showed a dependence upon Rattray's work. After further amendment in 1762–63 with help from Bishop Forbes, the Primus published this in 1764 on his own authority, although with the knowledge of his episcopal brethren. It therefore had no formal synodical approval; but it was rapidly accepted by the Episcopal Church in Scotland.

It owed something to the rites of 1637 and 1662, to the Nonjurors' rite of 1718 and to Rattray. Four significant elements came from 1637—the offertory sentences, the offertory rubric with its direction to "offer up" the bread and wine, the text of the prayer for the Church, and the text of the epiclesis. But the general structure of the rite and the internal structure of the eucharistic prayer showed the influence of the Nonjurors and Rattray. The prayer for the Church and the 1662 penitential material came between the eucharistic prayer and communion; while in the eucharistic prayer itself the act of oblation (printed in capital letters) and the epiclesis followed the Institution Narrative.

The Communion Office of 1764 marked the beginning of a new family of Anglican eucharistic liturgies which followed primitive patterns and could be regarded as derivatives of 1549 rather than of 1662. Within a short space of time the American Anglican liturgy of 1790 adopted the same pattern.

BIBLIOGRAPHY
J. Dowden, *The Scottish Communion Office of 1764* (1922).
D. Forrester and D. Murray (eds.), *Studies in the History of Worship in Scotland* (1984), pp. 66–67.
F. Goldie, *A Short History of the Episcopal Church in Scotland* (1976).
W. Jardine Grisbrooke, *Anglican Liturgies of the Seventeenth and Eighteenth Centuries* (Alcuin Club Collections no. 40, 1958), pp.150–159, 333–348.
P. Hall, *Fragmenta Liturgica*, vol. 5 (1848), pp. 193–224.

The sections of the office before the Exhortations were not printed in 1764: They here follow the reconstruction by Dowden.

LORD'S PRAYER
COLLECT FOR PURITY
TEN COMMANDMENTS or SUMMARY OF THE LAW
PRAYER FOR DIVINE HELP or PRAYER FOR THE KING/QUEEN
COLLECT OF THE DAY.

The Scottish Communion Office 1764   303

EPISTLE

GOSPEL

NICENE CREED

SERMON

EXHORTATION

OFFERTORY (Devotions, Bread, Wine) with SENTENCES

And the Presbyter shall then offer up, and place the bread and wine prepared for the sacrament upon the Lord's Table; and shall say,

The Lord be with you.
Answer: And with thy spirit.
Presbyter: Lift up your hearts.
Answer: We lift them up unto the Lord.
Presbyter: Let us give thanks unto our Lord God.
Answer: It is meet and right so to do.
Presbyter: It is very meet, right, and our bounden duty, that we should at all times, and in all places, give thanks unto thee, O Lord, *(holy Father), Almighty, everlasting God.

Here shall follow the proper preface, according to the time, if there be any especially appointed; or else immediately shall follow,

Therefore with angels and archangels, etc.

Proper Prefaces.

Upon Christmas-day, and seven days after.

Because thou didst give Jesus Christ. . . .

Upon Easter-day, and seven days after.

But chiefly are we bound to praise thee. . . .

Upon Ascension-day, and seven days after.

Through thy most dearly beloved Son, Jesus Christ. . . .

Upon Whitsunday, and six days after.

Through Jesus Christ our Lord, according. . . .

Upon the feast of Trinity only.

Who art one God, one Lord. . . .

* *These words* (holy Father) *must be omitted on Trinity Sunday.*

After which prefaces shall follow immediately this Doxology.

Therefore with angels and archangels, and with all the company of heaven, we laud and magnify thy glorious name, evermore praising thee, and saying, Holy, holy, holy, Lord God of hosts, heaven and earth are full of thy glory. Glory be to thee, O Lord most high. Amen.

Then the Presbyter, standing at such a part of the holy table as he may with the most ease and decency use both his hands, shall say the prayer of consecration, as followeth.

All glory be to thee, Almighty God, our heavenly Father, for that thou of thy tender mercy didst give thy only Son Jesus Christ to suffer death upon the cross for our redemption; who (by his own oblation of himself once offered) made a full, perfect, and sufficient sacrifice, oblation, and satisfaction, for the sins of the whole world, and did institute, and in his holy gospel command us to continue a perpetual memorial of that his precious death and sacrifice, until his coming again. For, in the night that he was betrayed, (a) he took bread; and when he had given thanks, (b) he brake it, and gave it to his disciples, saying, Take, eat, (c) THIS IS MY BODY, which is given for you: DO this in remembrance of me. Likewise after supper (d) he took the cup; and when he had given thanks, he gave it to them, saying, Drink ye all of this, for (e) THIS IS MY BLOOD, of the new testament, which is shed for you and for many, for the remission of sins: DO this as oft as ye shall drink it in remembrance of me.

The Oblation. Wherefore, O Lord, and heavenly Father, according to the institution of thy dearly beloved Son our Savior Jesus Christ, we thy humble servants do celebrate and make here before thy divine majesty, with these thy holy gifts, WHICH WE NOW OFFER UNTO THEE, the memorial thy Son hath commanded us to make; having in remembrance his blessed passion, and precious death, his mighty resurrection, and glorious ascen-

(a) *Here the Presbyter is to take the paten in his hands:*
(b) *And here to break the bread:*
(c) *And here to lay his hands upon all the bread.*
(d) *Here he is to take the cup into his hand:*
(e) *And here to lay his hand upon every vessel (be it chalice or flagon) in which there is any wine to be consecrated.*

The Scottish Communion Office 1764

sion; rendering unto thee most hearty thanks for the innumerable benefits procured unto us by the same. And we most humbly beseech . . .

The Invocation . . . thee, O merciful Father, to hear us, and of thy almighty goodness vouchsafe to bless and sanctify, with thy word and Holy Spirit, these thy gifts and creatures of bread and wine, that they may become the body and blood of thy most dearly beloved Son. And we earnestly desire thy fatherly goodness, mercifully to accept this our sacrifice of praise and thanksgiving, most humbly beseeching thee to grant, that by the merits and death of thy Son Jesus Christ, and through faith in his blood, we (and all thy whole Church) may obtain remission of our sins, and all other benefits of his passion. And here we humbly offer and present unto thee, O Lord, ourselves, our souls and bodies, to be a reasonable, holy and lively sacrifice unto thee, beseeching thee, that whosoever shall be partakers of this holy Communion, may worthily receive the most precious body and blood of thy Son Jesus Christ, and be filled with thy grace and heavenly benediction, and made one body with him, that he may dwell in them, and they in him. And although we are unworthy, through our manifold sins, to offer unto thee any sacrifice; yet we beseech thee to accept this our bounden duty and service, not weighing our merits, but pardoning our offences, through Jesus our Lord: by whom, and with whom, in the unity of the Holy Ghost, all honour and glory be unto thee, O Father Almighty, world without end. Amen.

PRAYER FOR THE CHURCH "Almighty and everliving God. . . ."
   (As in Scotland 1637, with minor variations).
LORD'S PRAYER
INVITATION "Ye that do truly. . . ."
CONFESSION "Almighty God, Father
   of our Lord. . . ."
ABSOLUTION "Almighty God, our   Texts as in
   heavenly Father. . . ."   Scotland 1637
COMFORTABLE WORDS
PRAYER OF HUMBLE ACCESS "We do
   not presume. . . ."

Then shall the Bishop, if he be present, or else the Presbyter that celebrateth, first receive the communion in both kinds himself, and next deliver it to other Bishops, Presbyters, and Deacons, (if there be any present), and after to the people, in due order, all humbly kneeling. And when he receiveth himself, or delivereth the sacrament of the body of Christ to others, he shall say,

The body of our Lord Jesus Christ, which was given for thee, preserve thy soul and body unto everlasting life.

Here the person receiving shall say, Amen.

And the Presbyter or Minister that receiveth the cup himself, or delivereth it to others, shall say this benediction.

The blood of our Lord Jesus Christ, which was shed for thee, preserve thy soul and body unto everlasting life.

Here the person receiving shall say, Amen.

If the consecrated bread or wine be all spent before all have communicated, the Presbyter is to consecrate more, according to the form before pre-scribed, beginning at the words, All glory be to thee, *etc. and ending with the words,* that they may become the body and blood of thy most dearly beloved Son.

When all have communicated, he that celebrates shall go to the Lord's table, and cover with a fair cloth that which remaineth of the consecrated elements, and then say,

Having now received the precious body and blood of Christ, let us give thanks to our Lord God, who hath graciously vouchsafed to admit us to the participation of his holy mysteries; and let us beg of him grace to perform our vows, and to persevere in our good resolutions; and that being made holy, we may obtain ever-lasting life, through the merits of the all-sufficient sacrifice of our Lord and Savior Jesus Christ.

COLLECT OF THANKSGIVING "Almighty and everliving
   God. . . ."
GLORIA IN EXCELSIS
BLESSING

43 *The Prayer Book of the Protestant Episcopal Church of the United States of America* 1790

At the time of the Declaration of Independence in 1776 Anglicans in America used the 1662 Prayer Book as their liturgy and were considered to be under the jurisdiction of the Bishop of London: but no bishop ever crossed the Atlantic to fulfill episcopal obligations. The first American state to seek a remedy for this defect was Connecticut, whose clergy elected Dr. Samuel Seabury as bishop in March 1783 and instructed him to seek consecration in England. The English bishops failed to cooperate, however: and eventually three Scottish bishops consecrated him in Aberdeen on November 14, 1784, expressing the hope in return that he would commend their 1764 rite to his brethren and sanction its use. In the following year a convention of seven states—New York, New Jersey, Pennsylvania, Delaware, Maryland, Virginia and South Carolina—drafted a constitution for the Protestant Episcopal Church in America and agreed to a revision of the 1662 Prayer Book in order to adapt it to the American scene. The original proposals, prepared by Dr. William Smith of Maryland and envisaging a shorter and more comprehensive book than 1662, met with a mixed reception. There is evidence that they were widely used, but there was also enough criticism to prevent their official endorsement. The English bishops, to whom they had been submitted for consideration, were also critical, commenting that they, i.e. the proposals, "showed less respect to our liturgy than its own excellence and your declared attachment to it, had led us to expect." A revised set of proposals in October 1789 were more successful, however: they were approved by the General Convention of that month and the first American Prayer Book came into use on October 1, 1790.

This book was a brave attempt to be more contemporary than 1662, with fewer archaisms, greater flexibility and abbreviation, a broader range of services, and drawing material from a wide variety of sources, including 1662, the Scottish rites of 1637 and 1764, Irish proposals made in 1711, and Dr. Smith's original proposals of 1786. The eucharistic rite was generally faithful in following the lines of the Scottish 1764 rite: but there was also evidence of a sturdy independence in showing a preference for 1662 or the Scottish rite of 1637 at significant points, or even in adopting a quite new line. For example, the prayer for the Church and the penitential material followed the offertory as in the Scottish rites of 1637 and 1662 rather than coming between the eucharistic prayer and communion as in the Scottish rite of 1764. The Prayer of Humble Access also came in its 1662 position between the Preface-Sanctus and the eucharistic prayer, thus differing from both the Scottish rites of 1637 and 1764. On the other hand the eucharistic prayer followed the Scottish 1764 rite in having an epiclesis after the Institution Narrative; but the text was that of the Scottish 1637 rite, although the salient words "that they may become the Body and Blood of thy most dearly beloved Son" were omitted. The preference at certain points for the Scottish 1637 rite is perhaps not so surprising in view of the fact that many of the clergy ministering in America had come from Scotland and had tended to use the Scottish "Wee Bookies" which contained the 1637 rite and had been in use in the country for some seventy-five years.

This first American rite can therefore be said to have freely followed Scottish patterns, marking a further development in the family of Anglican liturgies following 1549 rather than 1552–1662. Some minor corrections were made to the Book in 1793 and this later edition came to be known as the "Standard" text. This in its turn was subject to further minor changes on six occasions between 1793 and 1892: but all of these were essentially editions of the same Book.

BIBLIOGRAPHY

J. Dowden, *The Scottish Communion Office of 1764*, (1922).
P. Hall, *Reliquiae Liturgicae* vol.5,(1847), pp. 86–114 (the original proposals of 1786).
Marion J. Hatchett, *Commentary on the American Prayer Book*, (1980), and *The Making of the First American Book of Common Prayer 1776–89*, (1982).
William McGarvey, *Liturgicae Americanae*, (1895).
Massey H. Shepherd, *The Oxford American Prayer Book Commentary*, (1955).

The Order for the Administration of the Lord's Supper or Holy Communion.

INTRODUCTORY RUBRICS

LORD'S PRAYER (Priest) (Omission permitted if Morning Prayer immediately precedes)

COLLECT FOR PURITY (Priest)

TEN COMMANDMENTS

SUMMARY OF THE LAW (Optional)

PRAYER FOR DIVINE HELP

COLLECT OF THE DAY

EPISTLE

GOSPEL

APOSTLES' or NICENE CREED

NOTICES

SERMON

OFFERTORY (Alms, Bread, Wine) with SENTENCES

PRAYER FOR THE CHURCH MILITANT

EXHORTATIONS (3)

INVITATION "Ye that do truly. . . ."

CONFESSION "Almighty God, Father of our Lord. . . ."

ABSOLUTION "Almighty God, our heavenly Father. . . ."

COMFORTABLE WORDS

After which the Priest shall proceed, saying,

> Lift up your hearts.

Answer: We lift them up unto the Lord.

Priest: Let us give thanks unto our Lord God.

Answer: It is meet and right so to do.

Then shall the Priest turn to the Lord's Table, and say,

It is very meet, right, and our bounden duty, that we should at all times, and in all places, give thanks unto thee, O Lord, (*Holy Father), Almighty, Everlasting God:

Here shall follow the proper Preface, according to the time, if there be any specially appointed: or else immediately shall be said or sung by the Priest and People,

These words (Holy Father) must be omitted on Trinity Sunday.

Therefore with angels and archangels, and with all the company of heaven, we laud and magnify thy glorious Name; evermore praising thee, and saying, Holy, holy, holy, Lord God of Hosts, heaven and earth are full of thy glory: Glory be to thee, O Lord Most High. Amen.

Proper Prefaces.

Upon Christmas Day, and seven days after.

Because thou didst give Jesus Christ. . . .

Upon Easter Day, and seven days after.

But chiefly are we bound to praise thee. . . .

Upon Ascension Day, and seven days after.

Through thy most dearly beloved Son Jesus Christ. . . .

Upon Whitsunday, and six days after.

Through Jesus Christ our Lord; according. . . .

Upon the Feast of Trinity only, may be said,

Who art one God, one Lord. . . .

Or else this may be said, the words (Holy Father) being retained in the introductory Address.

For the precious death and merits of thy Son Jesus Christ our Lord, and for the sending to us of the Holy Ghost the Comforter; who are one with thee in thy eternal Godhead: Therefore with Angels, etc.

Then shall the Priest, kneeling down at the Lord's Table, say, in the name of all those who shall receive the Communion, this Prayer following.

PRAYER OF HUMBLE ACCESS "We do not presume. . . ."

When the Priest, standing before the Table, hath so ordered the Bread and Wine, that he may with the more readiness and decency break the Bread before the People, and take the Cup into his Hands, he shall say the Prayer of Consecration, as followeth.

Prayer Book of the Protestant Episcopal Church *1790*   311

All glory be to thee, Almighty God, our heavenly Father, for that thou, of thy tender mercy, didst give thine only Son Jesus Christ to suffer death upon the cross for our redemption; who made there (by his one oblation of himself once offered) a full, perfect, and sufficient sacrifice, oblation, and satisfaction, for the sins of the whole world; and did institute, and in his holy gospel command us to continue, a perpetual memory of that his precious death and sacrifice, until his coming again: For in the night in which he was betrayed, (a) he took Bread; and when he had given thanks, (b) he brake it, and gave it to his disciples, saying, Take, eat, (c) This is my Body, which is given for you; Do this in remembrance of me. Likewise, after supper, (d) he took the cup; and when he had given thanks, he gave it to them, saying, Drink ye all of this; for (e) This is my Blood of the New Testament, which is shed for you, and for many, for the remission of sins; Do this, as oft as ye shall drink it, in remembrance of me.

The Oblation. Wherefore, O Lord and heavenly Father, according to the institution of thy dearly beloved Son our Savior Jesus Christ, we, thy humble servants, do celebrate and make here before thy divine Majesty, with these thy holy gifts, which we now offer unto thee,[1] the memorial thy Son hath commanded us to make; having in remembrance his blessed Passion and precious death, his mighty resurrection and glorious ascension; rendering unto thee most hearty thanks for the innumerable benefits procured unto us by the same.

The Invocation. And we most humbly beseech thee, O merciful Father, to hear us; and, of thy almighty goodness, vouchsafe to bless and sanctify, with thy word[2] and Holy Spirit, these thy gifts and creatures of bread and wine; that we, receiving them according to thy Son our Savior Jesus Christ's holy institution, in re-

(a) *Here the Priest is to take the Paten into his hands.*
(b) *And here to break the Bread.*
(c) *And here to lay his hands upon all the Bread.* (1. corrected to *hand* in 1822).
(d) *Here he is to take the Cup into his hand.* (2. corrected to *hands* in 1892).
(e) *And here he is to lay his hand upon every Vessel in which there is any Wine to be consecrated.*
1. This phrase, capitalized inadvertently in 1789, was reduced to lower case in 1793.
2. "Word" was capitalized in 1793 to refer to the Incarnate Word.

membrance of his Death and Passion, may be partakers of his most blessed Body and Blood. And we earnestly desire thy fatherly goodness, mercifully to accept this our sacrifice of praise and thanksgiving, most humbly beseeching thee to grant, that by the merits and death of thy Son Jesus Christ, and through faith in his blood, we, and all thy whole Church, may obtain remission of our sins, and all other benefits of his Passion. And here we offer and present unto thee, O Lord, ourselves, our souls and bodies, to be a reasonable, holy, and living sacrifice unto thee; humbly beseeching thee, that we, and all others who shall be partakers of this holy Communion, may worthily receive the most precious Body and Blood of thy Son Jesus Christ, be filled with thy grace and heavenly benediction, and made one body with him, that he may dwell in them, and they in him. And although we are unworthy, through our manifold sins, to offer unto thee any sacrifice, yet we beseech thee to accept this our bounden duty and service; not weighing our merits, but pardoning our offences, through Jesus Christ our Lord; by whom, and with whom, in the unity of the Holy Ghost, all honor and glory be unto thee, O Father Almighty, world without end. Amen.

Here shall be sung a Hymn, or part of a Hymn, from the Selection for the Feast and Fasts, etc.

Then shall the Priest first receive the Communion in both kinds himself, and proceed to deliver the same to the Bishops, Priests, and Deacons, in like manner (if any be present) and, after that, to the People also in order, into their hands, all devoutly kneeling: And when he delivereth the Bread, he shall say,

The Body of our Lord Jesus Christ, which was given for thee, preserve thy body and soul unto everlasting life: Take and eat this in remembrance that Christ died for thee, and feed on him in thy heart by faith, with thanksgiving.

And the Minister who delivereth the Cup shall say,

The Blood of our Lord Jesus Christ, which was shed for thee, preserve thy body and soul unto everlasting life: Drink this in remembrance that Christ's Blood was shed for thee, and be thankful.

*If the consecrated Bread and³ Wine be spent before all have communi-
cated, the Priest is to consecrate more, according to the Form before prescribed, beginning at:* All glory be to Thee, Almighty God. . . . *and
ending with these words:* partakers of his most blessed Body and
Blood.

*When all have communicated, the Minister shall return to the Lord's
Table, and reverently place upon it what remaineth of the consecrated
Elements, covering the same with a fair Linen Cloth.*

LORD'S PRAYER

PRAYER OF THANKSGIVING "Almighty and everliving
    God. . . ."

GLORIA IN EXCELSIS or HYMN

BLESSING

FINAL COLLECTS AND RUBRICS

3. In 1845 *and* was changed to *or*.